The Audacity

Praise for

The Audacity

'A fearless origin story that shows women how to be absolutely fucking awesome at all times. Having Katherine Ryan as the new voice in your head might well be the next stage in women's evolution. If she can't be your best friend, this book is the next best option'
CAITLIN MORAN

'Outrageously brilliant! Katherine's straight-talking, no-nonsense book is the honesty we all need. I'm buying this for all my friends'
LAURA WHITMORE

'Like Katherine, this book is witty as hell, sharp as a razor and yet still sensitive, insightful and kind'
TOM ALLEN

'Massively recommend . . . I laughed, cried a little and ended up feeling proud to be a strange, small-town sister'
SCARLETT MOFFATT

'Katherine is one of the smartest, funniest voices in comedy . . . an icon of our time. This book is absolutely hilarious, deeply insightful and truly original. You will love and devour *The Audacity*'
LOU SANDERS

'Like Katherine Ryan herself, *The Audacity* is hilarious, sharp and brilliantly honest'
JOSH WIDDICOMBE

'I am in love with Katherine's writing. *The Audacity* is exhilarating – fierce, funny and brilliantly written, but there is so much tenderness, honesty and generosity too. I loved every joke but was also deeply moved by its frankness, and the story of contemporary womanhood. It's a book I want to give to every woman I love'
DAISY BUCHANAN

'There is nothing more powerful and dick shrivelling than an audaciously liberated woman living her truth. If there was a North Star for uncompromising confidence, it would be Katherine. This book feels like a hilarious and comforting hug from your best friend'
GRACE CAMPBELL

Katherine Ryan

The Audacity

BLINK

bringing you closer

First published in the UK by Blink Publishing
An imprint of Bonnier Books UK
4th Floor, Victoria House, Bloomsbury Square,
London, WC1B 4DA
Owned by Bonnier Books
Sveavägen 56, Stockholm, Sweden

facebook.com/blinkpublishing
twitter.com/blinkpublishing

Hardback – 978-1-788-703-98-7
Trade Paperback – 978-1-788-703-99-4
Signed – 978-1-788-704-49-6
eBook – 978-1-788-704-01-4
Audiobook – 978-1-788-704-02-1

A CIP catalogue of this book is available from the British Library.

Design by www.envydesign.co.uk
Typeset by IDSUK (Data Connection) Ltd
Printed and bound in Great Britain by Clays Ltd, Elcograf S.p.A.

1 3 5 7 9 10 8 6 4 2

Blink Publishing is an imprint of Bonnier Books UK
www.bonnierbooks.co.uk

Dedicated to Phil Mount

Contents

Introduction   1

How to Be Strange, Small-town Sisters   9

How to Become French, Fast   25

How to Be the Most Popular Girl in School   35

How to Let Your Friend's Murder Define All Your
    Relationships   45

How to Nearly Be in a Music Video   57

How to Be Crowned Miss Hooters Toronto   71

How to Get Started in Comedy   83

How to Waste All Your Money on Designer Dogs   93

How to Get Plastic Surgery   107

How to Skip Town for Good   123

How to Have a Baby   135

How to Potty Train Your Baby by Ten Months   141

How to Stay Booked and Busy   151

How to Break Up   165

How to Attract Toxic Men . . . AND Keep Them Interested!   183

How to Have Another Baby: Part One   199

How to Marry Your High School Boyfriend   207

How to Cut Off Your Problematic Auntie   225

How to Be a Real Piece of Shit to Your Grandma   239

How to Get Robbed by a Masked Man   245

How to Have Another Baby: Part Two   261

How to Impress Famous Celebrities   281

How to Survive Controversy   297

How to Redefine Family   307

Acknowledgements   319

Introduction

Hi, my name is TV's Katherine Ryan. I'm a comedian, writer, presenter, podcaster, excellent rapper and terrible actress, and now I'm writing this book for you. Maybe you've chosen it for yourself because you like my vibe and you plan on reading it snuggled up indoors with a warm mug of wine on a rainy day or outside in the sun on a government-sanctioned Covid-safe holiday. Maybe someone gifted it to you ironically, like the time my dad gave me Bill Cosby's *Love and Marriage* vintage manifesto from the late eighties as a wedding present. Let me tell you, that man was hiding in plain sight. Cosby, I mean – not my dad. Dad is still very much under the radar. Nah, Dad is pretty cool, actually. In fairness to him, and to my entire family, as you'll see, I was a complex child and they all did the best they could with me . . .

Maybe somebody who loves you gave you this book because you're hard to get presents for (code for 'not worth the research') but everyone knows you like comedy so tour tickets and autobiographies do the trick. I ADORE comedy and my favourite comics are the ones who unashamedly reveal truths about their unique worldview and about their personal lives as well. You should see me in a green room whenever gossip is shared and I gleefully get to find out that two comics I know might probably be fucking. You'll never know a happier woman. Especially when you know for a fact they'll regret it. A few years ago at the Edinburgh Fringe Festival, a photo went round of a very unlikely pair of comedians making out and the over-40 male comic who told me about it delivered the news with the giddiness of a sugared-up 12-year-old girl.

I like a mixture of high and low media. I'm moved by serious events in the news and I want to be active in what's going on but, equally, I'm not ashamed of my unquenchable thirst to find out how Bennifer got back together. Nobody wants to hear a secret more than I do and therefore this book is going to be full of them. Every week, when I record my podcast, *Telling Everybody Everything*, at home in my tiny office, I try to forget that newspapers exist and that a reporter can easily listen to what I say and print those words in an article. I'm also regularly affronted to discover that yet another one of my parents' friends has downloaded it. These are my private conversations that I've decided I'm okay with certain cool people being a part of. I think that's the best way to build friendships and to deliver my most authentic truth, so I'm writing this with a similar mindset. It's the exact Kris Jenner business policy that built the Kardashian reality empire as we know it today: Share Everything.

Stand-up isn't about telling the full story. There's a certain rhythm to delivering a stage set that demands sharpness and brevity. During my early days on the road, I once overheard another comic say, 'What we offer is a service. Your job as a comedian is to serve the punters laughter. It isn't about you.' It's a message I haven't forgotten. Of course, I get to be authentic on stage and weave in my agenda here and there but, ultimately, the crowd want to have a laugh, so I've got to come with some strong jokes that are relevant to their lives and give them a reprieve from the mundane during that precious hour in their company. It's a challenge and that's part of what makes it so much fun, but I think female comedians are told we have fewer punchlines compared to our male peers, plus we're expected to be EXTRA commanding, brash and alpha to hold an audience's attention. That the audience has got to be laughing every few seconds or it gets awkward. In the context of most short sets, there's limited room to stretch out ideas. That's fine, but there are also more long-form, earnest stories that I'm glad to have the opportunity to tell here. Comedy is, after all, a conversation, and I feel very honoured that people reach out to me for advice or connection. Through social media, letters or email, I get to hear directly from people who've seen my work and who ask for tips on how to match my lurid level of courage and assurance.

What they describe is:

Audacity

NOUN

courage or confidence of a kind that other people find
shocking or rude

Audacity is a word mostly used to indicate disapproval. Like, 'HOW DARE she carry herself with that wicked abundance of self-belief. How AUDACIOUS!' Any kind of audacity pisses people off sometimes, especially in middle-class England. The pearl-clutchers come out from time to time, voicing their ire that I should wear this or say that, but it doesn't bother me. I've never wanted to upset anyone and the truth is that I tried for a long time to be the kind of person who didn't ruffle any feathers. I failed miserably at that challenge. But, over the past decade in particular, I've come to peacefully accept that being audacious is a gift that I can't escape – and it's one that I'd like to share with you. This book is a collection of 'How-Tos' that led me towards the calm, contented woman I am today, who's come a long way from waitressing at Hooters. (Though I do miss the chicken from there and sometimes I view my move into comedy as a lateral one.)

I can always take a joke, I don't waste time worrying about things I can't control and I have zero anxiety about what strangers think of me. Sure, I care about people – their safety, wellbeing and access to free and legal abortions – and I'll always do my best to make others happy wherever reasonable. But I embrace the reality that you just can't please everyone. As my mother always said, 'Katherine, if we all liked the same thing, we'd all be married to your father.' I'm absolutely confounded as to why perfectly lovely people bother being wounded over criticism of their bodies, their choices, their art. Do you like everyone in the world? Be honest: you don't. So why even begin to give a toss about whether or not they like you? It's a ridiculous use of your energy. There are seven billion people in the world and I suspect you could fit every person I like into a single Starbucks.

Living with audacity isn't just about strength. I've learned that there's bravery in being vulnerable, too. In the past, I've run from challenges, withdrawn from loved ones and cheated on partners, all because I didn't have the courage I needed to face tough situations properly. Accepting who I used to be, admitting I was wrong and apologising for the mistakes I've made hasn't been easy, but you've got to forgive yourself and fix up if you want to move forward. I love the wild child who still exists in my stand-up and is woven through my writing. I tried to kill her a hundred thousand times before accepting that the angry-baby-musical-theatre-kid-weirdo is not only an inescapable part of who I am, but that it's maybe the best part. She's certainly got the most unique tools and is probably the entire reason I've been able to pursue this incredible life authentically.

Having young people – well, the ones who aren't busy trying to cancel me on TikTok – following me and listening to me is a great privilege that I don't take lightly. If you're young and you're frustrated and you're strange, I hope you feel encouraged by the stories in this book. It's totally normal to want to fit in but perfectly okay if you never really do. I promise you'll find your tribe and, when you do, you can look back at all the moments where you struggled and hopefully laugh at how far you've come. Imagine how boring life would be without a few memories that make you cringe. Laughing at yourself is so much fun.

At this point in my career, I realise that people have their own pretty fully formed ideas about who I am. They've watched my Netflix specials or they've seen *The Duchess* series and they've conflated my on-stage persona and that ballsy scripted character with me. For the most part, I don't correct them. They can think that my entire face is plastic, that I hate ALL men, that I'm high maintenance and a 24/7 bitch. Maybe a lot of them want me to be that person. I suspect it's something to do with boarding school and being spanked by a matron. TV commissioners also seem utterly gobsmacked when I manage to fulfil any kind of brief that's 'nice'. In reality, I'm progressive, I'm an advocate, I listen to contributors and I'm friendly, but because there's some chip inside them programmed to think 'Confident Female Comic Equals Dragon', they're surprised. TV execs are most satisfied when they're able to use the same words to describe me that they might use to sell a duvet. They'll ring my agent and say, 'Wow, we're thrilled that Katherine was so warm, comforting, soft and 100 per cent sourced in Canada.' I don't blame them. No matter what, there will always be something about me that reads as simply, outrageously audacious.

And I wouldn't have it any other way.

Some people
just aren't
cut out to
be babies.

How to Be Strange, Small-town Sisters

I was an angry baby. I only remember snapshots of my infancy, like the texture of my grandparents' carpet that I hated crawling on because it itched, or the time I had a cold and I gazed out the window dramatically thinking, 'I've had a sore throat for two whole years,' which I'd worked out because it was my second birthday party. I remember some kids still being in nappies at that age, which I judged them for. One afternoon, I was on a playdate with my friend Lindsay and, investigating a smell, her mother asked, 'Lindsay, did you poop your pants?' I felt mortified for her. I looked up from the floor mat at my mum as if to say, 'Who the hell poops their pants?!'

I accepted that some of my nursery friends could speak and some were still non-verbal. I had palpable contempt for a certain little boy who'd hit the rest of us with Lego bricks, so, one day, while he was taking far too long at the top of the slide, I shoved him down it. I rolled my eyes as he wailed and took position to go next, but the nursery school teacher scooped me up off the ladder and made me sit in time out. It was humiliating. Though cross on the inside, I'd built a reputation as a 'good girl' with intelligence and manners who was normally composed. I remember how foolish I felt to have thrown that all away for a fleeting moment of revenge. I hated being admonished and losing the respect of my peers – the teachers.

This is seared into my memory as the very first time I got into trouble and I felt that it was unjust. I remember feeling hugely disrespected again on the day my dad dropped me off with my grandma, Dorth, so that he and Mum could go to hospital to have a baby. I loved hanging out with Dorth – she taught me backgammon and gave me Oreos – but in this instance it was an effront to rudely exclude me from such a meaningful event. A day later, I seethed in the car on the way to meet my newborn sister, Joanne. I hadn't spent much time away from Mum and the bullshit gifts and cuddles I received during my special visit only made me more furious. I was three and a half. Yes, that's a vivid memory for three and a half, but what can I say? I was mentally alert; a step ahead. I wasn't ever *just* playing with my pretend kitchen, I was thinking, 'What if we knocked through into the pretend lounge?'

Even though I was an angry baby, I wasn't usually naughty in the traditional sense. Rather, I was consumed by the desire to please and impress my superiors. That's why it always felt shit when I chimed into an adult conversation in public or at my parents' friends' houses only to be met with disapproving looks. That never happened at home. I was funny at home.

Some people just aren't cut out to be babies. My best guess as to why I was such an ungrateful one is that I hated having zero control over anything and felt frustrated by my own pathetic limitations. I never had tantrums about it, just glared eerily at people a lot. Mum let me start answering the kitchen phone and saw that independence seemed to lift my mood, and that the more that I could do on my own, the happier I became. When I was old enough, I started going to proper school, which was entirely French Catholic because I think Mum decided that it would be best for me to start conducting my affairs in a completely separate language. Finally, I had a sense of fucking purpose.

I was born in Sarnia, a petrochemical town in south-western Ontario, Canada, that sits a small river's width away from Michigan, USA. I entered what I understand to be this world on 30th June 1983 and my very small mother describes my birth as the most horrendous experience of her life. That's saying something, considering that as a teenager working at the bank, she was felt up by her boss and routinely had to defend herself from his advances. So she's faced challenges in her life, but her labour and delivery with me stands out to her as having been the greatest one. I'm very punctual now but was two weeks late being born, so Mum was induced. If anyone's considering an induction, I've heard mixed reviews but generally speaking, the synthetic oxytocin the doctors give you doesn't come in waves with the counteractive endorphins your body would naturally create, but hits you quite abruptly with a steady pain instead. It's maybe tolerable with an epidural but Sarnia didn't offer that anaesthetic in 1983, so Mum coldly begged the nurse to kill her with a sledgehammer instead. She and I have always had a way of inadvertently upsetting people.

My parents both work in jobs that I don't fully understand. I've asked. They've explained. But I struggle to truly get it. I briefly considered fact-checking the following, but ultimately decided it's better to speak from the heart and deliver my unedited truth as I remember it. Mum is a computer systems analyst and a consultant. I gather she does securities and coding, but when she was 23 and I was born, she carried printers around a lot and was often covered in ink as a result. She worked for the chemical plant companies in Sarnia but upstairs in the office with the computers, or as she calls it today, 'chained to a desk for 35 years'. Mum worked mostly with men and did coding in the 1980s before people had home PCs, which I've always found pretty cool. Though I have wondered why she isn't Bill Gates. She's been in the game roughly as long as he has. If she were, she'd be equally dedicated to vaccines and philanthropy, but would definitely have punched Jeffrey Epstein in the dick when she met him.

My dad moved from Ireland with his best friend in the early 1980s to start a corporate engineering company in Sarnia. I should absolutely know what goes on in their office since I worked there for a summer during university but I was very busy having a romance with a colleague and scamming chocolate milk from the break room. All I was able to gather was that Dad's main role was to pop out and move the company cars every two hours to avoid parking tickets. He occupied the front office of the building and was stationed there to be a charming peacekeeper and everyone's friend. He's like a white Obama. He met with clients and went down to the chemical plants sometimes, but evidence suggests that he isn't an actual engineer. He's more of an engineer facilitator . . . or corporate concierge, of sorts. I think maybe he's a deal-maker and a problem-solver. We were asked to draw pictures of 'our parents at work' once in kindergarten (pre-school) and I sketched him golfing.

* * *

Joanne eventually grew into a toddler that I could boss around and Kerrie was born two years after her. Having a captive audience pleased me as director of the house. I was soft with them, read them stories, made up endless games, choreographed dance routines to Michael Jackson songs and made them watch *The Golden Girls*. I liked regular 1980s things like Barbies, My Little Pony and Rainbow Brite but most of all, I wanted to become Bea Arthur. My publisher has said that I now need to tell you who Bea Arthur is for anyone unfamiliar but, to be honest, it sickens me that you might not know. It's not that I'm annoyed, just disappointed. Besides, you're too late because she's dead. Bea Arthur was an iconic Emmy and Tony Award-winning comedian, actress and activist who starred in a number of sitcoms (including *The Golden Girls*), theatre shows and films. She was famous for her deadpan delivery and I loved her. She also worked as a truck driver, a medical assistant and was awarded the Victory

Medal as a Marine in the Second World War, but I'll leave you to uncover the rest of her genius at your leisure. Enjoy.

My sisters and I played our own artistically embellished version of *The Golden Girls* – a game called 'Harriette'. We pretended to be single neighbours in a retirement community set up in different rooms of our actual house and, for some reason, we all had babies that we would care for and bring to visit each other for chats. Women over 60 with robust reproductive systems and no men – everything I created was ahead of its time. Kerrie was the central character, Harriette, whose pretend house was my parents' bedroom. I was called 'Melissa' and I lived in my real-life bedroom with my infant son. Joanne was 'Derf Gale', named not after the Dorothy character that features in *The Golden Girls* but, confusingly, Dorothy Gale from *The Wizard of Oz*. It was a complex set up but we could get lost in it for hours a day. If Mum was making lunch, we'd pack up our dolls for an outing to the kitchen, which then became our local cafe. Mum had her own catalogue of excellent, layered waitress characters and blended in seamlessly with the game.

All of our games were about elevating Kerrie. I'd conceived one called 'Jacques', where Kerrie was a little princess and I was the queen, so we had employed Jacques the French butler to answer to the princess' every whim. Joanne was the butler and she'd spend most of the game dragging Kerrie around in a wagon carrying a parasol while I barked orders in a British accent. Another game was 'Earwig', where I was a mother ladybird looking after Kerrie, a baby ladybird called Tiny Tim. The earwig (Joanne) was a disgusting creature that we'd run from to avoid Tiny Tim being eaten alive. Poor Joanne. Our roles seemed to suit our personalities, though, and Joanne never objected to being under our rule.

It was the classic treatment of the middle child but Kerrie and I were just more sympatico. We were as weird as each other and even looked most alike. At three years old, Kerrie spoke often of 'Anne Land', a world inside the wardrobes that she'd disappear into and re-emerge as one of a host of characters – all of whom shared a southern American drawl. Kerry-Anne, Gary-Anne, Serri-Anne and Barrie-Anne were the most popular visitors to our dimension, and we'd address them accordingly all day or until they got bored and travelled back through the coats. One evening at dinner, Kerrie became overcome by guilt and tearfully confessed to the family that she had been acting as these Texan incarnations the entire time, and that Anne Land didn't actually exist. We'd been fooled. My mother dejectedly put her napkin over her plate, playing along by pretending to be disappointed, but comforting Kerrie by saying that she was forgiven and that we'd soon get over this great deception. Our family always committed to the bit.

As soon as we were old enough, my parents enrolled us in the local theatre groups to keep us entertained and make the most of the kind of imaginations that existed before iPads. There were very few men involved in the musical productions, so my dad offered himself up as bait to get us in. He was typecast as either a policeman or a vicar in every performance – oh, and Joseph's eldest brother, Reuben, in the story of his Technicolor Dreamcoat. We'd never have been accepted to the theatre roster if it hadn't been for Dad – they needed his tenor voice so badly that all three of us girls jumped the queue. He really took one for the team by joining. It was a delicious education in nepotism and I liked it.

Between Sarnia Little Theatre and Bluewater Musical Productions, we spent three or four evenings and every Saturday in rehearsals. It was serious business because, for an absolutely trash town, Sarnia actually continues to produce very high-quality shows.

There's no easy build up to this but after we'd been in the plays for a couple of years, it turned out that one of the adult actors we'd spent regular intervals of time with was quite a prolific paedophile. It was obviously shocking and sad, considering he'd dedicated his entire life to working with children and was even named on the Mayor's honour list. He seemed nice. He volunteered with disabled boys and was even the city's official Easter Bunny, dressing up in a pink costume and posing for pictures during the annual egg hunt. So many childhood photos lost. Nobody wants to reminisce like, 'And here's Grandma back in 1993, trading in the painted rocks she found for chocolate eggs from this giant rabbit who was convicted on 40 counts of molestation.' He exclusively preyed on boys, but my sisters and I had spent enough time in his company to know him well and it bothered me that I quite liked him. I wondered how monsters managed to seem so funny and great. Surely 'bad guys' should be more easily identifiable, I reasoned. I wished that I could have been more clever and warned people.

After he'd been arrested, there was a dedication to him printed in the pantomime programme. All our names and little faces above the final words included by his best friend, the theatre director, who wrote, 'Dedicated to . . .' Um, 'A FUCKING CHILD MOLESTER', HELLO?!?! Even then, I thought it was deeply inappropriate.

When I was ten, our theatre group announced auditions for a variety show. We could sing anything we wanted and I LOVED an open brief. The other girls prepared pretty songs from *Annie* or *Carousel* and wore sweet curls in their hair with floral dresses and white socks to the try-outs. I waited my turn alongside them in one of Dad's oversized flannel shirts, holding an empty pizza box prop that I'd brought along for my performance. When the judges called my name, I crept into the audition space already in character, calling out, 'Pizza! I've got a pizza for Mr Rossini?' I pretended to 'realise' that I'd accidentally stumbled into an audition and that all eyes were on me. Then, for dramatic effect, I threw the pizza box away and tore off the flannel shirt to reveal my regular shorts and top. In the deepest, manliest opera voice I could muster, I sang an a cappella version of Rossini's 'The Barber of Seville', as I'd seen Robin Williams do in the guise of a cartoon bird in the opening to *Mrs. Doubtfire*. Weird.

My uniqueness was rewarded, though, and I was invited to perform my exact audition piece in the variety show. I struggled all the time with the juxtaposition of wanting to be sweet and safe like the pretty girls, while also wanting to be funny and stand out. Being pretty was never going to win me a solo.

I was an odd and politically charged little girl. Later that year, I chose a poem for my school's French speech competition which was all about consent and how your parents shouldn't make you kiss aunties, uncles, babysitters, etc., just to be polite. 'Des Baisers' (French for 'Kisses') was a piece that I passionately connected with as I hated being made to embrace strangers and I knew that mine was a message worth sharing with the community. I delivered it enthusiastically, knowing instinctively to speed up or get louder in certain places and then soften up during others. I looked the audience and judges dead in their souls when I needed to and even injected comedy now and then to ease the tension. Mum has since uploaded a video of my winning performance to YouTube and looking back at it now, I was a perfect comedian. What have I been pissing away at for the past 27 years? That child is the comedian I'm working towards becoming now!

I was lucky to grow up with a few cherished and like-minded friends, but for the most part, I had to contend with bewildered gazes as very few people 'got me' in Sarnia. I can't blame them for that – I didn't understand most of those muggles either. We were very close with one amazing family though – my dad's friends, the MacSweeneys. They'd emigrated from Ireland around the same time as Dad and had two perfect children who were a little bit older than me. I loved and looked up to these kids, but I also knew that they carried themselves with a certain composure that I was lacking. The eldest girl, Orla, brimmed with intelligence and class. She was tall, beautiful, athletic and very happy to sit and play the piano wearing another showstopping tea dress whenever we popped round to their place. She didn't cry when asked or pointedly refuse like I did.

I noticed the pride on my dad's face watching Orla execute a number of helpful tasks, like presenting a homemade pavlova to the table or regaling the adults with a perfectly pitched, non-controversial story. I remember thinking to myself, 'You're killing me, Orla, take it down a notch, babe.' Any time I chimed in, things got weird.

One afternoon, the MacSweeneys had a neighbour round who was speaking about her new interiors business called 'Chintz'. Orla congratulated this woman and spoke graciously about how much she loved her style choices. Trying in my own way to be helpful, I offered the information that 'Chintz' might not be the most suitable name because my mother used the word 'chintzy' to describe clothes I wasn't allowed to buy due to their poor quality and cheap construction. Had I misunderstood that definition? While Mum quietly turned purple choking on her salad, the neighbour lady explained in quite a huff that 'chintz' was a type of colourful Indian fabric. I dropped it but the damage had been done. We were both right. Except I was wrong as she'd already registered the company name. I wished so badly that I had said nothing, or that I'd been able to offer something simple and kind like Orla had, but I always managed to be strange and offensive instead. Orla was magnificent and it's good that I had her around because her presence served as a bootcamp for learning to be unthreatened by another woman's excellence. There was no reason not to love her. She's a doctor now. SHOCK. I'm sure Dad loves that I write dick jokes while his best friend's daughter writes prescriptions. Once again, Dad, sorry.

I didn't have to worry about Orla being his favourite anyway. She had a brother called Conor who – in addition to being a dashingly handsome and charming basketball star – was, crucially, a BOY. Neither of us could compete with that. Back then, you could daintily serve as many puddings as you liked, but it was mere window dressing if you didn't have a dick.

I speak about my hometown in my stand-up often. Despite the growing fentanyl problem there, it's a pretty wholesome place to grow up. Sure, the chemical plants may very well be unproveably poisonous (my dad says they're safe) but you'd earn a nice income working in that industry, and there's a beautiful (though potentially toxic) lake. There are twin bridges over the river and you can go there to sit on a bench with the best chip truck fries. Sarnia provides a wonderful community backdrop for the majority of its families, but the way I describe it is a reflection of how I felt about myself in that setting. I was restless there. I knew better than to accept the general opinion that I didn't make sense and I trusted that I would one day make more sense elsewhere, and not just within the safety of a little theatre bubble.

I didn't make sense at Catholic church. From when I was pretty small, my sisters and I went to Sunday school together at our local place of worship. My mum even volunteered to teach a few classes there, which was awesome and subversive because she was a truly powerful witch pretending to be a dutiful religious wife. Like Hillary Clinton in the nineties. She did great work with the kids, though, and is excellent with small children, which is where I get my competency from. I was difficult to raise and she was less sure of how to handle me after about a decade. I'm also less confident as a parent with my own daughter than I was when she was small because it's harder to navigate their big ideas and unique opinions when they become headstrong enough to vehemently disagree with you, a 'boomer'. Infancy is where we shine. Oh, and if you don't know what 'boomer' means, it's an insult which degrades your ideology and worldview based on the varying levels of privilege enshrined within the generational divide. But worse still, it implies you look old.

Mum wanted to please people like I did. She wanted to do the right thing and project the proper image in our community, to an extent, but sometimes innocently got it wrong. She couldn't help making spicy comments once in a while but was chastised for ambiguous reasons too. Mum kept clothing and vintage coats for years. She wasn't bothered about driving a fancy car and took pride in being frugal. I remember a big controversy when, after Mass one day, one of the basic townswomen asked Mum where her winter jacket was from. She said, 'Oh, I found this at the charity shop!' I watched some women sneer and Dad later suggested that maybe Mum shouldn't be so vocal about bargain hunting. Why lie about something beautiful costing a few dollars? She just didn't get it and neither did I. Like Mum, I couldn't give a fuck about how things are perceived, I only care about how things are. The idea of church looks lovely but why bother going when you're going to be a judgemental bitch in the parking lot afterwards? Why show up when you clearly aren't listening to the sermons, heifer?

I knew how it felt to be alienated. One morning in Sunday school, a lady who was not my mother explained to us that Jesus wanted us to live without hate. I raised my hand and announced to the classroom of fellow eight-year-olds that we should be prepared to make some exceptions to that rule. When challenged, I replied that I hated Saddam Hussein and that my hatred was justified. I'd watched just enough of the news to have a US media-sponsored understanding of what was going on in the Middle East but was probably too young to be discussing it in such bold terms with the other children. I had a limited capability to grasp the nuance or scale of most of what I was watching. For example, when I first heard about the Gulf War, I'd assumed it was happening on our local golf course. I'd have nightmares about my dad and his friends happily teeing off one minute only to find themselves battling in a desert by the ninth hole. Sometimes, I'd see riots or fires on TV from, say, Chicago, and barricade myself in my bedroom, thinking our house was about to catch alight next. Mum would have to get the map out and explain just how big the world was. Regardless, I was passionate about indoctrinating my friends from Sunday school against an Iraqi president I'd seen on CNN.

'Well . . . no . . .' the lady began, 'Jesus loves Saddam Hussein too. He is a forgiving God.'

NOPE. I wasn't having that. 'Absolutely not!' I insisted. 'Saddam Hussein is an evil dictator who tortures people and I hate him and Jesus hates him, no matter what you say!'

Come to think of it, maybe I'm the entire reason why the church asked my mother to take over those lessons . . .

It pains me to admit that I don't actually hate Sarnia. I speak about it as though it's an irredeemable hellscape and in many ways, that's what it was to me, but deep down I'm fond of the memories I made there. I'm just sick of the boring narrative of people being humble about their roots. I find it much funnier to pick the fresh angle of being ungrateful instead, so EXCUSE ME for trying to be a badly needed breath of fresh air. Rappers are always shouting out their postcodes, 'repping' their hometowns. Kanye West even named one of his children 'Chicago' after his birthplace. Not only do I relentlessly disparage my city but I've taken the extra step of targeting its most famous export: a widely respected astronaut called Chris Hadfield. Finding fault with a space hero is a tough sell, which is what makes it ridiculous and fun for me. It's as ludicrous as if a British comic came for David Attenborough. (Makes mental note to come for David Attenborough.) I've found that the best angle is to take down the universe as a whole, to insist that celestial exploration is stupid and to argue that Chris Hadfield cannot be famous because he has a moustache. The entire premise is so dumb but what's even dumber is that people choose to take it seriously and let it make them cross. I obviously think he's great and the joke lies in the pettiness of my jealousy.

Mum, Kerrie and Joanne have all left Sarnia for greener pastures but they do enjoy a visit back now and then. I'm not sure I'd be welcome as displeasing the townsfolk with my unique sense of humour is a tradition that I have continued well into adulthood. I suppose I could just start being nice – but I figure, why ruin what we've built?

"I've **never** respected the creative opinions of **people** who create **nothing.**"

How to Become French, Fast

Neither my mum nor my dad spoke French but they decided to send my sisters and me to the French Catholic school in our town. Canada is officially a bilingual country and there are many pockets of Francophone communities outside Quebec. All schools teach a little bit of French but some are full-time French for every subject – no English. That was L'École St Thomas D'Aquin. Mum wisely predicted that being bilingual would help us become more well-rounded adults, and the easiest way to learn a language is to be immersed in it as a child. Earlier this year, I was a contestant on Michael McIntyre's hit gameshow *The Wheel* and I used my fluency to correctly answer a multiple-choice ballet question, so Mum's been proven right at least once.

As the oldest sister, I was the first to attend *l'école* and I remember walking into kindergarten and immediately clocking that people were speaking a different language to the one I understood. That's a headfuck no matter how old you are and it felt like some kind of prank. For a moment, I considered whether the whole world might be French and perhaps it was just my family and friends who spoke the way they did. Great. At four years old, I'd lost my ability to communicate and was reduced to being a baby all over again. I HATED BEING A BABY. (No offence to the baby community. Some of my best children have been babies.) So, I did what any baby would do and I cried. I refused to participate in whatever the teachers were asking me to participate in (how the hell would I know?) until they had no choice but to ring my dad. He came to collect me and I got to hang out in his office and solemnly photocopy my hand for the rest of the day. I put myself to bed without dinner that night, hoping a hunger strike would save me from being sent back to school the following day. Joanne was a year old by then and got to stay home with the babysitter, so surely I could do the same? Wrong. My mother – who'd been casually staging her own hunger strike since the mid-seventies – had no mercy. She walked me onto that school bus and assured me that she would do this every day until I relented. She was mentally stronger than I was so I knew she meant it. After returning to the classroom, I sat on the *tapis magique* (filthy carpet) with the other children and decided I'd better give things a go.

Most of the kids spoke French at home, though a few were from English-speaking families like mine. English was banned at school, as the teachers knew that using it would impede our learning immersion. You'd get a time out in the corner if you were heard speaking English and the teachers wouldn't translate for you either. I had no choice but to get on board with French if I wanted to have a voice and stay out of trouble, which happened to be the two things that mattered most to me in the world. Historically, it's having a voice that's gotten me into trouble, so laying low and holding my tongue in the French community might've done me some good, but some things just need to be articulated. Like when you need to ask for permission to use the toilet.

Around lunchtime on my second day, I was playing at the sand box table next to Chris, the boy I'd have a crush on for the next six years, and I realised that I needed a wee. Our teacher came past and I asked her, 'Excuse me, Tante Claire, may I please go to the washroom?' She smiled wryly and answered, 'En Français, Katherine.' For a kindergarten teacher, this chick was pretty merciless. She knew what I wanted but was so committed to the French cause that she was prepared to watch me squirm instead. 'La . . . washroom?' I offered. 'En Français, Katherine,' she warned once more. I hesitated, worried that I'd be sent for a time out on my third strike. Just then, she was distracted by another child smashing its face into something and scurried off.

Chris was francophone but I was too embarrassed to ask him for the words and risk looking stupid, and besides, I'd get us both into trouble if the teachers overheard us uttering the forbidden language. I didn't want to start off my first ever romance as 'the bad girl'. I guess I thought it better to become 'the girl who peed her pants'. Just like that, I was a four-year-old with the sensibilities of a 12-year-old who'd become mute and infantilised, and who'd wet herself in front of an entire room of strangers. It was humiliating. I stood frozen in the puddle until someone finally noticed and I was nonchalantly guided to the toilets, where Tante Claire helped me change out of my cute outfit and into a spare orange tracksuit from the lost-and-found bin. A knock-off prison uniform that identified me immediately as a failure. *Fantastique.*

At the end of the day, I tottered off the school bus and was greeted at home by our babysitter, Val. I held up my plastic bag of wet clothes almost pridefully, hoping that when Mum found out what had happened, she'd feel even more discredited than I had. 'Thought you'd send me to a French school, did you? Expected me to just go along with it, I'll bet! Well, look what you've done – I've brought shame upon us all and it's your fault!' But this was on me. No one spoke of the tracksuit incident at home. There wasn't even any banter about it. Mum put me on the bus the next day and the message was solidified that I'd need to assimilate – and fast.

I did. It only took about a month before I was fluent. It's amazing what a small child can achieve when given no other options. Either that, or I really felt that orange wasn't my colour. It baffles me when second language teachers use English during the lessons in schools today. My daughter's been studying French for years and hardly speaks a word of it for two clear reasons – one, all the worksheet instructions are in English and two, her mother is a lazy millennial cow who never bothered to teach her at home.

L'École St Thomas D'Aquin turned out to be a very flamboyant school and was probably my single greatest blessing growing up. I guess our little primary had a bigger arts budget than the English schools did because it was a separate system, so we had regular music and drama classes, creative writing contests, a radio show, pantomimes, speeches and opportunities to write and deliver original performances at monthly assemblies. Francophone culture and language was celebrated, so we were regularly encouraged to express ourselves, to get stuck in and to be competitive.

In the third grade when I was eight, my drawing was chosen as the best nativity scene to be framed and displayed in the church for Christmas Mass. I was very proud to show it off to my family but Mum burst out laughing when she saw it. Dad held his head in his hands while I tried to figure out what was funny about the holy family that I'd worked so hard recreating in colour pencil. Years later, I would learn that the Virgin Mary would likely not have been a buxom blonde wearing an extremely low-cut blue cocktail dress with chandelier diamond earrings and red lipstick. I had drawn her in the exact image of my own mother.

The teachers clearly didn't mind my whitewashed and glamorous interpretation as they were happy to hang it in the church. That's what I loved about early nineties French-Canadian culture – very non-judgemental. That faculty loved me. I was chatty, enthusiastic and deeply committed to pleasing them with my behaviour and top-notch grades. They even thought I was funny.

One morning, my dad decided to read us our horoscopes from the newspaper and that's when I learned that my June astrological sign was 'cancer'. I'd been aware of that word but only as a disease. (I am from Sarnia, after all. We're riddled.) Later that day, our teacher was correcting the class for their misuse of *je suis* and *j'ai*. It's something a lot of kids mix up grammatically but it's the difference between 'I am' and 'I have'. She said the correct way to indicate that you've finished a meal, for example, would be *J'ai fini*, meaning 'I have finished', while *Je suis fini* means 'I am finished' or, in other words, I'm dead. I thought it would be a laugh to approach the teacher's desk afterwards and tell her that '*J'ai le cancer*' or 'I have cancer'. Her jaw dropped before I rescued the moment by delivering my punchline of '*JE SUIS UN CANCER, MADAME!* Haha!', meaning 'I am a cancer', and explaining that I'd learned about star signs over breakfast. A sick, dark, horrible joke – and from a child?! Her reaction didn't make me feel strange – she actually liked it. It was of course a callback to her earlier 'I am dead'. These were the legends I was dealing with. I loved that school.

In the fourth grade, for no reason that made sense, I choreographed an 'I Dream of Jeannie' dance and performed it with my two best friends, Nathalie and Jessica, at a school assembly. At French school, you can be nine years old wearing harem pants and a bra top that shows your midriff! Again, very liberal. VERY French. There was never any talk of modesty or 'distracting the boys'. When it came to artistic expression, we could do whatever we wanted. I played on the chess team, became editor of the school newspaper and was generally respected as both a leader and an academic.

So far, so good. I'd had a few social bumps in the road, like in Sunday school or while visiting my parents' friends and their perfectly lovely children, but overall, I was well-liked in this community. I had theatre, I had French and was set up nicely to believe that acceptance would always be this easy.

Our headmistress was baller – a very tall, handsome woman with a platinum crew cut and a commanding presence. Madame Roi (which fittingly means 'king') was a boss role model and she liked me a lot. She knew that I took part in dance classes so one afternoon while I was in grade five, she asked whether I would be up for performing a dance at the grade six leavers' ceremony. A theatre kid never turns down a gig so I accepted without hesitation. I chose to perform 'Your Mama Don't Dance', a 1972 song by the rock duo Loggins and Messina because, you know, it's a terrible selection and a song that zero kids my age would like or have ever heard of. Looking back, I feel like Mme Roi was either prepping my ten-year-old ego for tougher challenges to come or she thought she'd throw the sixth graders one final treat for their superior amusement before releasing them to be small fish again in high school.

My timeless performance can be re-watched as it's basically a scene from *Jurassic Park* – the one where they introduce a small goat into the T-rex paddock as bait. The goat is me.

I picked out a neon colour block bodysuit – that's right, no regular school clothes would do – and crimped my hair for the event. Mme Roi booked me to headline so I went on right after the popular girl, who'd cried in her valedictorian speech about 'taking the next steps' and never wanting to abandon the special friendships they'd all made. Several of the sixth graders were sobbing contagiously and the last thing any of them wanted as a final memory of the school was for the grade five teacher's pet to dance on their scholastic graves. They seethed with disdain as I gyrated around, committed to keeping a wide nervous smile plastered to my face.

Songs are long. There were parents in attendance and even they were a largely unsupportive audience. Journalists often ask comedians about the harshest heckle of their career. For me, a bad heckle doesn't really exist as it can be turned into a funny interaction. What's worse than a heckle is resentful silence. Do you know what I would do if I witnessed a fifth grader dying on stage? As an empathic adult, I would whoop and cheer, or at least smile encouragingly, bopping along. I got nothing from these Sarnia people. Fucking drips. I was horrified to see that they existed even within the flamboyant francophone community.

The 'Your Mama Don't Dance' incident took place on a Monday, which gave the sixth graders four whole schooldays to bully me mercilessly before the summer holidays started. That week, whenever they saw me in the corridors or playground, they'd mimic my dance back at me and laugh. I can't say that I loved that experience but I didn't hate it either. I'd done what I'd been asked to do and tried to create something nice for them.

I've never respected the creative opinions of people who create nothing. If you spend more time criticising than creating, I can save you a whole lot of trouble now by letting you know that none of us give a shit what you say, so rather than reaching out to tell us, you might as well scream it into your pillow instead. Most of the kids who made fun of me weren't peers whom I looked up to, and they weren't exactly clever either. It was lucky that they didn't bother me much because there would be a whole lot more of them to come.

"

Why would I run
unless a killer was
chasing me?

"

How to Be the Most Popular Girl in School

Being a teenager is all about fitting in but I was increasingly bananas personality-wise while rapidly falling behind in attractiveness too. Some asshole famously once developed a hot/crazy ratio where you've got to be at a certain level of good-looking to get away with being nuts, and my ratio was audaciously out of balance. I started high school (we begin secondary at age 14 and you'll know from movies that we call it high school) with a gap between my two front teeth so big that I could comfortably stick my finger through it. It grew almost overnight, after I'd had an orthodontic retainer fitted to widen my small jaw. To add insult to injury, my mother had already bought my winter coat from the Gap and wouldn't get me a new one, despite corporate branding being emblazoned across the back. Mine were not the kind of parents who bought me shit just for the sake of it. So, I would become known as simply 'The Gap'.

I'd chosen not to continue in the French school system because, by then, the majority of my friends were from musical theatre or dance class and I wanted to pursue the rest of my education with them and in my first language. Besides, I thought the options for English-speaking high schools were 'cooler' and I was growing quite focused on becoming 'cool'. I went to the newly built English-speaking Catholic High School – the one my dad wanted me to attend because of its affiliations with the even greater institution of Heaven. I hardly knew any of the girls there, as most of my friends went to Northern, the godless public school nearer to my house. My best friend, Caitlin, was going to Northern but she only lived round the corner so I figured I could link up with her every weekend and after school.

We'd met in the musical theatre group and clicked in such an easy, familial way. Caitlin was the kind of friend who could come over just to take a nap and it wouldn't be awkward. She was close with my parents and even my sisters looked up to her as a bonus big sis. Caitlin is still my best friend today and she's as funny, tall, blonde and beautiful as she was then. She found me amusing for some reason and took me under her wing as a freckled troll sidekick. I was basically the Danny DeVito to her Arnold in *Twins*. But I'd be fine in high school without Caitlin, right? How bad could it be?

Very bad. St Christopher's was a terrible shock to my French-Canadian system. Athletics reigned supreme and I had no interest in sports. I still don't see what all the fuss is about. Why would I run unless a killer was chasing me? What would be the point in potentially hurting myself to stop a ball from going in the arbitrarily 'wrong' direction? I don't care where the ball goes AT ALL but there are people in this world who will get angry, sweaty or injured to try to make a ball fit into a net. WHY? Don't they realise it's only a BALL?! I'm ambitious, sure, but not competitive. I could care less who makes a ball do more things than someone else can make the ball do. I go to Wimbledon for the atmosphere and Henley for the Pimms.

All the popular kids at St Christopher's were athletic and they found my interest in comedy and musical theatre extra bizarre. None of the quirky tools I'd sharpened were any use to me there. Instead, I was classified as 'alternative' and dismissed. Again, I didn't blame them. I could see that I was an absolute wildcard who was going through a monumentally awkward phase, so I resigned myself to treating this period of my life like a halfway house to focus on academics and sort my teeth out.

It's not that I had a specific bully, there was just a general vibe that nobody liked me. A few years ago, I learned by watching the documentary *Blackfish* that killer whales are so intuitive that they think as a collective. The kids at my high school seemed to have that same ability. Even the ones I'd never had any previous interactions with appeared to instinctively detest me with a singular telepathic consciousness, like the alien Selenites used in H. G. Wells' *The First Men in the Moon*. It was destabilising but I clung on to the idea that my unpopularity had to be temporary.

By springtime, I'd found some acceptance with the other 'alternative' kids who played instruments and smoked weed. I didn't even drink alcohol at that age but these kids liked me, so I liked them. And now, I also liked Pearl Jam, Tool and Blind Melon. I developed a crush on a boy called Luke, who reminded me of

Adam Sandler and who was peculiar because he hung around me quite a lot but didn't fancy me whatsoever. He'd come to my house, go on day trips with my family, have me over to his and speak to me on the phone for hours but, contrary to what teen movies had taught me about boys that age, he seemed to be interested in my mind alone. It was the strangest thing because he was straight and routinely had girlfriends throughout our friendship. In retrospect, I'd have to put it down to that imbalance in my hot/crazy ratio.

The madness of puberty destabilised my values and I started to agree with the many messages I was receiving from the world telling me that the best thing that a girl could be was pretty and sweet. I was neither. It seemed like the more I tried to ingratiate myself with people, the more I offended them. One morning, our school cafeteria was set up to host citizenship testing and I was tardy for class because I'd been helping a lady with directions. When I entered the lesson, I said with a smile, 'Sorry I'm late, the corridors are full of immigrants!' A student took offence at that and it spread quickly around my grade that in addition to being uncoordinated and ugly with bad teeth, I was also an evil racist. But they *were* immigrants. My dad was an immigrant too. I didn't understand why saying it had such negative connotations.

Later, my history teacher assigned a project about the Second World War and I recorded a video for my presentation the way I always did. I loved writing sketches and editing videos. This time, I'd dressed Kerrie as a little seamstress and made her recite a script I'd written about her wartime experience in her sewing circle constructing items for the troops. Then, I'd used one of

Dad's old police uniforms from his many theatrical roles to dress Joanne as Hitler. That's right – Adolf Hitler. I'd even drawn a little mascara moustache on her and used black ice-hockey tape to authenticate the space with an incorrect attempt at a swastika. I taught her lines in a German accent (which she pulled off beautifully, by the way) to explain the timeline of his tyranny and genocide. I presented my film to the classroom and was accused of taking the piss out of the Holocaust. I hadn't been taking the piss! I looked at it as using the resources I had to complete an assignment and tell a story. Nope. Apparently, I was a monster.

The nail in the St Christopher's coffin came during a basketball game against our rivals, Northern Collegiate. My girlfriends from the opposition school invited me to attend with them and while I didn't care about sports, my entire social life was limited to fun weekends with these girls, so of course I agreed to go. We got ready for the game at Caitlin's house, where everyone tied spirited red and black pom poms into their hair and chose cute outfits in the same school colours. I wasn't about to turn up in the Northern section wearing St Christopher's blue, mainly because I had zero emotional ties to the school and I frankly wanted them to lose. I liked my friends, my friends liked me, so I matched them in red and black for our evening out together. Within minutes of us walking past the St Christopher's bleachers to our seats, someone from my school had recognised me and telepathically spread word round that not only was I an obnoxious loser but now I was a traitor as well. Those kids were really, REALLY invested in athletics and my red knee-high socks spat in the face of everything they held dear. Plus, they lost. Whoops.

Being in high school felt like I was starting kindergarten all over again – struggling to learn another new language from scratch. Only this time, it was even harder than French and there was no Tante Claire to teach it to me. How could I become fluent in 'cool teenager'? I'd need to swallow a bit of my personality, speak a whole lot less and, importantly, I had to get a boyfriend. All the cool girls had boyfriends. My self-confidence had reached an all-time low, which is the absolute most TERRIBLE time to choose a partner, by the way. It's akin to food shopping when you're hungover.

The horny teenaged boys were probably kicking themselves because I'd have been such an open goal in that state of vulnerability but, try as they might, they just couldn't get past the crazy, so no one was interested. If I wanted to find love, I'd have to find a boy with rock-bottom morals who'd throw me a bang regardless.

By the end of grade nine, I learned that trying to get revenge on a boy will only result in a sick backfire of self-revenge. By now, I'd met several of Luke's friends and, in an attempt to make him jealous, I started flirting with the least conventionally desirable one. We started sort of a physical relationship, though we weren't officially dating. We were friends who would make out at his mom's house. The sick twist is that Luke wasn't bothered in the slightest and I'd developed strong feelings for this hideous delinquent friend. His gift to me for my fifteenth birthday was a glob of hash oil stuck between two pennies that he had taped inside a card. I'd never used drugs and I wasn't about to start! But

I was operating on the system that if you liked me, then I liked you, so I was smitten.

Even today, some of my grown female friends believe that if they date a loser, he'll be so grateful that he'll cherish them and never leave. This isn't true. Deep down, losers know who they are and with whom they do not belong. A few months into our arrangement, this guy broke my heart by meeting a girl with whom he truly connected. They started dating exclusively and I was out, which is what I deserved. I found it so utterly demoralising to have been dumped by a boy I'd only liked for revenge that I started avoiding my favourite restaurant, Taco Bell, where he worked. It was the Sarnia hot spot where every teenager congregated late at night after house parties. (I told you – we were a quaint town with some trash interests.) So I was genuinely gutted to be missing out on queuing up for Mexican-inspired fast food famous for giving its patrons diarrhoea.

One evening, I was with Caitlin and my original group of girlfriends who rallied around me during this time of grief. Emboldened by their support, we all went into Taco Bell together to essentially cause a ruckus and to laugh in his face. We went into the toilets and sketched a caricature of him 'stealing all the tacos because he's fat' on the mirror in lipstick. On the way out, he marched after us, accompanied by his manager and informed JUST ME that I was banned for life from Taco Bell. My friend Lori argued, 'You can't ban her because you don't even work here.' To which he replied, 'Yes, I do,' and she erupted with laughter, like, 'Hahahaha you fucking loser, you work at Taco Bell!' It was funny, but so mean. I decided pretty much then and there that I liked being mean. It felt a whole lot better than being on the receiving end of any hurt. I was pissing people off either way, so I might as well be in control of it.

Come September, my dad relented and let me switch to Northern High School to be with my friends. I saw this as a fresh opportunity to reinvent myself and, after the tumultuous year I'd had, I was in desperate need of a do-over. My orthodontic journey finally came to an end and having straight teeth had actually changed the entire structure of my face. I started wearing make-up and even let my Natalie Imbruglia pixie haircut grow out. I discovered tanning beds, acrylic nails and was now considered to be borderline attractive. It turned out that being passably 'pretty' was half the battle in cracking the teenaged cool code and I was magically considered less strange. I was assimilating. I carried myself with a lot more confidence and kids who didn't know me just thought I was mean.

I was fifteen years old as I entered the tenth grade and, determined not to relive the hell of my first high school inauguration, I walked around those corridors like an absolute bitch. I never went out of my way to be unkind but if anyone dared to be less than gracious towards me, I came back at them like a lion. I had a very sinister ability of being able to cut to the core of someone and eviscerate them before they'd finished speaking . . .

Lying in wait was another weapon in my artillery: I could sit on an insult while holding a grudge for ages. I remember overhearing a grungy skater-type boy (yes, like the Avril Lavigne song) dismissively call my group of girlfriends 'stuck-up preps' and I said nothing until about a month later when he'd been vulnerable enough to play an original song on his guitar in front of the entire class. As soon as he finished and nervously looked up at us all, I said, 'At least he'll have a hobby in prison.' I thought it was cool to be a mean girl. People were rude to me, so how could I help it if being rude back hurt them more? I'd unknowingly positioned myself as the original Regina George.

Like any pendulum, I oscillated from one extreme to another before eventually landing in the middle. I'd been hurt and I'd been hurtful (more on that later), but by my final year of high school, I was pretty much indifferent towards my social standing. I cherished my friends but was confident enough in my own uniqueness to apply for universities without being influenced by their post-secondary plans. Most of them stayed close to home and close together, whereas I knew that I needed to take more of a risk and try yet another fresh start. I didn't care what I studied as long as I was living independently in a city condo rather than a campus. I just wanted to have adventures.

"

This **happens** all the **time.**

"

How to Let Your Friend's Murder
Define All Your Relationships

I'm deeply suspicious of mutually agreed splits. The likelihood of two people who share children, a house or maybe a pet, or who at the very least have seen each other naked, deciding at the exact same moment that they want to change those existing arrangements is LOW as hell. My own parents divorced when I was 15, which, in hindsight, was pretty great. It was definitely the best move for both of them, though it was initiated by my mother and not at all endorsed by my dad at the time. I think he objected more from a position of ego and logistics than out of any genuine love for my mum, but I could see where they were both coming from. They were never well suited yet married young because my mum was hot and my dad was funny and from Ireland, which was exotic to people from Sarnia in the early 1980s.

My parents each have unique and admirable qualities that I'm lucky to have inherited. I love them both for different reasons, so the stories I'm recalling now are from my limited perspective as they happened in 1998. It's also maybe useful to note that I was a dickhead teenager and somewhat preoccupied by the breakout success of All Saints, the release of the hit movie *Titanic* and Geri Halliwell quitting the Spice Girls at the time. Please proceed with that context in mind and an attitude of fairness with regards to any actions you may disagree with.

Dad probably won't mind me telling you that he called my mother a whore a few times while I was growing up, and he'd probably stand by using that expletive today. I remember walking around the shopping mall with my parents and two little sisters one afternoon, and noticing a man staring shamelessly at my mum's body as we passed. I laughed and said, 'Oh my God, did you SEE that man checking you out, Mom? He looked right at your boobs!' My dad didn't think it was funny. He said, 'Well, people wouldn't do that if your mother didn't dress like a slut.' She was wearing a fitted turtleneck. I watched my mum's expression fall and she quietly sobbed as we entered Toys R Us. A toy store is the right place to get emotional because everyone's crying, so it goes largely unnoticed.

That was a hurtful thing to say and Mum didn't deserve it but here's the truth: everyone's wrong in the wrong relationship. Mum's waist-to-hip ratio (which was one of the attributes that had probably attracted him to her in the first place) was not something that Dad could navigate long-term and in public. And Mum really should have done her research into the values held by Irish Catholic men born in the early 1950s before making a commitment to raising three children with one. They were too different. Doomed from the start. The plan was probably to hang in there and make the best of it but that changed when Mum turned 37 and my grandma died. The loss of her mother was the shock Mum needed to start living for herself but I doubt she was prepared for the misery and chaos involved in divorcing someone stubborn who'd rather stay married.

Mum didn't take divorce lightly so was never going to dissolve her marriage without applying due diligence first. She resolved to give things one last go or 'earn her way out' through couple's counselling which, from my personal and limited experience, is only helpful in the unlikely scenario that your differences are reconcilable but you both lack communication skills. It's a waste of time if you're already able to articulate quite clearly that you don't like each other and that you're unwilling or unable to change. Mum also had her own therapist, who asked that I come into a session one day to give my mother permission to divorce my dad. Even as a teenager, I knew that was pretty fucked up and was like, 'Excuse me, but this feels like quite a co-dependent and inappropriate strategy.' But nobody else seemed to mind, so I went along with it.

For the most part, I liked being treated like an adult. I liked that everybody confided in me and trusted me to keep confidentiality. The therapist told my mum to write a diary of all her memories, thoughts and feelings about the marriage, which I found and read with great interest. It was an absolute violation of boundaries and I'd do it again. I'm nosey like that. That's the trouble with kids who want to be treated like adults – they're only kids.

The whole house walked on eggshells during the separation proceedings. Dad was very hurt and angry. Mum was sad and scared. My sisters and I mostly tried to stay out of the way. We had never been notably dysfunctional as a family before but it felt like we had now unwittingly become part of the *Sex and the City* cast, forced to present the con of a united family while navigating an SJP/Kim Cattrall-stye feud behind the scenes. I could really have done without those final months. My parents had never been particularly affectionate but now they routinely kissed in the kitchen through resentful pursed lips just to show each other up. It was like watching both of them get simultaneously molested. No matter what veneer you whack on it, dissolution inevitably ends up one way – Oasis breaks up, so spare the roadies the tumultuous denouement and just get on with it.

Dad agreed to move out but child custody and financial dealings were viciously acrimonious. He point-blank refused to speak to my mum or be in the same room with her, so that left me to sort out a lot of the logistics with my sisters. In just a few months, Mum lost most of her friends and half her body weight through stress. She shrunk to my sister Kerrie's size, who was ten years old at the time. One might assume you'd look sick after such a rapid transformation but Mum just kinda morphed into a little pop star. It was like living with a white-knuckled version of Ariana Grande. It's actually amazing that I haven't got body issues as an adult because I remember her trying on my clothes and remarking, 'Isn't it funny, Katherine, your jeans are too big for me but your tops are too small!' Yes, Mum. You're a human Barbie doll while I'm 15 with a fat ass and no tits. That IS funny. (My fat ass was ahead of its time and had not yet become fashionable.)

My sisters and I hardly wanted to spend quality time with our dad, which understandably hurt his feelings. I found it frustrating that he was demanding any of my attention at all when I'd never been expected to give it to him when we'd lived together. Once he moved out, I'd only see him if I needed him to pick me up from friends' houses, drive me to the mall or basically ferry me anywhere around a small town without adequate public transport. It was the classic divorce hustle: we'd go to his place whenever we didn't get our way at Mum's. Dad let us eat anything we wanted and he gave us money. One day, in the car, he lost it and said I was selfish for using him. I gently explained that, 'Yes, of course I am, Dad. Because I'm a teenager. That's what we do. We use people.' I wish more dads knew this about connecting with their daughters. I think they've got this idea that we're over at Mum's bonding over scrapbooks and braiding each other's hair when, in reality, we're all just trying to get a ride. From ANYONE. So give us a ride or we'll find some high-school dropout in a 1978 Dodge Challenger to take us where we're going.

It wasn't just Dad who'd waged war against my mother, it was basically the whole town. As I've mentioned, my mum is, like me, the type of spicy individual who rubs freshwater conformists the wrong way just by existing. Initiating the split from my dad gave them more reason to see Mum as a villainous outlier. She was branded with a scarlet letter and I could see that she was disappointed and surprised at the fair-weatheredness of some friends who'd deserted her during such a difficult period. Life became chaotic for everyone but especially for Mum. Dad, by contrast, was regarded as a wounded and eligible local hunk.

My parents have each moved on with better-suited partners so their split was wholly the correct choice but they never became friends and haven't spoken since.

Having watched the whole thing play out, I was sure that I definitely wanted to avoid causing pain or chaos for any romantic partners in my future and certainly also for myself. I decided pretty early on that, in my own life, I wouldn't be breaking up with anyone, ever. I could see that it was too much hassle.

* * *

Trigger warning, there's some domestic homicide now.

Freshly 19, I'd successfully evaded the need to end any of my relationships by cleverly being undesirable and always dumped first. I'd recently started a job in Sarnia's best summer restaurant, where I was often paired on the bar with an older girl called Jessica. All the people who worked there were lovely but Jessica stood out as being the best-liked. She was open, beautiful, generous with her time and took great pride in doing things properly. I admired her 'cool girl' qualities as much as I respected her work ethic. She cared about logging the liquor counts meticulously, always left the equipment clean, was charming with customers and showed me tricks to make the best tomato cocktails. I learned from Jessica that no one is too good for their job and that no one is beneath anybody else. I wasn't in her friendship group but she treated me like her peer when we worked together and that meant a lot to me.

She'd tell me all about the dramatic ups and downs of her relationship, not leaving out any details. Some of what she said was quite private and tragic, but she'd shrug it off or say something funny a second later, the way my favourite confessional comedians do today. She could see lightness in the dark. I loved people who were candid with me. It made me feel valued. Some of the other girls would hide away to have private conversations with their closer friends but Jessica included anyone at the table without bias.

Her on-again, off-again boyfriend was well-known because he was athletic, which was a quality that people in our town admired. I wasn't exactly friends with him but he'd been on dates with a few of my close girlfriends and he acknowledged me enthusiastically whenever our paths crossed. He seemed cocky and not very bright but otherwise nice enough. I'd heard from Jessica that he'd also been abusive, which I found difficult to put together at that age. Surely only monsters are violent towards women and he really didn't seem like one – how could a man have two hugely conflicting personalities? (Drugs, Katherine. Narcissism. But I didn't understand those things then.) After a particularly dramatic incident, Jessica ended things for good and was granted a restraining order against her ex by the courts. I didn't (and still don't) know all the details of course, but she spoke about it at work and seemed genuinely relieved to be moving on.

Soon after, I was scheduled to open up the restaurant with Jessica for lunch. I arrived at ten in the morning to set up the covered patio bar for a private party. Jessica wasn't there but I filled the ice, set all the chairs up, wiped the tables and carefully prepared as she'd shown me. A manager came over a few moments later, holding the landline telephone and looking dubious. 'Your friend says she needs to speak to you and that it's an emergency.' He hovered over me to listen, not because he believed there was any real problem but because I was generally a little shit teenager who was probably lying and had liar pals.

'Jessica's dead,' my best friend Caitlin's voice said bluntly down the line. 'He killed her.' I argued that she was wrong and that Jessica was actually at work. I don't know why I decided that I had just seen her when I knew that I hadn't. I guess my instinct was to protect the idea of what I wanted to be true. I repeated what I'd been told to the manager, who took the phone and headed back into the restaurant, where other staff members were learning the same horrific information on other calls. Dread and confusion spread through the building before the worst was confirmed by police showing up to question Jessica's friends who'd last seen her. There are no secrets in a small town, so when we opened our doors, customers came in already privy to what had happened. Jessica's close friends at the restaurant were understandably hysterical, so many of them went either home or to the police station. The private party did go ahead but it became something of a sombre wake; people murmured quietly for a bit, offered their condolences to any crying staff and left early.

When I arrived home that evening, I recounted the dramatic events of the day to my mother, who'd unsurprisingly already been made aware. She was sick that someone had lost their daughter, and in such a violent attack, but she didn't seem overly shocked. Instead, it reinforced what she already knew: men are dangerous. Having not yet made this connection, I flew around the house in a furious rage, ranting about how the bar should have immediately closed for observance, about how international news cameras would soon be descending upon the town to cover the story and about how wild it was that a young woman we knew was killed by a man we were also familiar with. He wasn't a stranger or a demon or a masked intruder but a person Jessica had once trusted and loved. 'That's how it happens,' Mum answered bleakly. 'If you leave them, they sometimes kill you. No reporters will come. This happens all the time.' Duly fucking noted.

Jessica wasn't my sister or my best friend, and I realise I've centred myself quite a lot here but that's because I'm writing a book and because her life and brutal murder is something I still consider often, nearly 20 years later. I think traumatic events have a way of writing on the canvas of who you are, especially when your brain is still growing. I decided that night in our kitchen that I should be very frightened of men and that rejecting one would be more than just a painful hassle. It could cost me my life.

It was *perhaps* silly of me to think my ex-partners would kill me. But I had a solid framework telling me that it was a definite possibility. I could name two exes now who'd be quite satisfied if I was rubbed out today – of natural causes, at the very least. I suppose it's never ideal to 'scorn' someone. I have ended relationships in my life but I mostly did so in cowardly ways. And it took me about 18 months more than it should have to finish each one. I was afraid. I'd laugh at my own grandiosity and say, 'Get over yourself, Katherine. No one wants to murder you.' But deep down, I really believed that they might. I wish that I had been more honest and courageous in my exit strategies, but I know that I did the best I could at the time and I calculated risk based on the information I had.

Evidently, I'm still alive, despite having truly pissed off some men in the past. My best learned strategy for improvement has been not getting into relationships with hot-tempered, unpredictable characters in the first place. Also, I now remind myself that the vast majority of a woman's ex-partners are not murderers. Though some are. It's tough to know which ones to avoid without offending the rest.

I've tried to speak about my legitimate fears before and been punished for my vulnerability. My medium today is stand-up comedy, so I'll introduce an idea on stage like, 'Men are nature's gun because you're statistically most likely to be killed by the one in your house.' True. But rather than acknowledge the omnipresent threat that many women like me feel, HUNDREDS of men have opted to send me defensive and often very aggressive messages in response. I truly don't understand how saying 'I am afraid' provokes them but the reaction I get certainly doesn't give me any comfort.

As much as I liked to think of myself as an adult from birth, I was a teenager when this happened and it left quite a traumatic imprint that I've had to work very hard to overcome for the benefit of my healthy relationships with men.

Jessica's killer spent just a few years in prison, was then transferred to a 'healing house' and is now free. That's how it works.

"

I was born **curious** and **cursed** with relative indifference to judgement for it.

"

How to Nearly Be in a Music Video

In the autumn of 2002, I moved to Toronto to start the urban and regional planning programme that I'd been accepted into at Ryerson University. No, I didn't care whose permit for a porch extension was successful and I couldn't give a shit where the hospital was built, but Ryerson was situated smack in the middle of the city so it suited my geographic needs. I'd also applied for the journalism and radio and television arts programmes there but was only offered my failsafe. Fine. I loved writing, performance and media but knew that all I needed to pursue those interests was the buzz of a city. I could do the rest without a formal education in it.

My mum drove the three hours from Sarnia to drop me off and help build my flat-pack furniture in the apartment I'd found through an advert on the school website. While I waited for my mystery roommate to arrive, Mum and I went grocery shopping and I was genuinely touched when she bought me a 'going out' top from a nearby boutique. I've never felt comfortable with people buying me things or giving me gifts, but I accepted the gesture as I knew Mum wanted to share a special afternoon with me and that I wouldn't see her again until Christmas. Part of me wished that Mum could stay in Toronto and go to university herself because I know she felt the same way about Sarnia as I did and would have loved to have an adventure too, but we'd definitely had enough of living with each other. We hadn't been getting along very well since my parents' divorce a few years earlier and Mum wasted no time converting my basement bedroom into a second lounge. We both knew deep down that I would never be coming back permanently.

My roommate was called Katherine and I couldn't have dreamed of a more amazing match for my downtown explorations. We bonded straight away and threw ourselves into fun big city life. Katherine was beautiful and stylish; she was studying fashion and dressed the part. In contrast to my mother's respect for my independence and need for distance, Katherine's Polish mother routinely came to visit and to drop off cabbage rolls and Russian salad. One weekend, upon noticing that I was about to pop outside to the grocery store in my pyjamas, she stopped me and said, 'Why do you dress like this? You are a beautiful girl. You could meet husband in parking lot.' I decided that I'd better start making more of an effort if I wanted to win the affections of all the eligible men hanging out by the bakery bins. My mother also thought I might meet a man in a parking lot but her advice was to carry bear spray and a rape whistle to deter him.

I started dressing more like the other Katherine. We went out to clubs, drank cocktails and ate sushi on fancy rooftop patios, and we submitted applications to go on a dating show called *Matchmaker*. The format was that one best friend goes on a blind date while the other watches it unfold on closed-circuit television and delivers running commentary from inside a limousine with the presenter. It's not a bad show. Moments after I hit send on the email, we received a phone call from production asking if we'd come to their offices straight away for a meeting.

When we arrived, they were delighted with us. 'Katherine and Katherine . . . do you look like twin Barbies all the time?' they asked. 'Yes,' I told them without flinching. 'And we call ourselves K Squared.' We didn't but I was a dickhead, so I felt that it was important that we had a branding strategy right off the bat. I'd heard Britney Spears once say that when opportunity knocks, you've got to be ready and I wasn't prepared to let any chance of adventure pass us by in the big city.

They scheduled us to film our episode the following week. Katherine was still seeing her high school boyfriend from back home, so she chose to do the commentary while I went on the date. Full disclosure – I had a boyfriend too but he was in America on an ice hockey scholarship, which is where you basically get paid to punch people in skates and have threesomes with college girls afterwards. It was worth the risk to me. Besides, it was television. I knew it wasn't real.

There are conversations today about the duty of care on reality TV programmes and I can tell you from experience that the entire production is built around protecting the mental health and wellbeing of all contributors, but that's all very new. Nobody gave a shit in 2002, when a channel's idea of aftercare was a taxi ride to the station. That's when I swiftly learned that reality TV was not my forte. I didn't fancy the boy and it all just got awkward. The female producers gave us drinks and nudged me to be more flirtatious, but instead I chose the path of frigid standoffishness and, for some reason, kept mentioning my dad. When it was over, I could tell that I had disappointed them. But I'd also picked up on the entire reality TV hustle. Producers lavish you with praise and affection to earn your trust, then withdraw their sisterly approval when you stop doing what they want. I worried about having let them down for several months afterwards and I felt embarrassed when the episode came out. In his wrap-up interview, the boy described me as being 'good from far, but far from good'. That was a blow and I heard from friends that many of my naysayers back in Sarnia thought I was totally cringe, but I was still glad that I'd tried it. The experience simply proved that I had a lot more to learn if I was ever going to work in television again.

A few weeks later, and having learned absolutely fuck all, I then arranged for K Squared to try out for a national TV show called *Electric Circus*. This time, things would be different. This time, we'd be podium dancing. *Electric Circus* was broadcast on the MuchMusic channel every Friday night from a studio set that was designed to look like a nightclub. Cameras cut back and forth between popular music videos and live dancers wearing very little clothing. Growing up, we didn't have access to Wi-Fi or pornography, and it was common knowledge that this is what all the boys wanked to in desperation. It was exactly the kind of project I was looking to get involved in.

K Squared chose incredible club outfits for our big audition. Fuzzy Kangol caps, low-rise mini-skirts that might as well have been denim belts, crimped hair and barely there boobs engineered up to our necks using sports socks in our bras and masking tape. On the short walk to the downtown studio, a car pulled over and I saw that the driver had his pants open with his erect penis in his hand. 'How much?' he asked sincerely. Katherine and I burst into fits of laughter while trying to run away in the snow, using our stilettos like tiny ice picks for traction. This was great. The public was wanking already! We'd definitely be getting the (no fee) job.

When we arrived, we didn't even have to dance to get the gig. The producer, John Paul (still my friend), liked the look of us and, from there, we started turning up every Friday night to dance for all of Canada. We met fun people and I actually got to do a few extra bits for the channel. They let me (and a few other select dancers who were comfortable doing so) speak every now and then, like when I was on my podium and the presenter put the microphone in front of me and asked, 'Got a message for the people partying at home?' and I said, 'Toronto needs affordable housing!' which was important and true, though probably made for some challenging wanks at home.

With my politically charged professional non-paying dance career going strong, I applied for bartending jobs around the city and was invited for several interviews. We didn't have smartphones back then, so I'd have to use a map to figure out how to get to each restaurant on time, like when Tyra gave the models go-see challenges on *America's Next Top Model*. En route to my first appointment, I took the subway in the wrong direction, then back in the right direction but one stop too far, then I got too cold walking for ages. My legs were also sore from the many weekends of having dropped it like it was hot for my fans. My pet peeve is being lost and the frustration that comes with it is one of the only things that actually makes me cry. So, like generations of white women at traffic stops before me, I sobbed in the street. Tearfully, I kept going, squinting through the snow flurries to make out the road signs. Then I saw it. Like an orange beacon of respite. Finally, a landmark. A warm, iconic brand that called out to me to come inside out of the storm. I practically ran to the front door, pushed it open and, with gratitude, shook the snowflakes off my hair and jacket. A cheerful brunette wearing orange shorts skipped towards me and shouted, 'Hi, babe! Welcome to Hooters!'

She introduced herself as Emily, pointing to her name tag. It said 'Emily'. Her story checked out. Emily was beautiful and innocent-looking – just a friendly girl-next-door type with long tanned legs. I noticed immediately that her boobs were small like mine! It's a misconception that you need massive breasts to work at Hooters. Sure, it's not exclusively about your personality and academic credentials, but in those orange shorts the bum can't be discounted. The brand is mostly aiming for a cheerleader vibe.

They want sweet young women who are generally physically fit and from a variety of ethnic backgrounds. (Blonde does help during pageant season, though.)

I explained to my new friend Emily that I was late for an interview and I asked for directions to the pub I couldn't find. 'Forget that!' she said. 'If you worked here, you'd already be at work by now.' This girl was a logistical genius. She called the manager over, who shook my hand and offered me a job. Which I took. Brilliant. Life is really easy when everyone says 'yes'.

I appreciate that there is great privilege in walking into rooms and gaining access to your dreams based solely on the way that you look, but bear in mind that my goals were all quite pathetic. The double-edged sword of being a young woman at that moment in culture was that I'd learned to value being well-liked and pretty, which meant that my realm of dreams included aspirations like 'dance on a block of wood' and 'work at Hooters'.

There's absolutely something to be said for getting in the door but the glass ceiling for this type of wilful exploitation is low and sinks lower with age. Positioning yourself as a 'pretty young thing' means living like an avocado: you're delicious for a very brief window of time so you'd better also be cultivating more substantial, imperishable skills and characteristics for the future. But at least for the moment, I was armed to the teeny tits with 'Yesses'.

A month into the job, I'd become popular with the other Hooters girls and was thriving in their friendly, collaborative environment. So far, I had everything I thought I'd ever wanted. I had real friends, a fake tan, independence, cashflow and a Friday night gig dancing on TV for teenaged wankers. University wasn't difficult, so I popped in there every once in a while to achieve a barely passing grade on written exams. I felt busy and fulfilled; I didn't have a long-term plan for my life but I had confidence in the choices that I was making and loved the potential that Toronto offered me. I couldn't imagine being stuck in a dormitory eating pizza in a study group, which is how I envisaged regular campus life to be. I was living authentically and feeling stimulated by more and more interesting, open-minded friends and acquaintances all the time.

* * *

That spring, in what should have become a viral meme for entitlement, I convinced the other Katherine that we should audition to be in the next big Sean Paul hip hop video. I'd seen the casting call for 'Get Busy' stuck to the door in the *Electric Circus* dressing rooms and I loved that Director X was attached, who was then Toronto-based and known as 'Little X'. He'd made Sisqo's 'Thong Song' video, a bunch of Usher hits, had worked with R Kelly (yikes), Rihanna, Foxy Brown and even Destiny's Child. What I lacked in self-awareness, I made up for in early 2000s hip hop fandom – this was the music I loved. Ever the dutiful wing woman, Katherine came on board for another K Squared adventure and got to work on our outfits.

On the day of the audition, we turned up at the designated hotel and joined about a hundred stunning non-white dancers along the corridors outside a conference room. I tugged on my pink marabou feather tube top, noticing that most of our competition were very, VERY curvaceous by comparison. Some wore kneepads and running shoes while they stretched into full splits against the walls. There were a lot of Jamaican flag-print leggings, gold chains and vibrant dancehall looks. The women seemed to know each other, chatting and laughing animatedly with a confidence that showed they'd been here a thousand times before. There were only a brief few seconds of politely bewildered silence as K Squared teetered in, looking like a couple of extras from *Clueless*. Katherine had gone for a pretty pink 'bling' aesthetic with our trademark pointy heels. Skinny and afraid, it was as though we'd been booked for *Toddlers in Tiaras* and wandered in to find our mums.

While she was applying another coat of pastel glitter lip gloss as we waited, the reality hit Katherine, who nudged my arm and whispered, 'How about I pretend to go to the washroom, then you wait a few minutes and follow me outside?' But I was no quitter. I convinced Katherine that we should see this through, as it would be character-building, if nothing else. I promised her that it would be quick and painless. I could see that producers had been taking girls into the conference room in groups and then sending them back out within minutes. We hadn't heard any music, so it's not like they'd been making people dance. 'They'll just want to take a look at us,' I soothed, 'like our *Electric Circus* audition.'

A large black man wearing sunglasses bellowed 'K Squared' and called us inside. Katherine shot me a panicked look, probably regretting that she'd ever participated in the absolute indignity of this ridiculous nickname. Once through the door, we were confronted by a boardroom table filled with the ten most underwhelmed and disappointed men I'd ever seen in my life. Little X wasn't actually there – THANK THE LORD – but his producers patiently went through the absolute charade of letting us try out. They asked how old we were (so not R Kelly's team, then), what kind of music we listened to and then – either to punish his colleagues for some earlier infraction I knew nothing about, or maybe just out of sheer curiosity – one of them turned on some reggae music and asked us to dance. It's never appropriate to be the only person dancing in an otherwise static boardroom, and in daylight no less. But I was all in, so with a haunting smile on my face and courage in my heart, I managed to wiggle around on the spot. Katherine stood frozen, looking like she might cry, so I thought I'd ameliorate the situation by grinding against her a bit, just to bring her into the energy of the performance. I wondered when they'd stop the music but it just kept going. By about minute three, I was running out of moves, so I pulled up an empty chair and incorporated it into my freestyle choreography, like I'd seen the Backstreet Boys do.

This was a massacre. These innocent men were being harshly oppressed by structures of white privilege right in front of my eyes – the audacity I had, to think for a minute that I should be subjecting them to my freestyle. Wow. When the song finished, I ended in a back-facing squat, looking at them over my shoulder, still smiling. Admirably, they didn't laugh. They didn't react at all. Instead, they compassionately thanked and dismissed us. Katherine practically shoved me out the door. 'Why did you do that?!' she gasped.

I'll tell you now what I told Katherine then: I did it because I saw an opportunity and thought, 'Why not me?' I would always rather try something fun than back out for fear of someone having a negative reaction. I was born curious and cursed with relative indifference to judgement for it. People ask me all the time whether stand-up comedy scares me and yes, a lot of my experiences have been frightening, embarrassing or ill-conceived, but each has also served to prepare me for the next one, and sometimes the next one goes well. If you're really that consumed by the fear of failure or criticism, then you'd better hide yourself away for eternity. If not, people in your school will talk shit about you, people in your office will talk shit about you, people on the internet will talk shit about you, *Variety* magazine will talk shit about you – it's all the same and it is all inevitable. Nobody cares about your bad reviews more than you do, so you might as well just get over it.

I look back on that day as a fun memory. Katherine and I went to lunch afterwards; we had cocktails and laughed ourselves out of our chairs. I still smile fondly every time a Sean Paul song comes on the radio. I turn to my daughter and say, 'You know, I was nearly in this music video,' and that's true. I made it all the way to the top one hundred.

In the words of Samantha Jones from a season five episode of *Sex and the City*, 'If I worried what every bitch in New York was saying about me, I'd never leave the house.'

"

I seemed to be getting in trouble just as often as I was being rewarded for my sharp tongue.

"

How to Be Crowned
Miss Hooters Toronto

For a busy young woman shortly after the turn of the century, Hooters was the best job ever. The schedule was unique because every week, you'd request time ON rather than time OFF. That way, management could see who was available for any given shift and strategically choose girls based on how busy the restaurant would be. You'd make the most money during major sport events, weekends, evenings and working on the patio in the summer, so the best girls would choose those shifts and usually get them. If you weren't well-liked or weren't a strong server, your boss might only stick you on one or two slower lunch shifts and you could expect to earn much less. We tip at least 20 per cent in Canada because we're not animals, so naturally the more you sold, the more you earned.

This system meant that you could take a holiday or have time off to study for exams just by leaving your requests blank. There would usually be enough girls eager to cover you. Equally, this created major financial and logistical incentives to working hard and performing well – being at the top meant getting the shifts you wanted. And that meant being rich.

Admittedly, I'd expected that a lot of the Hooters girls would be useless bimbos; some were and those came and went. But the ones who lasted were smart, funny, fascinating, collaborative and truly special women, many of whom remain my close friends today. It may sound like the old cliché of 'I was stripping to pay for my medical degree', but it was like working in any other sports bar, apart from there were no male waiters to contend with. Plus, it had the added twist of making you feel like a bit of a celebrity because the brand is world-famous. Sure, it may not be the perfect feminist environment for a variety of reasons but I cherish the memories I made there – both good and bad.

I got the opportunity to meet women from all over the world while working at Hooters. I flew in a helicopter, became a corporate trainer and even helped open their new UK location. Hooters even saved my life. One day, my friend Jordan spotted an odd-looking mole on my leg while we hula-hooped on the patio in our orange shorts. She suggested I go to the dermatologist, who confirmed it to be stage two melanoma, which required immediate surgery and could have spread.

The managers mostly hid from us upstairs in the office and we ran things ourselves. It was a matriarchy. People often assume that Hooters was a seedy environment, but we had a very mixed clientele. (Kids eat free at weekends!) Sure, some absolute serial killers came in now and then but we grew to tolerate them as regulars. Fish & Chips was a young guy in his early twenties who carried a hidden camera inside a thick CD case. We told him all the time: 'We know you're filming us and you're not allowed.' He'd deny it so we just learned to avoid passing or congregating near his table for too long. Some regulars asked for permission to take photos and we'd happily oblige. One man in particular collected them in a book he carried but there didn't seem to be an ounce of sexual gratification in it for him. We might as well have been antique coins or baseball cards, and he visited once a week to update his catalogue. But then, on the other hand, I was convinced by a balloon fetishist who rang the restaurant to take loads of pictures of myself with inflated Hooters pantyhose. I was stalked for weeks by that man, turned up on balloon sex websites and learned all about inflatophilia.

Rarely, men would ask to buy a girl's sweaty sports socks or dirty underwear, but no one ever asked me. They targeted girls like Carrot, whose name was actually 'Karen' but she mumbled the day her name tag was being made and just answered to it forever rather than correcting the mistake. That's what you get in the real world for being softly spoken. You've got to either grow a backbone or be prepared to live as a root vegetable. Carrot was so beautiful and sweet that she never got told off. She didn't say much, so she never offended anyone. Sometimes I thought about what my life would be like if I were Carrot instead of myself. My lips were too thin and my face was angular, not delicate and pretty like Carrot's was. I could see that my favourite celebrity women, like Britney Spears, Jessica Simpson and Beyoncé, were rewarded for being gentle and innocent. Meanwhile, I seemed to be getting in trouble just as often as I was being rewarded for my sharp tongue.

I loved to draw and took pride in creating the chalkboard designs around the restaurant every day. I would turn up early just to make them extra special. Hooters loves a tacky slogan, like 'Girls Are Flattery Operated', and I had to fit the lunch specials on there as well. Our location had a roof terrace and people would ask how to access it no fewer than ten thousand times per day. To help them, I put a chalkboard indicating towards the stairs with a uniformed Hooters Girl going up, next to the words, 'Don't Be a Fattio, Climb To The Patio'. (I wouldn't write that today but it was 2003 and I hadn't heard of the Fat Acceptance movement.)

Miss Hooters Toronto was our annual pageant and it was a hilarious concept to me. We'd transform the restaurant by moving tables and erecting a stage along which the girls who chose to put themselves forward would strut in different bikinis, answering questions like, 'If you could be any wing sauce, what flavour would you be and why?' The desired answer was 'hot sauce' with the odd 'BBQ – because I'm spicy AND sweet' added in for good measure, but I admired the girls who'd deviate from the norm and give responses to make each other laugh. It was a sure-fire way to confuse the crowd but never seemed to negatively impact your actual scores. I loved it when my friend Athena said, 'I'd be honey mustard because I'm a ubiquitous condiment with infinite potential!' I chose to be 'mild' on account of how 'I am bland and well tolerated by sensitive Europeans.' Pageant season was the best because groups of us got to visit different Hooters locations to cheer on their girls, to do photo signings or just to build brand recognition caddying golf tournaments and putting on charity car washes.

You might reasonably assume that the prettiest girl or the one with the biggest boobs would be crowned the winner. Wrong. Or at least, that didn't happen in my case. Each restaurant location's aim is to send its strongest representative to compete in the next heat of Hooters' pageants and to pose for the provincial posters and national calendars. It's a whole fun branding recognition thing. I wasn't the most beautiful by any stretch and I won Miss Hooters Toronto at my branch in 2003 as an A-cup without breast implants based on my PERSONALITY ALONE.

You're as shocked as I was. Hooters has a reputation – I know. And yes, to work there in the first place you've got to fit a certain image. But the judges were a mixture of the owner's friends and regular customers, and they liked me for my banter. The boss appreciated the hard work that I put in and he knew that he could trust me not to misbehave on the trip to Florida for the winners' photoshoot. He even liked that I had been on television and that I could interview so well. (In your face, shy, beautiful Carrot!) I considered it a win for the strange girls everywhere and thought that maybe I was blending in as one of the nice pretty-enough ones after all.

* * *

I felt like Kate Moss on the flight to meet the other winners in St Petersburg (the Florida one, not Russia). I'd fake tanned to within an inch of my life and packed the entire collection of K Squared bikinis that Katherine and I owned between us. When I gathered my bags after landing and walked out into the airport arrivals area, I immediately identified my group by the orange glow that shone off them in their low-rise Juicy Couture velour tracksuits and giant sunglasses. I love how much men unanimously hated the sunnies we wore in the early 2000s. You know, the massive ones that covered an entire socialite's face? Everyone's boyfriend said they made us look like insects but we persevered and wore them anyway, probably to offset our whisper-thin eyebrows. What a time for fashion. I approached the girls and introduced myself, complimenting Krista, a girl from Ottawa, on her sunglasses. She took them right off her face and tried to give them to me. That's the level of benevolent sisterhood we were working with.

The other girls were stunning. Calgary, Alberta, had been very canny to send HOT TWINS as their entry. Everyone was super friendly and it felt powerful to move around the city in a huge, intimidating pack of what looked like a glamorous Canadian hen-do.

When it came to the actual photoshoot, I wasn't the best. Most of the other girls had modelled in swimsuits before and were a lot more photogenic. I preferred to be moving and talking on camera, and I'm still that way now. Having my picture taken makes me nervous. I look annoyed and self-conscious in the final image, and I didn't even place in the top five at the Miss Hooters Canada pageant that followed. I loved the adventure but needed to think of a way to refine it so that it worked better for me. I wondered whether there was a version of events where I could speak and keep my ass covered.

It struck me that at every pageant level the hosts were rubbish – random men wearing cheap tuxedos reading out the same tired questions and struggling to breathe in ill-fitting bow ties. As the local winner in Toronto, it was my role to crown my successor the following year but because I loved the hustle, I asked my manager whether I could host the pageant instead. 'PLEASE,' I begged him, 'I'll wear a nice dress and do a respectful job.'

I was touched when he agreed because he said he thought I was funny and talented. Now, I had been sleeping with him for a few months but I swear that was just a coincidence. Throughout my life, I've never had sex with anyone I didn't genuinely have feelings for. This is an illness. It would be far more prudent to use sex as a currency with which to manipulate men but I never figured out how. If you're of a similar sensibility, you've got to be extremely careful about who you fuck because, like it or not, you'll be emotionally attached to them for a few months, minimum. I'm pretty sure the first official encounter we had was the day I walked up to the office and said, 'I'll suck your dick if I can leave early' – half joking, half serious. I appreciate how incriminating this sounds, especially considering he was technically my superior at work, but I fancied him and it was totally my idea so he shouldn't be blamed. We were never an item and he was sleeping with other women from work too.

Looking back, I find it funny those of us sleeping with the manager considered ourselves to be the clever ones in our arrangements. From our perspective, this poor husk of a man-whore had to contend with being passed around a bit when all he probably wanted was a nice relaxing wife. I imagined this dehydrated fellow in the impossible position of working out the schedule with so few girls available, his shift calendar like a chalkboard out of *Good Will Hunting*. As my feelings for him developed, it did start to sting – not literally, though, I was routinely tested – when I heard about him with other girls or saw them flirting, so I stopped having sex with him. We remained friends and he didn't put any pressure on me to continue. After all, he had loads of options and I was just one less girl leaving early to worry about.

Besides all that, he absolutely changed my life by green-lighting me to host the pageant. I loved it. I asked the girls meaningful questions on their turn around the stage, like, 'Alicia, where do we keep the bin bags?' This truly tested the contestants' commitment to teamwork, as the useless ones never took the trash out. Everyone agreed that the energy was better with a woman hosting and my investment in the girls was genuine. I adored having clothes on and getting to hold the microphone. It gave me a sense of authority that I cherished and I took it as my very serious responsibility to deliver a well-rounded, entertaining show. I did a bit of rudimentary 'crowd work' while the girls disappeared to the ladies toilets for their outfit changes and I used my 360 perspective of the restaurant to call out the men trying to peek inside with cameras. I was mistress of ceremonies and security all in one. A customer had been eating chicken wings and decided to start pelting me with moist towelettes at one point. Picking one up, I tutted, 'This is the closest you'll ever come to getting a woman wet.' Sure, it was a simple beginner's slam but the crowd erupted and I was hooked.

One afternoon after my pageant triumph, I heard on the radio that Pamela Anderson had spoken out about cruelty to animals and highlighted seal clubbing as a violent injustice. This news inspired me to make a topical chalkboard, which read, 'Club Sandwiches, Not Seals', not realising that an indigenous Canadian family were having lunch in the restaurant while their son was receiving cancer treatment at the nearby hospital. I found out because they made a formal complaint with corporate headquarters that a Hooters Girl had racially profiled and abused them. I hadn't noticed them as another waitress was looking after them and I was so focused on my art, nor was I aware that seal meat is the main staple of traditional diets in almost every Inuit community.

Because this was classed as 'political terrorism' by corporate office (and the addition of the sick child probably did me no favours), our owner flew in the following day to read me the riot act. I remember he was shorter than I was because he screamed inches from my face in the middle of the busy restaurant and had to look up at me to do it. 'Why, Katherine?! Why do you have to be such a fucking FREAK all the time?!' he bellowed. My eyes filled with tears in agreement and my face burned with shame and remorse for having accidentally kicked an ethnic minority family while they'd been down.

This owner, who'd liked me enough to crown me queen of his chicken restaurant only a year before, had slowly been withdrawing his approval as he got to know me better. 'Shhhh . . . not everybody gets it,' he would say, pretty much half the time I spoke. I'd taken it too far this time and, evidently, he didn't like me at all anymore. He fired me that day but I was back within a couple of weeks under caution. I promised to be quiet and not to make chalkboards, and I wasn't allowed to host pageants anymore. I tried my hardest to be a 'good girl' and stay under his radar because I loved my job.

I'd been toying with the idea of trying stand-up comedy, not just because I liked watching it on TV but also because I passed the biggest Canadian comedy club chain every day while on my walk to Hooters. Yuk Yuks was a stone's throw away from the restaurant and I'd read on the sign outside that they hosted an amateur night. I thought I could pop on stage there and use it as a sort of exorcism to get my audacity out in an environment where it was considered appropriate. I owe the start of my stand-up career to Hooters.

"

I can't imagine
the hell of living
one's entire life in
boring earnest.

"

How to Get Started in Comedy

Funny people were always valued in our house when I was growing up. It's difficult to explain how important a sense of humour was because that would be like justifying sleep or a working toilet – they are simply necessary for a civilised existence. I cannot remember a time or a scenario where people weren't having a laugh, either generally in conversation, as a coping mechanism or just for the joy and camaraderie of slagging someone off.

I've met people who are utterly lacking in any sense of whimsy and, honestly, they creep me right out. God, they're a nuisance to be around. I can't imagine the hell of living one's entire life in boring earnest. I've encountered people who say things like, 'Oh, I can't watch comedies, I hate that genre.' And that's the quickest way to tell me that you're a tiresome moron. That's not to say we must all share the SAME sense of humour, but to have zero interest in being amused makes you – and I say this with the greatest respect – a dangerous fucking psychopath. I'd rather spend the day with a mountain lion. At least then there'd be a story to tell if I survived.

I've known people to get offended by jokes about serious or sad subjects, but I think they misunderstand that comedy isn't meant to take the piss out of that stuff in any way that exploits pain or makes it worse. It's meant to be trauma-ADJACENT to lift you up out of the darkness.

Growing up, Mum's impressions of my alcoholic grandad transformed him into quite a warm, almost adorable character. 'Goddamn broads!' she'd snarl, lurching around the kitchen, shaking her fist with an imaginary cigarette in the opposite hand, 'That's the ugliest goddamn baby I've ever seen!' Those had been his first words as he held me after I was born – very funny and he hadn't been wrong. That story always made me smile and taught me that I'd needed to be able to laugh at myself from my first day in this life. Having a sense of humour isn't only about making jokes, it's about knowing how to take it on the chin with grace and resilience.

I'm routinely asked in interviews, 'When did you know you wanted to be a comedian?' and 'How did you get into comedy?' The underwhelming truth is that it just sort of slowly happened and, mercifully, continues to happen. When I was little, I wanted to please people and become a doctor. I was effortlessly academic and thought that saving lives might be the most heroic use of my time. I envisioned myself as 1995's newly released Baby Doctor Barbie (because girls are too stupid to know what a paediatrician is), wearing cocktail earrings, an impossibly short skirt and royal blue court heels while cradling newborn black, white and Asian triplets. The box came with one of each and also a cute pink stethoscope. Whatever I was going to do, I knew that I definitely wanted to be the boss and that I wanted to be wealthy and glamorous while doing it.

Most of our television came from the local Detroit channel feeds, so I had access to a stellar comedy line-up that included the sketch show *In Living Colour*, *The Cosby Show*, *The Golden Girls*, *The Fresh Prince of Bel-Air*, *Def Comedy Jam* on BET and Martin Lawrence's namesake sitcom, *Martin*. That was one of my favourites and from about age nine I used our family camcorder to film my sisters acting out spec *Martin* episodes that I had written. On reflection, they were deeply inappropriate but I loved making them and my sisters always took direction well.

Sometimes, Mum would let me stay up and watch *Saturday Night Live* or *The Late Show* with David Letterman. We'd laugh at the opening monologues and she'd say, 'You could do that,' but I never paid much attention. Mum pointed at everything and suggested I could do it. Letterman's Canadian sidekick, Paul Shaffer, offered little quips and played intro music or riffs on the piano and she'd say, 'You play piano, you could do that!' She'd notice our prime minister refusing to send troops into Iraq and say, 'You could do that!' Singers, builders, architects, inventors, astronauts – Mum insisted that I could do it and become it. She was eerily silent during the televised bikini rounds in the Miss America pageants, though, and whenever my dad watched organised sports. Mum had ambition for me while maintaining a realistic outlook regarding my short legs.

Thanks to my many experiences in plays, dance recitals and school poetry competitions as a child, I'd figured out from a young age that an audience could only be comfortable when the person on stage was comfortable. All performance is actually a great demonstration of and lesson in consent, because it's immediately clear when someone is nervous or not into it, and that's excruciating to watch. Being confident is half the battle. What I might've lacked in grace or talent, I always made up for in reckless abandon. My great friend, comedian/writer/ actor/legend Roisin Conaty describes it beautifully when she says, 'Comedy is all about the sizzle, not the sausage.' If I'd decided to do something, I always gave it my best sizzle, and I wanted it to be funny. That's why I cast my sisters in all my school assignment films – I wanted to give people a show, and I liked the challenge of taking mundane information from the curriculum and presenting it in a fresh, surprising way. I think a lot of what makes comedy special is the element of juxtaposition and surprise. A lot of the time, I'd been mostly amusing myself, so I was pretty comfortable on stage whether people laughed along with me or not.

* * *

I'd watched her on television but it was during my first year at Ryerson University that I properly discovered Sarah Silverman's stand-up online. That's when something just clicked. I loved her and, for the first time, fantasies entered my head about what writing and performing an actual comedy set could be like. Living in a big city after growing up in Sarnia where everyone was in your business made me feel anonymous, so I thought I'd have nothing to lose by putting my name down for the comedy club's amateur night. I figured that it would be a rush to get up on stage and indulge my demons, with the added bonus that I could then get back to my main goal of becoming a 'nice' lady like Baby Doctor Barbie. It could be the perfect creative outlet.

The procedure for signing up to amateur open mic was a lottery. The night before, you rang a number that went to voicemail and you recorded your full name, asking for a spot. You then had to ring back after 4pm the following day and listen to the new recording for your name to see if you'd been picked for the show. I got lucky on my very first try.

I was allocated a five-minute spot and spent an hour before the show throwing up. I loved feeling nervous because it wasn't an emotion that I got to experience very often and it gave me an unfamiliar rush. My mouth went dry as I delivered my planned set (about my school, my life in Toronto and my favourite TV show at the time, *Dr. Phil*) to a small room of college boys who were waiting to go on next and a handful of punters who'd paid maybe three dollars to watch newcomers bomb. It wasn't great and I'm certain the sparse crowd could smell the fear on me. But still I liked it. Nothing else had made me feel so shit and so alive all at once.

I rang again the following week and put my name on the list to do it again. I wanted to get better. As the weeks went by, I absorbed the general vibe of the room and I received a ton of unsolicited advice from the other amateur comedians, which actually made me much worse. I got terrible for a while, subscribing to the climate of comedy at the time by talking too much about race and putting myself down on stage. I loved comics like Chris Rock, Joan Rivers, Adam Sandler and those I'd seen as a child on *Def Comedy Jam*. I was drawn to the edginess of their jokes but lacking the understanding of the sophisticated misdirection that made their work compelling. So I floundered trying to copy them and ended up coming off as crass instead.

My stuff was really offensive without being funny because I hadn't learned the nuance needed to tackle contentious issues with the context and respect they deserve. I was like a toddler running around with a steak knife. I think that early on, a lot of comics panic about not getting laughs so they settle for any reaction instead. Shock is a reaction. Disgust is a reaction. Nervous laughter is . . . a form of laughter. I'd take whatever I could get and struggled embarrassingly to find my authentic voice. I'd take months off to gather my thoughts and then go back to the club, still dreadful.

Stand-up comedy was just a hobby and in my mind, that's all it would ever be – but still, I wanted to be good at it. The adrenaline it delivers is certainly addictive. I was in university full-time and working at Hooters as much as ever, so the weekly five-minute spot didn't disrupt my 'real life' at all. It was just another thing I was doing.

A lot has changed. My legs haven't.

Above: I still make this face. Mum still has this face.

Left: Two weeks old.

Below: Five months old. Smiling for the haters who say I've had a nose job.

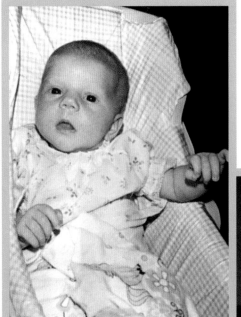

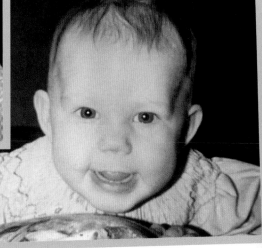

Right: FASHION POLICE: pre-stylist, dressed as a Christmas tree skirt.

Left: I had bars from an early age.

Above: When they told us most of the future jobs we were training for would be taken by robots…

Happily camouflaging into Mum's eighties blouse and kitten collar.

Comparatively livid to be now saddled with the responsibility
of entertaining two sisters 24/7.

All icons wear power suits.

A pic worth chasing this cat barefoot through the streets for.

Lost my appetite coming in second place.

Early nineties T-ball: the pinnacle of my athletic career.

Left: Another power suit as Joanne tries to outshine me in my own dress.

Right: Still, I showed her the good life – playing in autumn leaves.

Left: 1988, livid at Mum's sexual incontinence as we met newborn Kerrie for the first time in hospital.

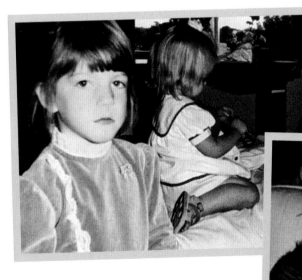

Right: Coming round to the idea of having another sister.

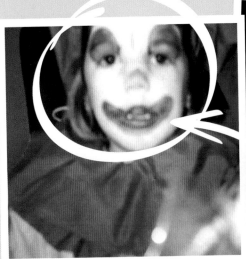

Early auditions for an invite to Jonathan Ross' iconic Halloween parties.

Below left: Dorth and her immaculate pussy.

But because I was new and different – therefore surprising – I was given a few opportunities to participate in open mic competitions and sometimes I'd be paid a small fee to travel to a suburb with a better comic and do a short set before they went on. I was learning. Eventually, the manager added me to a list of up-and-comers who were given extra stage time to practise on Wednesday nights. It was a step up from the amateur night and it meant that I started to make proper friends with other comics on the circuit.

There were two other women in my fast track group – Rhonda and Lianne. Rhonda talked about being overweight (she wasn't) and joked about how her boyfriend never bothered to remove her clothes entirely, just took a boob out, played with it and put it back, for example. Lianne talked about being overweight (she wasn't) and had a dark bit about men always asking to ejaculate onto her glasses, and how if she were a superhero, her power would be that she could be wiped clean. Her uniform would be a trash bag. Whenever I referred to myself on stage, I mostly giggled and talked about what a dumb, useless girl I was. Even my hero Sarah Silverman did an awkward little laugh early in her career. I guess we did that because maybe we felt like we had to undermine ourselves to be likeable. Sarah Silverman was adorable but that didn't stop her being called 'the Queen of Mean'. The boys certainly aren't assessed by their perceived kindness on stage as much because while they're expected to be funny, women have to calculate how to project good-natured appeal too. You only have to look at how Jo Brand started her career with the stage name 'the Sea Monster' to understand just how self-deprecating women had learned to be.

We made do, though, and soon I started doing more alternative gigs for free in pubs and even got to perform at fellow comic Andrew Johnston's bespoke comedy night, Bitch Salad. His tagline was 'comedy for bitchy queens, by bitchy queens' and he put it on at an iconic theatre in Toronto's queer district. Doing Andrew's show was a lightbulb moment. For the first time, I felt capable of telling the truth on stage and of relaxing into an actual comedy conversation. The audience didn't seem hostile like many other crowds had been. When I think about it now, the difference might've been that this community already believed that women could be funny, so I went on without feeling a need to apologise or qualify my existence by putting myself down to gain their approval. Another woman on the bill did her entire set as Little Richie from one of my favourite nineties TV shows, *Family Matters*. It was super niche, but she fully committed because it was meaningful to her and everyone else in the room trusted her on this basis. It killed. Rhonda joined two friends, Lilly and Mike, in a drag trio called 'The Cheeto Girls', who performed hilarious pop star song parodies.

Before Bitch Salad, I'd only ever seen the things I loved – celebrity, divas, Britney Spears, reality TV – being mocked or sneered at. This was still the era where paparazzi could chase people down and sell their pictures to tabloid magazines for their mean-spirited articles. My favourite weeklies featured a back page where comedians were employed to write quickfire nasty captions underneath images of my favourite celebrities. It aimed to be roast comedy but it lacked the all-important layer of love for the subject matter. I had a genuine love for pop culture but I'd never thought that what interested me might also resonate with other people. Andrew's Bitch Salad night showed me that I didn't have to follow a trend or put myself down – that I could joke about anything that mattered enough to me, as long as I learned how to do it well.

"

I became
obsessed by
teacup **dogs.**

"

How to Waste All Your Money on Designer Dogs

Up until the mid-1990s, we'd been a cat family. My parents captured Eddie, a wounded kitten they'd found in the street, while trick-or-treating with me on the night of my first proper Halloween in 1984. Eddie was missing his tail and had been through the sort of trauma that turns you into a violent asshole with zero desire to be domesticated. For this reason, I can't exactly call our actions a 'rescue' but more of a well-meaning midnight abduction. We held this feral creature hostage for nearly three years and all I remember is that Eddie tried to kill me every single day of his life until he was able to escape one night while under my grandfather's idle care. I respected Eddie. He exploited my grandad's only weakness – alcoholism – and grabbed his opportunity for freedom by darting out an open door. That, or my grandad got rid of him. If the latter is true, no one's ever told me and I'm pretty confident they would have fessed up to it by now. In any case, Eddie was swiftly replaced by an absolute princess called Roxanne.

She was a gorgeous snow-white Turkish Angora whose gentle demeanour charmed anyone who came to the house. Roxanne was famous in the neighbourhood, where she roamed around making friends without ever running off as she was proud to remain our trophy cat. Also, Roxanne was trans. The vet said she was a boy when he neutered her but we knew that she wanted to live as a glamorous woman and respected her true spirit from the start. I know what you're thinking – maybe he was just gay, and honestly, how dare you. I think it's sad that you don't know the difference and I hope you use this moment as an opportunity for personal growth. You're cancelled.

Innocent of the horrors of Eddie, my sisters were born knowing only Roxanne. It was the first of many times I bore the brunt of my parents' first try while the younger girls got to experience the smooth, refined second try. Roxanne enjoyed nearly a decade of bliss before my dad ruined things by bringing home Jake.

On that day, I could barely see the sheet music through the usual floods of tears pouring from my eyes while I dutifully practised the piano in our basement. I hated that I played piano. I hated that everyone in the house could hear me making mistakes. I hated that my mother weaponised my talents against me by collecting me late from chess club and saying things like, 'You are naturally more gifted than your sisters and that's why we are forcing you to work the most and try the hardest.' This was my poisoned chalice. If I were a ten-year-old child today, I would simply refuse to play piano and initiate a standoff until my parents relented but in the 1990s, I was unaware that I could opt out of following the rules. If no one's told you that lately, it's true – you are allowed to challenge authority. But I didn't know that as a little girl. Sometimes I think they didn't want to let women in on the hotly guarded secret of imaginary barriers, but I'm encouraged to see how many of us have found our voices and since figured it out.

My music teacher only egged on my mother further by taunting, 'The Chinese aren't afraid to make their kids work!' I didn't understand why I was being punished for my advanced fine motor skills and for not being Chinese, but I tried my best not to disappoint anyone and seethed with rage as I banged on the keys as hard as I could.

Despite the aggressive noise of my angsty minor scales, I could hear that my dad had arrived home early and that my sisters were laughing with him in the garden. 'These fucking pricks,' I thought to myself about a couple of innocent toddlers, 'squealing in the winter sunshine while I'm stuck down here like the Phantom of the Opera!' My dad called for me to come up, so I decided to martyr myself and stay glued to the piano I hated instead. With complete disregard for my commitments, he called again. And again. Finally, I abandoned my music theory and stomped up the stairs to find out what couldn't wait. That's when I saw Jake, a four-year-old medium-sized cocker spaniel gleefully tearing around the backyard and wrestling my sisters to the ground by their mittens. Already, Jake was doing God's work.

I loved him. He was blond and beautiful like my mum, who hovered nearby looking suitably concerned. My dad definitely hadn't discussed getting another pet with her. This was a spontaneous decision to adopt a work colleague's dog, deemed unsuitable for their home 'because he kept attacking the kids'. In fairness to Jake, that family had teenaged boys who'd put on their ice hockey gloves and let him bite their hands for mutual entertainment. Dad assured us he could train Jake out of the delicious habit of mangling mitts but soon that responsibility fell to my mother, who prioritised toilet training him first. Night after night, Mum stood in the garden clutching reward ham optimistically, waiting for Jake to do his business in the preferred location. Roxanne, who'd become a counter-top cat since Jake's commandeering of her formerly floor-level territory, gazed out scornfully from her window ledge, remembering a more sympathetic time before the chaos of man.

Eventually, Jake improved but he would still wee in the house if he felt like it. He wasn't massive but was certainly big enough to destroy things. Shoes, toys, books, orthodontic retainers, blankets, birthday cakes – if left unattended, Jake could reach and demolish it all in seconds. The general ordinance of the house became, 'Hide it, or Jake will have it,' which certainly encouraged us to tidy our rooms a bit more as we got older. He was, however, a very competent musical theatre performer. Jake joined us at our tri-weekly rehearsals for the local production of *Annie* in 1996, where he studied to play Sandy, her loyal canine companion. Strategically, the stage version sees stray Sandy abandoned when Hooverville is raided, whereas in the film, he makes it into Daddy Warbucks' mansion with Annie. That meant Jake wrapped early and hung out with all the kids backstage while the rest of us finished the show. It also avoided the laborious and impossible task of achieving a rags-to-riches makeover on a dog every night.

Mum loved Jake the most. She sang to him and cuddled him and took him on long walks because stunning blondes are stronger in numbers. I'll bet Jake absorbed some of the street harassment Mum was used to weathering on her own. Whereas I liked Jake fine but he was honestly too exuberant for me and came with a lot of trouble. I thought maybe dogs just weren't my vibe.

One Easter Sunday, we arrived home from church and waited in the garden for family friends to arrive for brunch. Easter was actually lit because it made my parents really happy to host their friends and those friends always brought chocolate bunnies and gifts for us. North Americans know how to commercialise a religious holiday. Kerrie by this point had reached her pinnacle of Disney glam. At five years old, she wore ballgowns daily. More often than you'd expect, she'd emerge from her bedroom stark naked, adorned in just the plastic costume jewellery set from 1994's iconic 'Pretty Pretty Princess' fantasy/roleplay boardgame. The object of this was to move around the spaces collecting rings, necklaces and bracelets, culminating in the final prize of securing the grand tiara – basically, the Meghan Markle Project. Kerrie chucked away the dice early doors and committed to wearing the entire collection of *bijouterie* – tiara et al. – and rejected any gameplay. Her tiny bare legs looking like they could buckle under the weight of fake gold and gemstones, she'd swan around the house soaking up admiration until the Canadian cold coaxed her back into pants.

Suitably, on this particular afternoon, we all wore pastel dresses, Easter bonnets and frilly white socks with matching patent shoes. Kerrie's dress was the most 'Kerrie' of all, obviously, complete with a tulle petticoat for fullness and elbow-length pink satin gloves. She loved making an elegant first impression. However, just as our guests arrived, my sister bounced towards the gate and accidentally ran through a huge pile of Jake's wet poo, sliding forwards and then off her feet entirely. Every inch of that little girl made contact with the hot excrement as she hit the dirt. To this day, I have no idea how she got so much of it on her. I suppose it didn't help that she made several attempts to lift herself out of the mess, slipping back down harder and at a new angle each time. Or the fact that Jake had spotted the gloves and was now yanking on the left one and wagging his tail, absolutely delighted to be involved in his favourite game. Eventually, Mum was able to snatch Kerrie up, physically unharmed but wailing dramatically as I'd seen her train herself to do into the mirror more than once before. Showered and straight into the Pretty Pretty Princess set, she was allowed to do the egg hunt naked after that.

It's the classic 'dogginess' of dogs that wasn't for me. Jake smelled like death. He needed his anal glands routinely expressed by the groomer and would scoot himself along the carpet afterwards. He'd shake his head whenever he got an ear infection, spraying a cocktail of medicine and pus across my bedroom. He antagonised the cat, ruined my stuff, caused my mother to drop to her knees and scream things in the night like, 'I refuse to live in an animal's toilet!' and, worst of all, he landed better roles in the local musicals than I could. I loved him but I didn't 'like' him all that much and the feeling seemed mutual. Jake was Mum's dog.

My freshman year of university was the first time that I'd lived without any pets at all and after two years, I couldn't take it anymore. I missed them. It was 2004 and American socialite Paris Hilton was newly famous and often photographed carrying tiny chihuahuas in the crook of her arm like they were living handbags. They weren't just regular small, these were micro-mini, teeny mouselike apple-headed little creatures whose defiance of nature raised many important questions about the flouting of ethical breeding standards. The most pressing one being: 'WHERE can I get one of those for myself?!' They were adorable, easy to keep clean, always dressed immaculately and swiftly became the go-to status symbol for shallow little bitches like me. But they cost thousands and I happened to be poor and saving up for a boob job. Typical.

Nevertheless, I became obsessed by teacup dogs. I imagined fitting one with a tiny hoodie and cradling him at my desk in my English class, toting him through the mall, kissing his little lips, never letting him touch the floor and basically being best friends forever. I now wonder whether some of this was the result of being the first generation to approach childbearing carefully and critically. Did young women born in the 1980s start treating sickly puppies as babies because their ancestors would have all had human children by the same age? It's troubling.

But what's more troubling is that I eventually found a lovely woman in a Mennonite community nearby who apparently missed the memo on the teacup dog trend and agreed over the phone to sell me the runt of her shih tzu litter at a discount for being 'too small'. Sucker! By then, I'd done loads of research into exactly what size a puppy needed to be at eight weeks for its projected adult size to remain below 3lbs and this wee boy was tracking perfectly. She told me that another girl was interested so whoever got there first could take the puppy. Immediately, I threw my landline phone receiver across the room, printed off a map to her village (if you don't understand, ask your parents) and set off in my trademark pink velour Juicy Couture tracksuit. The boob job would have to wait.

Two hours and eight wrong turns later, I reached the farmhouse and was let into a tidy kitchen, where I laid eyes upon the absolute smallest dog I'd ever seen in my frivolous young life. He was smaller than I imagined he would be. Too little, I worried. As this hamster-sized pup tentatively crawled out from under a muslin cloth and shuffled towards me, I wondered whether I was making a terrible error. I did that a lot in my twenties: identified bad choices in real-time as I followed through and made those mistakes anyway out of politeness. Like the time I agreed to pose as an older producer's girlfriend and travel to California with him under the guise of 'holiday' for a work trip that I wasn't being paid for. (Though I did draw the line when the TV company suggested I stay in his hotel room.) Or the hundreds of occasions when I laughed at a stranger's off-colour jokes so they wouldn't feel embarrassed. We've all sat through terrible haircuts silently calculating how long it would take to grow back – then tipped. I'd committed to making this mistake too and hoped that this would be the time I got it right.

The woman scooped this puppy up easily in both hands and his entire jet-black body disappeared in her fingertips. His little wet nose poked out from between her thumbs as she presented him to me and I struggled to find his face beneath the fur. I held out my palms and she carefully parted hers to slip him out, like she was passing me a handful of sand. He was SMALL like the length of an iPhone; SMALL like an empty loo roll; SMALL like the actual wad of cash I gave her to pay for him. He cost 500 Canadian dollars. That's 15,000 dollars less than Paris Hilton's dog. Comparatively, it was still a fuck tonne of money to me. But here's the hustle with teacup puppies: their cost of sale is only the beginning.

I called him 'Biggie', after American rapper and songwriter Christopher Wallace (RIP) because I liked the juxtaposition of it and I also liked the New York gangster rap scene. Biggie became so much more to me than a trendy accessory. He was the absolute most important person in my life. He didn't act like a dog at all. He smelled of delicious cherry lip gloss from always being kissed and carried so close to my face; he never barked; he was easily trained to do little wees on an indoor toilet mat in my condo so I didn't have to take his little bladder outside too often; he slept on my pillow and he taught me to be gentle. With such a fragile guy around, I learned to make slow and considered movements, to watch my footing wherever I walked, to speak softly and to sleep stock-still so that I never disturbed him. He was so special and handsome.

Looking after Biggie transformed me from being a bit of a brat into a softer and more premeditated person. Sure, I loved adventure and independence but found that I enjoyed those things even more as a young single mother. My heart burst with love for him and he was pretty indifferent to everyone apart from me so our relationship became very intense and co-dependent. And then Biggie got sick.

It started with little ailments. Digestive issues, eye problems and, after about three years, Biggie just started to look old. I couldn't put my finger on it; he just got less confident walking on uncarpeted surfaces, testing the floor as though he might be stepping into a lake. He shook more often and his tongue started sticking out all the time. Public admiration turned into mocking and I'd notice people pointing and whispering, 'OMG, what's wrong with that THING?!' His eyes got cloudy and his balance seemed off. Again and again, I brought him to a vet, who ran expensive X-rays and treated him for ear infections that he didn't actually have. Over the next year, my expenditure crept up well into the thousands but, by that point, I'd have sold my right leg to fix Biggie.

Biggie came to England with me when I moved but one afternoon, after about a year in London, he had a minor seizure at home and I pleaded with the vet to investigate what was actually wrong. I was 25 at this point and heavily pregnant. I had absolutely no money but took out a loan to pay the vet whatever it took to help my dog. I explained that I certainly loved this dog more than my partner and maybe even more than my unborn child and that saving him was absolutely paramount. This is the wrong thing to confess to a charlatan.

It's not worth me getting sued, so I can't name him, but if anyone privately asks me, I'll tell you how much I hate this idiot. The vet I stupidly trusted ran more and more tests, saying each time that he couldn't really interpret them and that I needed to pay even more so that he could consult with a specialist. As my dog got sicker, the results remained inconclusive. Looking back, I'm sure he knew what was wrong.

By the time my daughter was born, Biggie could barely walk, he'd lost weight and stopped eating entirely. He was only five years old and basically catatonic. In a fit of mama rage, I walked to the vet, pushing Biggie in the pram and with my newborn daughter strapped to my body in her carrier. The situation had reached a crisis point and I was done waiting for answers. I demanded they give me his entire file. I brought those documents to a different vet a few miles away. The moment this new doctor clipped Biggie's X-rays up on the light, he saw the problem.

'I'm so sorry,' he said. 'This would be obvious to any student of mine from across the room. This dog has very little brain left. It's very clear.' When he pointed it out, I saw it too. He told me that teacups are prone to hydrocephalus, a congenital condition where fluid builds up in the skull. If diagnosed early, it can sometimes be resolved by surgically inserting a shunt but that this case had progressed too far beyond that and the prognosis was fatal. I ugly-cried all the way home. You'd think that would have caused alarm but people are less bothered by a young mother's public meltdown than you'd expect. The same vet kindly offered to come put Biggie to sleep at home in his own bed (my bed) a couple of days later, following another seizure. His paw print was taken and pressed into a stone made with his ashes, which sits on my dresser now.

The bereavement period was shocking. Losing Biggie was the first real pain I'd ever experienced and it took me almost a decade before I could even speak about it. Without Violet as a distraction, I think it's possible I'd have ended up losing my actual mind from the grief. It hurt so viscerally that I wanted to run away from my body to escape it and it still hurts to think about now. But over time, I've just learned to think about it less often. He was my very best dog ever.

I hate feeling sad. I can't stand it so I'll do anything I can not to bother with it at all. That's the main reason why I've never watched *The Revenant*, *Moonlight*, *The Color Purple*, *Dead Poets Society* . . . basically anything that moves people. (The Oscars are a very confusing time of year for me.) I've grown to trust that distance from any traumatic event is always promised and comes with waiting patiently; I think disassociation gets a bad rap and is a pretty decent way of dealing with grief. Comedy's great for it too. You know how TV and film depictions of therapists often show them using puppets to communicate with bereaved children? Swap those puppets for jokes and that's how to deal with me. God bless it.

I have four other dogs now (maybe five by publication) and I have to admit, I have extra fondness for the littlest ones. They're all small but none are as delicate as Biggie was – thank God. The trouble with pets is that they don't outlive you. But you can do yourself a favour and try to adopt the most hearty and ethically bred ones you can find. Always insist on getting a look at one of the parents, definitely don't order a dog online and please don't prioritise breed or size. It can cost you more heartache than you can afford. Personally, I struggle every day not to get more. I want to become an old eccentric woman with crystal chandeliers and a menagerie of tiny manicured dogs in pink diamanté collars. I want to drink champagne with Paris Hilton, wearing our Juicy tracksuits and laugh about the fake tans we used to get. But deep down, I know the dogs I've got are enough and I need to stop. Ultimately, I'm just searching for another Biggie, but I know I'm just chasing my tail.

"

I'd seen a **hundred dicks** before I ever saw an up-close **vagina.**

"

How to Get Plastic Surgery

My sister Joanne grew breasts before I did. I'd spotted them getting bigger as I entered high school flat-chested while she, not yet a teenager, started wearing a bra. I chose to believe she was using padding until the day Mum took us to a Backstreet Boys concert in Toronto and I could no longer deny their mocking existence. She'd tied a handkerchief around her body as a top, which, apart from the knot to hold it together, was completely backless. It was obvious now that Joanne had actual boobs because if there'd been a way to fake this kind of natural busty aesthetic, I'd have figured it out first. I had layered a padded bra AND my padded bikini underneath a low-cut tank top. I'd also used bronzer to cheat a fake cleavage by strategically shading my bony clavicle. Still, mine were just a blatant attempt at breasts while my little sister had the real deal. It was an outrage.

I had accepted that most of the girls my age had developed ahead of me and I assumed my body was just youthful and that I'd eventually catch up. By that logic, I'd probably live longer than they would, remain fertile well into my fifties and be the last to get wrinkles. (That last one has come true.) So it was okay that my friends had beat me to breasts but being leapfrogged by Joanne meant I definitely had a very serious genetic problem. Mum had massive boobs for her frame and not the saggy liability kind that cause people back pain. Mum's boobs absolutely looked like perky round implants and I remember her routinely defending their authenticity. She's the type of person who would have just been honest about them being fake, not that it's anyone's business, but they weren't. They were just incredibly commercially acceptable-looking boobs. Where were mine?

Our trademark family vaginas are like that too, though it took me till I was 35 to know this. Girls don't really see each other naked that often growing up. Or at least, I certainly didn't see anyone naked and if I did, I wasn't looking up their crotches with a torch. We aren't swinging them around in locker rooms or at house parties, or flashing them at strangers in car parks the way boys do with their willies. Unless you watch porn, girls mature with nearly no reference of what other vaginas look like. I'd seen a hundred dicks before I ever saw an up-close vagina. And I only saw that recently while watching Channel 4's *Naked Attraction*. If you haven't seen it, *Naked Attraction* is a British dating show where real single people agree to go on national television to judge or be judged by their genitalia alone. The weekly contestant doing the choosing eventually gets to see the potential suitors' faces but not before they've had a good long look at the dicks and fannies first. It's illuminating and the format is very body positive. The idea is to say, 'Look! There's no wrong shape or size! Everyone's different and that's normal!' which is true . . . But my reaction was more like, 'What the hell is up with these vaginas?!?!'

I'm sorry for what I'm about to write because I know it isn't 'woke' and saying it out loud has offended and bewildered people in the past, but it's true, so: my vagina is genuinely stunning. I might've grown up thinking I was more beautiful if anyone had bothered to tell me sooner but at least I know it now. I wish all women felt that way about the part of their bodies that modesty tells us is an unpleasant secret. I sort of wish mine was on my face.

I'd been confused many times before by vadges in pop culture. Like when Eugene Levy's character in the *American Pie* films tells his son, 'It looks like some sort of underwater plant, doesn't it?' Wait, what does? That baffled me. Or when Lauren Conrad was upset with Heidi and Spencer for calling her 'beef curtains' on the dramatic season three of MTV's *The Hills*. I couldn't conceptualise exactly what they were cruelly making fun of her for. My vagina is basically invisible to the naked eye. As a teenager, I used to think that maybe I was missing something or that mine was an anomaly. What I have now learned thanks to *Naked Attraction* is that mine isn't weird at all. It's actually the only thing about me that's considered 'textbook'. It's actually called a 'textbook vagina', meaning 'well thumbed through in college'. NO! I guess it just means that's what a standard one looks like in books – tucked away, not too anatomical. I suppose you would call it 'demure'. It figures that all my weird qualities are displayed for everyone to see on the outside and the one very ordinary thing I have going for me is imperceptible.

I've not got long left with it in its current state. I expect to have more children and who knows? It might hit a wall soon so I'd better rush myself into a plaster cast – and quick. The social platform OnlyFans seems to be a big money-maker for people looking to monetise nudes nowadays and I feel like I've got to make up for lost time by advertising my hidden normalcy. I'll say 'Look! You all thought I was strange but I'm typically, unremarkably, quintessentially TEXTBOOK!'

What has my most 'textbook' quality ever done for me? Sweet fuck all. Meanwhile, being unusual has bought me a house. It's such a shame that many of us spend so much energy trying to fit in.

I'm aware that my approach towards advertising my ordinary vagina isn't ordinary at all because I've been punished for discussing it. One sick evening that I'll forever regret, I was back at Mum's for Christmas and happened to casually mention to my sisters what I'd learned about my textbook vag. Joanne was at the table and this was my chance to get my revenge for the Backstreet Boobs. 'Yeah, I have that too,' she said. Kerrie confirmed her own vag as being textbook as well. My stepdad was in the kitchen with us, because we didn't see any reason to rudely exclude him from our conversations and, without thinking, he piped up with, 'Everyone in your family has that!' meaning my mother of course but definitely sounding like he'd examined all my extended female relatives naked. Poor Abe. Mortified, he blushed and retreated to the dishwasher. But that's how I found out that the women in my immediate family have identical vaginas. A sobering lesson for me on why some things are better kept private. The breasts, however, skipped me entirely. Kerrie spent many years studying as a ballerina. She's tall and thin but even SHE ended up with bigger boobs than mine.

In my teens, I resolved that I would one day move from my small town to a big city and have breast implants. Not exactly the Michelle Obama childhood story but nevertheless a worthy individual dream. They were all the rage at the time and there was even gossip that Britney Spears' parents had signed a consent form for her to get a boob job at age 16.

Inspired, I asked Mum if she would consider paying for my implants and she confessed that when she'd met my dad's family, she'd resigned herself to one day paying for her children's nose jobs in the event that we inherited his ancestral bump, but that she wouldn't condone any 16-year-old getting breast implants. 'Fine,' I said, 'so you'll pay for my nose job then?' Mum declined on the grounds that, 'Sorry, Katherine, but your nose just isn't bad enough.' (*ENOUGH?*)

Journalists have asked me, 'Katherine, how can you have said, done, dated, or believed (BLANK) and claim to be a feminist today?' The answer is because I was a little culture sponge and I didn't have a crystal ball with which to gaze upon the future. The turn of the century was a very peculiar time to be a young woman, dominated by a hypersexualised faux brand of 'girl power'. We were doing the best we could, but many like me got swept up in the purposeless belts and exposed thongs.

I've always been fascinated by both the science and culture of cosmetic surgery. And I've openly discussed it and been transparent about contemplating having procedures, so people can be forgiven for assuming that I've had more surgery than I've actually had. As I started to become more well-known in comedy, doing roast battles on TV and such, the subject of me looking very glam and 'done' often came up. We exaggerate in comedy and I have zero objection to being the punchline of anyone's proper joke. I've always been honest about lip fillers, Botox and my general interest in cosmetic tweakage, so that swiftly translated to 'Katherine is 100 per cent fake' in the context of any comedy diss. I've even capitalised on that joke myself by suggesting that, due to the existing amounts of plastic in the ocean posing a health risk to turtles, I don't meet the criteria for being buried at sea, etc.

It's fun! What strikes me, though, being on the receiving end of many accusations related to my appearance, is that the vast majority of the population feel a gross entitlement to comment on the way a woman looks. Print and digital media will do this thing where they publish photos of you from 15 years before and compare them to current pics. NOBODY looks exactly the same as they did over a decade ago! And what irks me is they lack the expertise to comment on procedures knowledgeably in the first place. If you're going to make assumptions, AT LEAST will you learn the difference between Botox and fillers first?!

For a start, I didn't have my incredibly talented make-up artist or money for hair extensions and beautiful clothes a decade and a half ago. My face has been changed slightly by injectable fillers but also because of gravity. Plus, I'm older and fatter than I used to be. I drink wine now! The *Daily Mail* should ring my mum and ask to get their hands on some of my ultrasound photos to really help them crack the existential case of 'What is time? And what biological impact does it have on cellular turnover in humans?' It makes me laugh because it's so dumb. If I'd had a nose job or anything else, I would just say it. Not because I feel that strangers are owed an explanation but because I am a shameless delinquent who thinks transparency helps people to understand the realities, limitations and dangers of this growing trend for cosmetic intervention. I just treat people the way I would like to be treated, and I would very much like for the Kardashians to tell me exactly what type of dark sorcery has transformed them into the most striking coven I've ever seen. I've been to see a couple of their dermatologists but these men are smokescreens for what's really going on. 'Hey guys, here I am getting a facial at Dr Ourian's!' That's nice, Kim, but WHO is doing your ASS?!

* * *

By my second year of university in 2003, several of my friends had lip injections and breast implants. Not just girls from work but girls at school, at *Electric Circus*, everywhere. Plastic surgery was normalised and aspirational; certainly nothing to deny or to be ashamed of. I was hard-working and well-liked at Hooters so I was getting all the best shifts and had saved a tonne of money, which meant I could just about afford to do it too. Though I resisted getting surgery at first, deciding it might be a bit 'on the nose' for a Hooters girl to have fake boobs. You certainly didn't need them to be successful there and remember, I'd already been crowned Miss Hooters Toronto in the annual pageant as an A cup!

My plan became to wait until my time at Hooters was over to get breast implants but as the months passed, I never wanted to leave. By this point, I'd seen enough good and bad examples of surgery, but none as formidable as my friend Kate's. When she walked back into work seven days after her procedure, I decided then and there that I couldn't wait any longer and that I had to visit her doctor. Her breasts were soft, perfect for her frame and looked totally natural – not bolted on under the skin like a few I'd seen before. I was impetuous at that age. Within minutes, I'd gone from firmly putting off surgery to ringing Kate's private clinic from the break room to book my consultation.

It was still dark when I crept out of our condo so as not to wake Katherine on the morning of my breast augmentation. I wore pale pink pyjamas and clutched the pillow I'd been instructed to bring to soften the bumps on the car ride home. I'd booked a taxi to the clinic and the driver complemented me on being a young woman with such a great work ethic to be heading to my job before dawn. 'Well, it's my passion,' I told him. 'Literally my dream job.'

In the eyes of an older cosmetic surgery nurse, 20-year-old women must look like children. I turned up all thin and fresh and probably had the loveliest little breasts, but I was still in the habit of throwing my uniqueness away to become this idea of what I thought was better. I often wished that I was less odd, less curious and that my caustic sense of humour would take a day off. I had fun but I wasn't sure of my place in the world and I hated disappointing people. I was definitely getting breast implants for myself but I can't deny that I also hoped they might help people to react more positively towards me. At that moment, I was just a dumb girl with a sharp tongue but I would walk out a grown woman with a boob job.

The nurses gave me a hospital gown and socks to change into and asked for the name of my chaperone who'd be taking me home. Following a general anaesthetic, they won't let you leave alone in case you're still high and wander off to a casino or something. I said that my friend Jameson would collect me and it struck me for the first time that I didn't know any of the Hooters girls' surnames. These were my confidantes, my closest girlfriends (apart from Katherine, who had school commitments that day), but we never had a reason to learn each other's full names. Only a select few of us even knew Carrot's real name! I was too embarrassed to confess the truth, so I gave the nurse a fake last name and hoped that they wouldn't give Jameson the third degree about it.

The doctor arrived to draw markings on my chest before surgery and I felt completely at ease. It wasn't until I lay on the actual operating table that I started to cry a little, briefly considering my potential obituary: 'Stupid Girl Dies Getting Frivolous Boob Job – Next of Kin Oblivious to Surname'. But I didn't die. What felt like seconds later, I woke up feeling happy and fully alert. (I know the drugs make some people puke but I react brilliantly to an anaesthetic.) I sat up to sip a ginger ale and overheard my doctor greeting another patient in recovery behind a curtain. 'You're a rock starrrr,' she slurred. 'You look just like Bon Jovi.' He did but this lady was mashed and laying it on thick. She gushed about how much she loved her new boobs. That's when I remembered, 'OMG, my boobs!' I threw off my blanket and looked down at the bandages which held actual cleavage. I wouldn't properly be able to see them for a while but I was thrilled that my very own breasts finally existed.

Jameson arrived with ice lollies and they let her straight in without an ID check. I felt so awake and pain-free that we decided to forego the cab and walk back to mine. We exchanged surnames. Recovery was relatively easy and, in the days that followed, I mitigated the pain in my chest by reminding myself, 'This would hurt more if it was inside my face.' Imagining that kind of inescapable tender swelling so close to my brain is how I decided never to have a nose job. I healed quickly and immediately loved my boobs – LOVED them.

I realise that as a flawless role model, my ethically responsible duty now is to set an example and say that your body is not a trend and that there are better things you could be spending your time and money on than cosmetic surgery – but it would have been unrealistic to expect me to believe that at the time. I'd been overexposed to Chernobyl levels of pop culture. The truth is that getting breast implants was a positive experience for me and I've never regretted them. They made me feel as though my body was more balanced and greatly improved my self-esteem.

In a perfect world, I would have been born 100 per cent comfortable in the body gifted to me by the universe but this was not a perfect world: this was the early 2000s and we were comfortable with a giant python being draped across a pop star's abs while she sang about being a slave. 'Nipplegate' saw Janet Jackson cancelled and slut-shamed for allowing her right breast to be revealed, even though I'm pretty sure Justin Timberlake was there too. As a culture, we hadn't even begun to discuss mental health. Women's bodies and actions were scrutinised on the cover of every magazine and in many conversations, which is why plenty of people on television, or even in your circle of friends, have had cosmetic surgery but choose not to advertise it, and that's fine. It's a deeply personal choice. I don't even think the culture of objectification has improved that much. We've just got better at concealing it. Funny that . . .

I've actually been considering having my implants removed because I have an autoimmune disease which we'll never really know whether it's related to having foreign objects in my body or not. Either way, we've had a good run and I made the best decision that I could with the information that was available to me at the time.

* * *

On a roll, I went back to my same trusted cosmetic surgeon for lip injections. He did a consultation and quoted a thousand dollars! I couldn't believe how expensive it was for a small syringe of temporary filler that would disappear within a few months. Undeterred, I lay back in his office chair, clutching a stress ball as he attentively and expertly injected my lips. He made lots of tiny jabs, layering the filler and firmly pulling it along my mouth through his fingers but I couldn't feel anything because he had used a numbing solution. Afterwards, I was obsessed with the result. My lips were swollen but the shape was beautiful and they looked natural. I was on the road to becoming quite stunning, actually. I'd had basically zero top lip before the treatment and now I looked like a small child had smashed a brick upwards into my face. Gorgeous.

When it faded away, a very dodgy new Hooters girl suggested that I go see her friend for a top-up. This girl's lips were awful but I figured lip injections were way less risky than breast implants, so why was I spending top dollar for an actual surgeon when, by my estimation, any idiot could do a fine job from their basement?

My close work friend Athena went with me to the appointment to investigate the possibility of having her own lips done on the cheap. In hindsight, I am utterly amazed that the many red flags that followed didn't raise either of our suspicions. First, we were following a map that had been scribbled on the back of a napkin to a residential address. Upon arrival, we were asked through a chain across the door whether we 'had the cash' and were subsequently led down a staircase littered with cats towards a woman's makeshift home office. I forget her name but I do recall she wasn't wearing gloves.

She greeted us warmly in an Eastern European accent and invited me to sit down in a chair already occupied by a rabbit. 'He's my office bunny,' she explained, as though that made any sense whatsoever. She picked up the rabbit and plopped him back on my knee once I'd sat. The cost was 400 Canadian dollars but she insisted this was 'permanent' filler. It didn't occur to me to question the brand, what the product was made of or what made it last forever. I foolishly assumed there were only good types of lip filler and that when she disappeared into the closet, this lady was collecting certified, clean equipment. She re-emerged with the needle and told me to take a deep breath as she plunged it into my bottom lip. It stung and she didn't have the same repetitive technique as my other doctor; she just pushed in a bunch of fluid once, then withdrew and did the same on the other side. Top and bottom. I had just four long jabs in all. I found that strange, as I'd had about 20 little injections before and that doctor had spent a long time studying and manipulating each additional amount. This lady finished up and proudly offered the word, 'Juicy?' Then she asked Athena whether she should add more filler. I swiftly interrupted, 'Don't ask her! You're the doctor.' She corrected me with, 'Oh, I'm not a doctor at all.' Great.

Athena had seen enough and decided not to take her turn that day. That evening, I went out with the girls after work, where I was drinking Bloody Marys through a straw. The top right side of my lip got really itchy and swelled so I rang the lady's mobile number but she didn't answer. She didn't answer the next day or the day after that but I blamed myself for using the straw. Maybe I wasn't meant to do that and I'd ruined my lips forever. She was right – the filler was permanent and I've since discovered it was silicone, a product medical professionals no longer use for the purpose of lip enhancement.

Now I get filler injected BY A DOCTOR about once a year or so, just to even the wonkiness out in my smile. It's not ideal but I was lucky to have trusted a real doctor to perform the surgery that really mattered, rather than agreeing to be put to sleep in a basement by a cash-only amateur. Things could have ended up a lot worse for me.

I worry that secrecy leads to a lack of understanding about the potential medical severity of these procedures and the need for regulated, decent practitioners. Besides, people will find a way to get what they want no matter how many times you try to point them in a more worthy direction so they might as well have all the facts to make the most informed and empowered decision. Officially, I don't advocate hurting yourself to change the way you look. Every single procedure hurts a bit. I hate to think of my daughter clutching a stress ball with tears streaming down her face while anything breaks her sweet, perfect skin. But ultimately, that isn't up to me. So you can bet your fake ass I'll at least be keeping her away from any laymen with a home office in a petting zoo.

"

My family had expected me to be successful, so I'd grown up fully expecting the same.

"

How to Skip Town for Good

I got sick when I first moved to London in 2007. I was nearly 24 years old and, for the first time, I had absolutely nothing constructive to do. I'd had so many hobbies, interests and friends in Toronto but my then-boyfriend wanted to relocate to London and I said I was up for it. Secretly, my plan was for him to go ahead to the UK while I stayed back in Canada and found a new place to live.

We'd actually met in a comedy club, which is where the warning, 'Ladies, whatever you do, DO NOT date the comics' comes from. I got on pretty well with him for the most part but cracks were starting to show in the relationship. Every few weeks, I'd get drunk and tell him how much I hated him. I never remembered saying any of it but he'd wake up very hurt and recite all the venomous words I'd spat at him back to me. I'd listen, stunned by Drunk Katherine's honesty and courage. She was normally the kindest drunk person ever! She'd make friends and lavish praise on everyone we knew, but for some reason, she had nasty words for him exclusively. I'm the toxic person in this story and I acknowledge that it's a terrible way to treat someone. I felt badly about it but I'm not a mean alcoholic – I just didn't like this guy anymore and drunk me managed to figure that out long before sober me noticed.

I was captivated by him in the beginning because he was different to all the boys from my town. He was stimulating, older, smart, funny and always told amazing stories, many of which later turned out to be either exaggerations or full-blown fantasies. The lie that I believed for the longest is that he'd been walking down the road with his ex-girlfriend's dog when it darted off into traffic after a squirrel and was hit by a car. The dog lay on the road injured and a huge celebrity got out of the vehicle to apologise. 'That man,' he said, 'was none other than . . . Canadian retail giant, philanthropist and theatrical impresario, Ed Mirvish.'

It now seems such a niche and implausible scenario that the legendary proprietor of Honest Ed's Famous Bargain House in Canada could've possibly been behind the wheel on that fateful afternoon. He would have been about 85 at the time – that could easily have been any old man! Do people even drive at that age? Wouldn't he have had a chauffeur? In retrospect, it's a hefty accusation to hoist against a beloved institution like Honest Ed Mirvish. Or maybe there never was a dog to begin with. I'd get lost in a variety of brain puzzles like this one during our relationship but I definitely subscribed to the 'Honest Ed Killed My Dog' narrative for an embarrassing number of years. The genius of it is that it can be neither proved nor disproved.

During the months of our Canadian courtship, I tried to end it a few times unsuccessfully. He'd have a charming counter-argument or he'd get upset and I'd bottle it. I struggled with confrontation so when he mentioned moving to London, I figured the best way to get out was to wait until he was an ocean away and then fake my own death. If that didn't work, my back-up excuse was to announce that I was a lesbian. That's offensive from a minimum of ten different angles today but in the early 2000s, I think it made a fine and impenetrable defence. In the context of that era, 'I can't be with you. I'm a lesbian' avoids the gentleman feeling inadequate because it renders him simply TOO MANLY to fuck. I wouldn't even have to prove it by dating actual women because I was already dabbling in stand-up comedy so I'd just need to get a smart blazer and everyone would be like, 'Ah, makes sense.'

Then-Boyfriend did indeed go ahead to the UK, scouting for flats to let in London, and, from a distance, I remembered our relationship as being better than it actually was. I do the same thing with Taco Bell. That's the danger of dispositional optimism. When I don't have immediate access to Taco Bell, my opinion of how delicious it is skyrockets. I long for it, I discuss it with my friends, I fixate on how to get tacos back into my life. It's not until I'm actually eating Taco Bell that I see clearly how utterly underwhelming it is. It may not even be food. But I haven't got any tacos now so, naturally, I want some.

Like a Crunchwrap Supreme, I missed Then-Boyfriend and I worried that I was being left behind in Canada to go-go dance and serve chicken wings for the rest of my life. I realised that I'd made the terrible mistake of backing myself into a job corner where my value diminished sharply with age. I was already 23, which in podium years is 65. Hooters starts cutting your hours or hiding you behind the bar once you're on the wrong side of 28 and a powerful intuition told me that I needed to go to the UK. Then-Boyfriend and I of course had lovely times as well as bad and this seemed like it could be our perfect fresh start. Plus, he needed my extra income to live there. I acted impulsively and did what I'd always done – I took a leap of faith for the adventure alone. If it went wrong, I could always try something else.

I arrived at Heathrow with $15,000 in my bank account to contribute towards the tiny north London studio flat he had found. (I keep telling you: waitressing in Canada can make you rich.) Landlords often make you pay six months upfront when you're foreign, which we identified as, despite being white in a structurally prejudiced nation that favoured our race. The British pound just about cut the Canadian dollar in half and rent was £1,000 per month, so my life savings were sucked up by that deposit. TB (Then-Boyfriend) started work and I waited around for my Irish citizenship to come through so that I could start attending job interviews too.

I no longer had the disposable income, social circle or comforts of home that I had taken for granted in Toronto. I was miserable, aimless, my joints hurt all the time and I developed unsightly ring-shaped lesions on my face. They popped up the same week Amy Winehouse infamously stubbed out a lit cigarette on her own cheek in a restaurant after a bartender asked her to stop smoking and gruesome photos of her injury featured on the cover of every UK tabloid. Suitably, I looked like some mad copycat tribute act. I felt self-conscious and expected people to stare, so it surprised me when they did the opposite and actually looked away. I had never realised how often strangers used to make eye contact and exchange smiles with me before. Now, the sight of my face was upsetting them to the point that they'd rather avert their gaze entirely and look at the floor.

I'd just helped open the Hooters in Nottingham, England, and trained the girls there for a few weeks, so I'd learned from that experience that the UK tipping culture wasn't robust enough to pay our bills. I continued dabbling in stand-up comedy for fun but, ultimately, I needed to start bringing money in and I saw myself doing that in a pencil skirt. I decided to apply to an agency for office work. I got sicker and more depressed but I was somehow successful in an interview for a sales company. All my paperwork had come through so, with a job and an NHS number, I felt politically justified in going to the doctor to see what was making me ill.

For six months they got it wrong. I was misdiagnosed with ringworm and, while the rash was in the shape of perfect rings, I thought it odd that I could get a persistent fungal infection like that on my face as an adult who wasn't a wrestler or enrolled in a nursery. I tried medications and anti-fungal creams that actually made it worse. Several further appointments produced the most notable guess: leprosy, which made me wish I could go back to just having ringworm again. I'd been to Catholic school and participated in the local musical production of *Jesus Christ Superstar* so I had a deep understanding of how inconvenient it was to be a leper.

How had I let my life unravel to such biblical proportions? I'd gone from being spoiled in my happy, comfortable life near my friends and family to working long days in excruciating pain trying to manage a potential host of infectious diseases in a new country. I had to wake up early and join a civilised queue for the bus at 7am for my morning commute, then try to hit sales targets all day, everyday, while nobody tipped me for flirting or asked me to participate in a single bikini pageant because – guess what? – I wasn't pretty anymore! And I had to pay taxes. Feminism sucked.

The silver lining is that I'd made friends at work and one afternoon with a searing headache, I broke down and they ushered me into the toilets. 'I'm just so sick of being sick!' I wailed. 'And people are scared of my face! They won't even look at me.' The British girls gently explained that nobody smiles in London and on public transport, looking anywhere apart from the floor was an act of aggression. Oh. There I'd gone, making it all about me again.

* * *

One Sunday a few weeks later, I went outside to cry on a bench so that TB could entertain a friend in the flat. I'd removed myself because I was livid that he didn't seem to understand just how desperate I'd been feeling and I wasn't about to put on a brave face for this pal, who happened to be the sort of man you'd see outside a kebab shop racially abusing a road sign. I'd been crying all the time, I had persistent fevers and I wasn't sleeping well, and not knowing what was wrong with me was making me nuts. 'Look at yourself, Katherine,' I whined, 'sat here covered in open sores, sobbing in the street.' Maybe, in true leper form, I was waiting for Jesus to come heal me so that I could return to the village. After a while, I guess I decided he wasn't coming and I walked to the nearest hospital and presented myself at the A&E reception desk. I would cry there all day instead.

'You know you shouldn't be here,' the doctor on duty scolded, after all the actual emergencies ahead of me had been dealt with. 'We treat accidents, broken bones, urgent problems . . .' I offered to go outside and bike down a stairwell or something so that I could come back and get some medical attention. I was very sick and I felt quite strongly that I required immediate help. 'I tried the GP,' I explained. 'I went to a homeopath, a private dermatologist and back to the GP again. What if this thing is contagious? I'm on packed busses and trains every day!'

The doctor could see that I was distressed but there was little she could do. She gave me paracetamol for the fever and, as I got up to leave, she said, 'You know, it might be lupus.' This freaking bitch right here. How dare she playfully quote Dr Gregory House, the beloved, misanthropic New Jersey doctor played by Hugh Laurie in FOX's American medical drama *House*. He offered this differential diagnosis dozens of times throughout the show without success. I left in a huff and without a solid answer but at least I'd spent the day doing something more proactive than wallowing on a bench. Out of curiosity, I googled 'lupus' when I got home.

Fuck. I had fucking lupus.

The diagnosis was confirmed by a rheumatologist a few weeks later, who listed off the implications of living with systemic lupus, a manageable but incurable autoimmune disease. I had to start taking hydroxychloroquine, the anti-malarial drug since made famous in its misapplication by Donald Trump. I might need dialysis, kidney transplants, have brain involvement, liver damage, need chemotherapy or have difficulty in pregnancy. The path of lupus is unpredictable but at least I now knew what was wrong. Instead of fighting viruses and other invaders like it's meant to do, my immune system was attacking healthy cells and organs. A sort of dramatic self-sabotage.

I'd been so stressed in those short few months since moving to London and my hunch was that alarm bells were going off in my body in response to that upheaval. I'd hated the first lonely weeks of not working and the office job I was able to get paid very little and left us with nothing before the end of the month. I managed a constant, low-level anxiety that I might've ruined my life by coming to London but I was too stubborn to return with my tail between my legs. For as long as I could remember, my family had expected me to be successful, so I'd grown up fully expecting the same. I couldn't recall my mother ever pointing to a leper crying on a dilapidated London bench and saying, 'You could do that!'

Everything I'd set my mind to had been working out for me until recently. So why not now? I wasn't happy in my relationship but I wasn't unhappy enough to risk getting out. We still had good days together and I let my optimism take over, refusing to admit how bad my situation had become. I missed my friends, my parents, Kerrie and sort of Joanne, but I couldn't confront that sadness either. I was a bit like the cartoon meme of the dog calmly drinking tea at the kitchen table while the house that surrounds him is engulfed in flames. That fire was lupus. My body knew better.

Hydroxychloroquine (and perhaps the relief of having an answer) helped ease the inflammation quite quickly. Telling someone with a chronic illness to 'relax' is maddeningly patronising so that's not what I'm trying to say but for me, calmness was a huge factor in my recovery. That was the infancy of the Zen 'no fucks given' mantra that I live by happily and manage lupus with today.

The relief washed over me and I stopped stressing about basically everything, transforming myself into the most chilled out person on earth. It helped. Sure, TB lost his job at the start of the 2009 recession but it's not like that was any indication that he'd be persistently unemployed on and off for the rest of our relationship. We'd been getting along better, playing card games in the flat and devouring British television series in the evenings: *The X Factor*, *Big Brother*, *Ladette to Lady*, *Totally Jodie Marsh: Who'll Take Her Up the Aisle?*, Channel 5 'documentaries', anything 'Katie & Peter' related on ITV – mostly whatever trashiness I could get my hands on, and I say that with love.

For the first time since moving to London, I was joyful – purely ecstatic and grateful for my rediscovered health. In late 2008, nudged along by living in a very nappy-valley-yummy-mummies neighbourhood (albeit in our same tiny flat), I'd reasoned that if I hadn't broken up with TB by now, then I never would, so we might as well go ahead and have a baby. Romantic, right? Like it was ripped straight out of a country song. TB loved the idea of starting a family and I feared that if I didn't try right away, that lupus might take the choice away from me in the future.

"I sucked back as much soothing laughing gas as I could, as a special treat to myself.
"

How to Have a Baby

You know how your parents said, 'Don't have sex. You'll get pregnant'? That's not actually true. You've got maybe a 30 per cent chance – at best – every month and that's only if you do it within a specific five-day window. But I had just turned 24, so I had sex and I got pregnant. It's a very apt warning when you're young.

I told my parents the news (separately) over phone calls and I can't remember my mum's specific reaction, but it was one of general resigned acceptance. She had the wisdom to conserve her energy for the things that she had the power to influence. She wasn't thrilled but she reacted appropriately enough on the phone because I was having a baby irrespective of what anyone said and I'm sure she knew her reservations about my relationship or financial standing weren't worth bringing up. My dad definitely cried though and they were not tears of joy. As he's an Irish Catholic, I'm assuming he is pro-life but he asked how far along I was, and I could tell he wanted to know if this was a done deal or not.

I was in a good place with TB. I mean, I purposely got pregnant by him and I did that with the full intention of moving forward as a family. As far as I was concerned, we'd had bumps in the road and we'd overcome them. Surely, him becoming a father would solve any residual issues I'd been having about some of his behaviour? He'd probably knuckle down, get into a stable career and we'd live a harmonious life. After Violet was born and her arrival didn't miraculously transform a grown man, I joked that we'd wanted a 'save the relationship' baby, but we'd ended up with a regular one instead.

No one in my family or friendship group had ever been a massive fan of TB but I stand by his good qualities now like I did then. He's not a terrible person, just a bit of a dreamer, and we were wrong for each other, but I guess my daughter just really wanted to be born. Souls can do that, you know. From, I dunno, space or wherever, they can match you up with a random person, drag you from Canada to the UK, strike you down with lupus and keep you in an unsuitable relationship just so that they can exist on earth. It's all part of their journey and I would never resent Violet for what she had to do to get here. If anything, I respect the hustle.

I was tacky, so I found out she was a girl as early as I could and I bought all Barbie pink baby stuff. I picked the name 'Dolly' after my grandma and embroidered it into everything. My dad bought us an expensive – though hot pink – baby buggy and apart from throwing up 24/7, I had a pretty uneventful pregnancy. I learned to line the inside of my backpack with plastic carrier bags that I could puke into on the way to work. I didn't look pregnant until my third trimester, so no one expressed sympathy for me; they might've just assumed I was a drug addict on a comedown. The drinking culture in England means that you're never the only young woman being sick on public transport in the morning, so I felt supported that way. And, of course, nobody stares.

Three days past my due date, I sat up in bed and realised that my waters had broken overnight. TB was working in a new job so he went off for the day and I set about getting the flat ready. I cleaned obsessively, then walked to the grocery store to buy dog food for Biggie, coffee beans for us and lilies to welcome Dolly home. More water leaked out as I moved around and contractions had started, but I was living in a post-lupus diagnosis state of Zen, so rather than be alarmed, I walked into town once more to get my nails done. I knew my hands would be in all the zoomed-in photos of me holding my daughter and I needed a manicure to honour her beautiful, fat, blonde babyface. The nail tech asked when I was having the baby and I happily chirped, 'Today!'

Back at home, I rang the hospital to fill them in on the progress of my labour. It was nearly dinnertime and I reported that my contractions were quite painful and close together now. TB would allegedly be home shortly and perhaps we should go in? 'No,' she said, 'you're speaking to me clearly so I can tell you've got a long way to go. Just take a paracetamol tonight and go to sleep.'

What is it with this country and paracetamol? Lupus? Paracetamol. The bones in your pelvis slowly prising themselves apart to accommodate the escape of a human head? Paracetamol. But I was still young and obedient, so I figured things were about to get a whole lot worse and I'd better just suck it up and prepare for a rough night.

A rough night it was indeed. By the time TB got home, I was experiencing what I can only describe as the worst full-body food poisoning of my life. Women always ask whether you poo yourself when you give birth and I can tell you that if you stay home long enough, you absolutely won't because there will be nothing left. Your body is in fight-or-flight mode, so it voids itself of everything you've got in preparation for battle. I tried to take a bath but decided I'd be more comfortable in the bedroom. I turned off all the lights and writhed around on the bed, mooing deeply like a cow. I was in terrible pain but I wanted to be tough because the midwife on the phone had said that I wouldn't have this baby until tomorrow, so this was just the beginning.

Rolling in and out of consciousness, I could hear TB baking sausage rolls for himself while he played video games and I worried that he wouldn't wash the oven tray and that the kitchen would be dirty when I eventually brought Dolly home from the hospital. That's my stand-out memory of my labour – the sausage rolls. I eat neither pork nor pastry but all I could smell in my newly sanitised flat was greasy, disgusting fucking sausage rolls.

That's when my body started pushing on its own. That wasn't supposed to happen so, through excruciating pain, I called for TB, who ordered a taxi. Only it wasn't an actual taxi, it was a crappy car from a dodgy minicab company. (Think 2000s

Uber but cash-only and without tracking or phones or licences or windscreens or brake fluid.) I limped to the car and saw the driver's eyes widen as he realised he might soon have to deliver a baby. 'I will go slowly over the bumps!' is all his panicked voice could offer. 'NO. BE FAST,' I growled back. I can't remember the journey now, just the searing image of a dirty sausage roll pan sat festering on my countertop.

We made it to the hospital just in time; the midwives knew when they saw me crawling towards the nurses' station that I probably shouldn't have been advised to stay home. I was more concerned with vindication than I was with having the baby, so I kept repeating, 'I told you . . . I told you . . . Paracetamol?! . . . but I told you . . .' as they hoisted me onto a bed. I pushed the baby out a few moments later and asked for gas and air while the doctor checked her over.

'But . . . you've already had the baby,' the nurse explained. 'True,' I said, 'but I would like some drugs now as well, please.' So even though the pain had stopped, I sucked back as much soothing laughing gas as I could, as a special treat to myself. They handed my daughter to me and she wasn't at all as I imagined she would be. She had black hair, black eyes and seemed pretty pissed off, to be honest. She certainly wasn't a sweet Dolly. Holding this nameless stranger, I felt sad for her.

'Oh no . . .' I whispered, 'this baby has no mother!' The midwife smiled knowingly, then softly suggested that maybe I could look after the baby and become her mother. I called her Violet and agreed that I would try.

The **absence** of training is a form of **training.**

How to Potty Train Your Baby
by Ten Months

As I was an ocean away from anyone who loved me, Violet swiftly became my best and only friend. During my pregnancy, I'd chosen not to attend NCT classes because it was hard enough getting the time off work for antenatal appointments. By evening, I was usually too tired to drag myself to a comedy gig, so there was no chance I'd be sitting in a two-hour swaddling class when I knew I could get that info in my own time online.

Stand-up comedy was not my first priority but I liked doing it, so I fit it in when I could. I'd briefly considered that a career being funny might work out for me but I simply didn't have the self-belief or energy to give it the push it requires. I certainly wasn't in high demand for gigs so it's not as though the circuit mourned or even noticed when the office job and pregnancy became too much to continue.

So when Violet was born, I hadn't met any 'mum friends' and most of the mothers in my neighbourhood seemed to be much older than I was and on their second or third child. My best friend, Caitlin – a kindred spirit and another rare Sarnia breakout – happened to be teaching in London at the time so she was a huge support on weekends but we were quite young and poor so it was difficult see her during the week, what with the million bus changes between our flats. Basically, Violet was on deck as my go-to-girl.

With no in-laws or grandparents around to tell you what to do, raising a child becomes beautifully instinctive. In Canada, we would normally decorate a nursery and stick a newborn in there to sleep all alone but, to me, that seemed like a foolish Western construct so I kept Violet in my bed. It's not as though we had the luxury of a spare room to make hers in the first place but she didn't even sleep in her own cot. Why would she? We are the only animals in the world who put our young far away in a separate nest when they are born. Even a snake would treat its eggs better. It never made sense in my head. Plus, I'd had practice not suffocating a little teacup dog who stayed in the crook of my arm all night so I knew that I'd never roll onto a baby. Co-sleeping worked for us and it gave me an opportunity to breastfeed on demand while laying on my side, which also meant that I got a lot more sleep than I would have if I'd been getting up every time she roused to feed her.

Violet took to screaming in her pram, so instead of pushing her around in that, I strapped her to myself and carried her mostly everywhere we went. She was held for most of the day, every day. I didn't know it at the time but I've since learned that I was raising her by 'attachment parenting' – a philosophy based on empathy, responsiveness, closeness and touch. Another element of this practice is called 'elimination communication' but I only recently learned it had a name. I'd seen toddlers struggle with potty training and often thought to myself, 'Sure. By the time they're 18 months old, they seem really headstrong. No wonder some of them resist a change to what they know.' Once, while I was working at Hooters, I witnessed a mother changing her VERY LARGE (probable four-year-old) child's soiled diaper right on the restaurant table. This kid had been drinking soda and eating chicken wings. In fairness, I'll now assume she was staging a social protest over the fact that our washrooms didn't have changing tables but nevertheless, no child (apart from in the cases of special needs) should be in a nappy at that age. I'm sorry, no.

I always put myself in Violet's shoes – or little pram boots – and I shuddered at the imagined indignity of having a stranger change my nappy. Even at three months, Violet was pretty switched-on and I decided that rather than train her to go in a diaper, I would skip it and go straight to the potty instead. This is the bit people miss. My friends have often said, 'Three months is too young to train them.' But even the absence of training is a form of training. They get used to nappies and then you move the goal posts once they become toddlers! Can you blame so many of them for feeling weird about it and going to hide behind the sofa to poop? I cannot stress this enough – EVERYTHING you do is training, even when you think you're doing nothing.

Nappies are useful for working parents, people on the move with their children, understaffed nurseries and, well, nappy companies. It's not realistic for most families to be on hand and responsive as regularly as it takes to potty train early and I absolutely don't judge them for that. But I had the luxury of being at home or near my daughter 24/7, so as soon as she started on solid foods, I could tell by the look on her face if she needed the toilet and quickly whipped off her nappy to hold her over the potty. I thought it was probably easier to go that way than it would be strapped in a chair. Poos are the easiest at first because you get a warning via facial expression. If my instincts were right and she went then I'd praise her and leave the nappy off for a while as a comfort reward. We'd sit on the potty to read a story first thing every morning when she woke up and that usually resulted in a wee. We'd do the same maybe hourly or so and always before bed. I started taking the buggy with us to the park and keeping a small potty in the grocery basket underneath, so Violet always had somewhere to go. She wasn't punished for 'accidents' or anything, we just incorporated the potty into our daily routine and it slowly took over nappies on its own.

I'd stumbled across articles and YouTube videos of parents who'd taught sign language to their infants and decided to buy a book about it. I spoke to Violet all the time and couldn't wait for her to talk back (she's 12 now and yes, I'm frantically trying to derail this training), so I thought it would be a good idea to sign meaningful things to her during regular chit-chat. My mum had always told me that babies know exactly what you're saying, they just lack the fine muscle dexterity in their mouths to form sounds and make words back. Mum hadn't taught me any sign language as a baby – largely because she got straight back to work when I was three weeks old – but I spoke to her on the phone quite a lot and she wholly approved of my methods.

By the time Violet was six months, I'd learned the signs for hungry, thirsty, potty, cold, hot, tired, happy, help, careful, finished, more, milk, cheese, cracker, apple, Mama, Dada and a bunch of animals that she liked. Violet didn't sign back for a few weeks but, at around seven months, she clearly signed 'finished' when she'd gotten annoyed by a hat. Typical Violet. Still won't tell you what she wants but is glad to denounce all that she abhors. I signed 'finished' to explain that an activity was coming to an end or a mealtime was over, but Violet ran with it and would sign it at anyone apart from me who dared to hold her or even gaze in her direction if she happened to be in the wrong mood. She used it exclusively as a command, which I thought was funny. Anything Violet didn't like was FINISHED. She was an early proponent of cancel culture.

I could see that she was grasping the power of communication and more signs, like 'milk', 'more' and 'help', quickly followed. Soon, Violet was signing 'potty' to let me know when she needed the loo so that I had to do less guessing. She was completely out of nappies by ten months, even at night, but I'd still occasionally stick one on her as a precaution if we were flying somewhere or majorly deviating from our usual routine. I don't think I ever bought a pack bigger than a year though as we didn't need them at all beyond that age. It just wasn't a stress for us and my favourite part about potty training was the personal empowerment that came with it for her.

From a very early age, Violet was less physically vulnerable than other children, knew that her words carried meaning and was seldom frustrated by the limitations that come with being a baby. She could tell us what she was thinking and we could respond. That girl never had a single tantrum. (NOTE: my therapist said this might be a bad thing, as apparently tantrums are necessary to regulate their central nervous system or something? Just telling you for the sake of full disclosure here – make of that what you will.) People have asked whether sign language delays speech, which to me is as ridiculous as thinking that crawling would delay walking. I suppose babies might not learn to speak as quickly if you were silent but I always said everything out loud as I was signing it. That's important.

I'm not sure when it started but Violet definitely spoke early and in full sentences. She could certainly carry a very meaningful conversation with me around 18 months. She was a funny toddler and a great friend. She was great at imaginary play and created little personalities and different voices for all her tiny toy characters. Just like my sisters would do, Violet committed to games for hours on end and constantly surprised me with her clever observations and sharp comedic timing. I was her very favourite person and it made me feel special that such a cool girl loved me so much.

Violet wouldn't eat anything with a face. Not meat but equally, not a cookie with a face drawn on; not a cake, not a cupcake or gingerbread in the shape of an animal or decorated with icing animals – NOTHING that might feel pain in some realm if she bit into it. I admired her, I trusted her and I received a lot of comfort from her, even though she was only a baby. She was genuinely zero trouble for me.

Violet stopped signing eventually but we still used 'careful', often across a crowded playground, which came in handy as a warning a lot more often than you'd think. It saved me shouting, anyway. I'm sure I'll be dropping her at a nightclub one day soon and signing 'careful' through the driver's window as she rolls her eyes and canters off inside with her friends.

I've mentioned early potty training in passing on TV and it's probably one of the things I get asked about the most by new parents. 'You should write a book about it!' they'll say but I think it's straightforward enough for one chapter. It won't be for everyone and it might not even be for me with the next baby! I work a whole lot more than I did before. I'm old, lazy and spoiled now. I'll have to ask for help this time and I have a husband who'll want to do things his way when he's minding the baby. Crucially, this baby might not go along with it as effortlessly as Violet happened to. They're all different. Attachment parenting worked for us at the time and I won't pretend not to have enjoyed the smug sense of superiority that came with it. One-year-old Violet, kicking her legs up in the buggy, wearing a summer dress with culottes, would make mothers literally stop and exclaim, 'Oh my GOD, I've heard about this baby but I didn't believe it! She's really not in a nappy, is she?' and I'd blush, basking in their jealous admiration and reply, 'No . . . she's potty trained.' They might've been rich and yummy, but I had this.

What I truly deserve next is a little boy who shits behind the sofa until he's four.

Comedians **knew** a lot about **a lot.**

How to Stay Booked and Busy

I didn't make an effort at stand-up in England to begin with. I turned up to clubs with TB now and then but asked to go on stage maybe a third of the time. We'd agreed that him securing gigs was more important because comedy was his career and I was only really doing it for fun. But I watched a lot and I loved so much of what I saw.

Sara Pascoe and Andi Osho were two of the first acts that jumped out to me as being amazingly fresh, smart and honest. I'd noted that they would probably have been considered 'alternative' at the club back in Canada but that they achieved mainstream attention in the UK. I started watching panel shows, which didn't exist where I'd grown up, and it struck me how clever everyone seemed to be. It wasn't just jokes about race, sex and shit marriages here – comedians knew a lot about a lot. It took me a few months to understand any of the literary or political references but straightaway I began devouring pop culture. I caught up on all the popular television series and found out from magazines about Cheryl Cole, Susan Boyle and Kerry Katona. I was building a reference catalogue of my own. This place was fucking awesome.

The few gigs that I managed to get booked on went okay but at that time I was tired from my office job and too sick from lupus to work at the circuit very hard. I entered a few new act competitions and TB was really supportive when I won or reached the finals. These contests are a good way for managers to see you and I was invited to sign with United Agents in early 2009. I was newly pregnant with Violet at the time and I wondered what this prestigious agency wanted with me. It felt exciting that they thought that I was talented enough to sign me and so I went for it and hoped that I'd be able to give them some kind of a return on their investment one day. It would be embarrassing otherwise. 'Maybe . . . ' I considered, 'I might be able to do some TV in this country like I did before in Canada.' I largely kept my excitement to myself and managed my expectations.

My agent, Hannah Begbie, and her then-assistant, Kitty Laing, encouraged me to write and gig more, and said that I should aim to build up enough material to perform an hour-long show at the Edinburgh Fringe Festival. I shrugged it off, never imagining that anyone would ever want to come see me on purpose or listen to me speak for a whole hour. Headliners in Canada were expected to do 45 minutes, and even that seemed long, so I put that idea right out of my head. I had a pretty hot ten minutes and that was about it.

Soon after, I was invited to audition for an all-female sketch show with a major production company for a main channel. The days in my office chair had become increasingly difficult as I was about six months pregnant and I started to wonder how I'd ever be able to return to full-time work after maternity leave. I'd started researching nurseries and found that all the nice ones cost way more than I was earning at my job in the city. This audition felt like a real chance to start taking comedy more seriously and make it my actual career. Maybe I'd be successful and leave my low-wage sales job for good? I made it all the way to the final round and was gutted to receive an email from the casting director that said, 'We would have chosen you but the only reason that we can't is because you're pregnant and we cannot insure you.' People used to put shit like that IN WRITING. These days, they'd still pass you over for the job but they'd usually be clever enough to lie about why. I'd opened the personal email at work because I'm deeply unprofessional and tears of frustration and anger ran down my cheeks.

I'm a brat with an unwavering commitment to justice so I started trying harder after that, just to spite them. I worked on my act and I was developing a more confident voice. Yes, I turned up at a pub open mic and sang and danced as Sarah Palin to a Pussycat Dolls parody I'd written, and yes, I insisted on delivering material about my favourite MTV show *Teen Mom* and a family no one in the UK had heard of called the Kardashians, but I was starting to be rewarded for my authenticity with a teeny tiny cult following. I hadn't left my office job for maternity leave yet but, fuelled by vengeance, I was unwittingly laying plans and building bridges for my future career.

* * *

I was invited to perform in a new act showcase at Latitude Festival on 16th July 2009. It was in the main comedy tent and would be the biggest gig I'd ever done, but it was less than a month after my due date. I figured that would be fine and put it in the diary because I'd caught the stand-up bug and wanted to do the show. I predicted that having a baby was easy and that they were probably very portable.

On the day of the showcase, I travelled by train to Suffolk with Violet and was mercifully collected from the station by Flo, who is now my friend and fellow comic Romesh Ranganathan's manager. Everyone was really accommodating and supportive about me having brought such a tiny guest but I learned that the general public aren't used to seeing babies that new. The boy comedians hovered around curiously and a few asked, 'Um, is your baby too small?' or 'Is that how little her legs are meant to be?' I just said, 'Yeah, she's regular size for a three-week-old.' Violet and I had started as we meant to go on – touring together and making people uncomfortable while doing it.

When people ask what my 'breakthrough moment' was in comedy, I can confidently tell them that it's been a series of baby steps. That's anticlimactic but true. Showcases turned into bookings; open mic nights turned into a bit of paid work and a few auditions turned into jobs. I brought Violet nearly everywhere – notably to a casting for Victoria Pile's newest comedy series for Channel 4, *Campus*. Violet was six months old when I carried her into the room and plopped her at my feet so that I could read for producers. She was fine until one of them instinctively offered to pick her up. She read in his face that he was about to do so and wailed, nearly blowing the whole thing. Luckily, I was able to calm her down and as I placed her back on the floor to start reading again, I said, 'Maybe please just don't look at her.' Violet was a tricky one-woman baby but she managed to charm them with her independence and we booked the job.

A few months later, I was scheduled to do a week of gigs at The Stand in Edinburgh, Scotland. It's an iconic comedy club with a great atmosphere opened by Tommy Sheppard in 1996. I wasn't in any position to be writing an hour for the festival, but I could manage a few short gigs. Violet was ten months old when we went and because I'd only be on stage for roughly 40 minutes total per evening across two shows, I borrowed a local comedian's babysitter for that time and explored the city with Violet the rest of the day. I didn't know the babysitter and I'd recently seen a story on the news about a nursery school teacher who'd taken and distributed indecent images of infants, which made me paranoid. So I devised a technique of buttoning up Violet's sleeper all wrong. That way, if it was buttoned back properly when I returned, I would know and could immediately ring Scotland Yard. That's the level of protective madness I was working with.

Edinburgh wasn't exactly wheelchair or pushchair accessible at the time and our hotel room was atop a narrow winding staircase, so I hoisted Violet and all of her accoutrements up and down them every day. I found a lovely mother and baby group for soft play in a church hall down the road and, since our hotel didn't have a fridge or a kitchen, I walked her to McDonald's for breakfast when she woke up at 6am every morning. I know it sounds grim but nothing else appeared to be open that early. I asked the girl at the counter, 'Is the egg in your Egg McMuffin made of . . . egg?' She looked at me like I was wasting her time with a trick question and stiffly answered 'Aye', which I'm told can be Scottish for 'go fuck yourself'. I removed it from the muffin and chopped up a bit of plain cooked egg alongside apple slices for Violet, and we sat in the restaurant watching the weekend drunks sober up for their early morning wander home. Afterwards, we'd visit museums, stop to look at street buskers and play with the toys in John Lewis. We had the best time.

I didn't really earn much money from that week of gigs when you factor in paying the babysitter, taking Violet to appropriately healthy restaurants for lunch and dinner and upgrading my train tickets to first class. I just wanted the experience of doing the shows and I wanted Violet to be comfortable. I wasn't sure how she would do on a five-hour train ride in coach, and I'd already experienced packed carriages where my seat reservation was cancelled and I'd had to hold her standing up the entire time, so I decided to give her as much room as I could.

On the way home, we found our seats and I laid out her books, small toys and a snack. Violet was playing quietly when, within the first few minutes of the journey, another passenger in a suit approached us and said, 'Hi, how old are you?' I thought he was referring to Violet so I answered, 'Uh, she's ten months.' But he persisted with, 'No, how old are YOU?' I'd turned 26 that year. As though he'd set out that morning to ruin my day, he moved a seat closer to us and said, 'Just so you know, this is first class. No judgement.'

He'd absolutely applied judgement. I swear there are men without anywhere to actually go who book first class train tickets back and forth just to bask in the smug thrill of loudly declaring who should and should not be in their exclusive carriage. I was nice back then, so rather than telling him where he should fuck off to and how, I entertained his many questions when all I'd wanted was to be left alone to play with my daughter. As soon as he learned I'd been doing comedy, he was off on a tangent about what type of jokes I should be telling and which comedians he liked best – mostly dead men. Without being asked, he announced that he was an important MP. I can't remember for what party but I know he wasn't Alex Salmond or anyone I'd seen on TV. I wasn't well-versed in politics at all but I swiftly decided that in future, I'd better beware of these pricks as a general rule of thumb.

The train journeys are a huge part of stand-up comedy. We spend more time travelling than we spend on stage and women have to factor in that they'll be harassed at some point, if not often. I think one of the reasons why there are fewer of us on the circuit is that many prioritise their safety on the road or just get fed up with bullshit from jackasses on trains. We can't fall asleep on a night bus the same way a man can. We can't just flop on any booker's sofa for a weekend without second-guessing his intentions. I knew male comics who'd all pitch in for a disgusting hotel room together and sleep on the floor. I would never do that and most certainly not with Violet. My then-boyfriend could do it. An incredible comedian and my friend Nikki Glaser posts her tour dates to social media with a sinister layer of dark humour when she says, 'Come kill me in Jacksonville, Florida, on August 21st at 9pm!' 'Come kill me for half-price in Atlanta, Georgia, the weekend of June 4th!' We are vulnerable when we are alone at night, having publicised exactly where we will be and at what time. We have to consider that you might follow us home.

* * *

If I had to pinpoint one transformative moment in my career, it would be my 2012 appearance on Jimmy Carr's *8 Out of 10 Cats*. Before filming each new series, the production company hosts office run-throughs of the show format, where select up-and-coming comedians are invited to 'audition' by playing the game for a small audience. They send out news packs a couple of days before so that you know what you've got to prepare in terms of angles and jokes for the show. When I was chosen to try out, I prepared until the very last second, sitting on the living room floor with Violet and her toys while squeezing ideas into a notepad. Seemingly out of nowhere, a mouse scurried across the playmat and I screamed, scooping my toddler up and bolting from the room. I stood on my bed and rang Kitty, my agent's assistant, to say that I was probably too stressed to go and that I should instead stay home and deal with the mouse. Kitty basically gave me the classic Old Hollywood advice that I should 'pull myself together, splash cold water on my face and go outside'.

I'm glad I did. I dropped Violet off at the babysitter's, delivered my jokes at the run-through and got booked for the show. This was an extremely big deal. An appearance on *8 Out of 10 Cats* could make or break my career. I don't remember all of the topics but I know I had watched the programme enough to be aware that I had to arm myself with more one-liners than I'd get the chance to say. There was definitely a question round about 'Things my parents taught me growing up' and I said something like, 'How to tie my shoes . . . together and throw them over power lines to indicate the location of a crack house.' Misdirection. Works every time.

On the evening of the taping of the show, I panicked just a little bit in the green room. I'd just been introduced to Jimmy Carr* and the other comics on the show – Sean Lock, Jon Richardson and Hannibal Buress. It dawned on me that I might actually be humiliated on a national scale here and that everything I'd done before had been a laugh but I had no hope of being as funny or accomplished as these men were. I decided that I had two choices: climb out the window or just try to sell myself for exactly who I was. I could never do a convincing impression of anyone else – I'd proved that by being terrible at the start of my career. I looked down at the brown wellies I had paired with my yellow dress because I knew they'd be hidden under the desk and realised that if I was going to have any chance at all, I had to deliver the angles that mattered to me and just hope that they made sense to someone watching.

I knew that at some point, the singing competition show *The Voice* would come up because one of the guests had been on it and I'd conceived this idea of hosting my own reality programme called *The Ass*. I'd noticed an early trend in celebrities' bums getting bigger during this time. Where the focus had once been on boobs, now everyone was talking about J-Lo's bum and Beyoncé's bum, and this was just when the Kardashians were becoming mainstream. When Jimmy mentioned *The Voice*, I invited everyone to 'come on *The Ass*' and explained my format. This, of course, had a glaring sexual implication that I pretended not to notice but it certainly got attention and made my 'filthy with a knowing innocence' vibe clear. Basic stuff but it was enough to get respect from the audience and they paid attention to my jokes after that.

The phone hasn't stopped ringing since that fateful appearance in 2012. That snap decision was the key to everything. I've seen it since from comedians making their debuts on the same star-making show. Those who walk into it owning their space, not trying to compete necessarily, but just bringing their clarity and uniqueness to the table, are the ones who shine. Love me or hate me, I'm pretty explicit about what I'm selling and I think that's a big predictor of success for comedians.

The comedy industry is going through one of its many evolutions at the moment, which is inevitable and usually necessary. Live audiences and a whole new breadth of online audiences from social media and streaming platforms are re-evaluating what they'll accept as progressive comedy versus mean-spirited jokes. When I started stand-up, it was absolutely fine to take the piss out of basically anyone and participate in comedy roasts, where a target willingly receives smartly written insults from other comedians. To me, roast battles are a huge demonstration of consent and that's a big part of why I love them and did four series of *Roast Battle UK*, alongside Jimmy Carr, but the show was taken off Comedy Central UK last year.

From 2017–2019, I filmed six seasons of a 'Tinder-inspired' gameshow for Comedy Central UK alongside Jimmy Carr again, called *Your Face or Mine*. The couples-based comedy format involved us bringing on real partners who had to rate each other's looks in the hopes of winning cash. Contestants had to be ruthlessly truthful because if they lied, their answers about how hot their mate was wouldn't match the audience poll and they'd lose the money. It became a cult classic because viewers could see that the heart of the show wasn't about looks at all but about getting to know the true essence of people during their short time on the screen and how their personalities could influence the public vote. For example, we might have a stunning woman on who belittled her boyfriend and refused to accept her own critiques with an ounce of humility. The audience would respond by voting her lower than all his exes. Similarly, if a primped gym-bunny disrespected his partner or took himself too seriously, the room turned on him and he'd start to lose their favour. *Your Face or Mine* wasn't about looks at all, it was entirely about displaying a good sense of humour. So I'm baffled when I spot complaints on social media about the show being shallow. I have to keep reminding myself that there are people in the world who look out at the ocean and can't imagine that there might be anything below the water's surface.

Violet tells me I don't get it because I'm 'a boomer' and maybe she's right. I can have all the best intentions in the world but ultimately, if we plan on sticking around, we all have to adjust somewhat to suit and reflect the culture we are serving. I actually find it exciting that the parameters of what's acceptable in comedy are always evolving. It keeps things fresh and challenging.

* I love Jimmy Carr. I'm grateful to him for putting me forward for a bunch of cool projects as much as I admire him for his attitude and work ethic. I think we're quite similarly minded, and I've modelled a lot of my career business plan after things I've learned by watching him.

Jimmy is glam. I love that. He's transparent and unapologetic about investing in his look. He's got the suits, the hair, the teeth and the workout regime that says, 'Hi, I'm a television star'. Jimmy is not only very naturally funny but works hard at the craft of stand-up, and if he hasn't got a filming commitment, he fills theatres every night of the week on tour. I've overheard punters tease him for being ubiquitously on our screens and he'll say, 'Most people I know work every day'. It's a really down-to-earth way of explaining away his popularity. Everyone knows what they're doing on Jimmy's TV shows and they run smoothly. If they didn't, you can bet that Jimmy would give calm, clear instructions on how to make it right. It's so relaxing to work with a leader like that. Jimmy is a solid booking, every show, every time. He'll be around forever because he's undeniable. You've got to be undeniable. Professionally, he gives no trouble and takes no shit. I want to be that way, too, and while I certainly give no trouble, I'm learning how to politely navigate taking less shit. My favourite of Jimmy's work mottos is, 'Never complain, never explain'.

Jimmy is kind and generous, which I'm not sure many would guess from seeing his act. I've heard him respond to a heckler with, 'If you want my comeback, you'll have to scrape it off your mum's teeth'. Adorable. My theory is that bad men can't talk like that. Instead, they'll craft a 'family man' image or start a podcast about enlightenment. Jimmy's act isn't trying to prove anything to anyone. He's there to make you laugh, and I think being a genuinely wonderful person offstage is what gives him the freedom to do that. He's a fixer. Great in a crisis. Jimmy's 'got a guy' for everything. If his friends are in trouble, Jimmy can be counted on to guide them to a resolution. He'd give them the Gucci shirt off his back.

The most common question that I get asked about Jimmy is whether he ever changes into casual clothes. He does. Just like you and me, he'll relax and sit, chatting in loungewear, playing fetch with his dog in the garden. The difference is that it's designer loungewear. And, sometimes, the ball lands on the tennis courts, and Jimmy's butler helpfully tosses it back.

"

Why you gotta be with such DIABOLICAL men?

"

How to Break Up

I've been bad with men. It's fine, though, because, by some miracle, I seem to have married the world's most wonderful, funny and utterly decent one. I firmly believe that my maturity is responsible for attracting him as much as my childish vulnerability was to blame for attracting the diabolical ones.

A girlfriend pointed that out to me once. 'Why you gotta be with such DIABOLICAL men?' she said. 'I mean, there are trash men, stupid men, violent men, lazy men, but you gotta be with the DIABOLICAL ones. Why?' My guess is that I used to find toxicity intoxicating. I sought out mental stimulation and attention (positive or negative) above stability simply out of boredom. Diabolical men are very complicated and require vigilance, saving and understanding. Plus, they tallied with my early suspicions that men were very dangerous and I think I have always quite liked being right. What you seek, after all, is what you shall find. To my credit, each time I put a message out into the universe that I was deserving of a scoundrel, I found one.

My daughter's father is a lovely person but we were wrong for each other from the start. I started dating him when I was a part-time amateur comedian and university student in my early twenties and he was a 30-something-year-old man. I began seeing him immediately following my entanglement with the Hooters manager, around the same time that I decided to dye my hair white and tan my body orange. It was generally a period defined by bad choices. Some of us still have underdeveloped brains in our twenties, which is one of the reasons why I encourage young women not to make life-determining decisions in a hurry: you're only half-cooked and you'll be lucky if it works out.

My decision to finally leave him after a couple years of relationship deterioration while living in the UK was a difficult one. I'd foolishly assumed that we would improve as a couple once Violet was born but I now see that having a baby is like going to war – sometimes you bond with your comrade and grow stronger as a unit out of mutual respect, but other times you find yourself deserted and with PTSD.

Suffice to say, I'd felt unsupported for a stretch of time. I'd reached out to mutual friends and family for help but the general consensus was that I should basically shut the fuck up and learn to live with it because he wasn't hitting me and he wasn't evil. Annoyingly, these instructions came from older women who thought sending me lingerie would help solve my problems. They suggested positive reinforcement for the behaviours that I hoped to encourage rather than raising complaints about what I wanted changed. I tried that for a while but resented the effort that it took. In the end, I told one of the women that I wouldn't settle for my current situation and that she shouldn't settle for hers. She was appalled when I suggested that she should follow my lead and split from her partner because I could see that she'd be better off alone, too. This chick couldn't believe the audacity of me squaring up to her normalised bullshit with a little progressive advice of my own. I don't know why she got so offended. It was meant to be a compliment!

I literally lost my voice in that relationship. I don't mean 'figuratively', like how Gen Z means it when they say 'literally': I mean literally, for real. I had a big lump in my throat and I couldn't speak properly for a couple of years. If you can be bothered to find any old stand-up footage of me from 2010–2012, or watch the sitcom *Campus* on Netflix, you won't recognise my voice. It sounds scratchy and it was audibly painful for me to speak. At the time, I tolerated cameras up my nose and down my throat (a gig's a gig), a biopsy of a bulge in my neck and the frustratingly familiar diagnosis that nothing was wrong.

It also made me angry that my voice – the tool I was trying to use to claw my way to independence – seemed to be broken and I didn't know how to fix it. I was heavy with the guilt of breaking up our family and I really did wonder whether I was nuts to be doing it. I wished so badly that I could snap out of it and somehow love him again but, ultimately, the respect was gone. The easiest thing in the short term is to stay and be miserable but I knew deep down that it would eat me alive. I'd also read a lot about mental development in children and I decided that if I was definitely going to get out, I needed to do it while Violet was young enough not to remember or blame herself.

Between all the conversations, broken promises and genuine attempts to repair things, it probably took just over a year to actually end it. I spent most of that year crying on the phone to my family and getting anxiously thin. During that period, I allowed someone to enter my life for comfort and protection, which I like to call 'overlapping', though it's essentially cheating, even if you're not sleeping with both of them at the same time. Looking back, I can see I felt like a lonely, bad person who was deserving of punishment – otherwise I never would have entertained such an utterly humiliating clown. We will call said clown 'The Overlap'.

It's the classic love story really; we met on a train when he insisted that I remove my headphones to give him my attention. I'd just been on stage at my friend Tania's new material gig in Great Portland Street in London and, as usual, I had left in a hurry to get home. I'd downloaded an episode of Louis C.K.'s new comedy series onto my phone and was looking forward to a few child-free moments on public transport to watch it. As I settled into the show, I noticed a very small blond man chatting at me from the opposite seat. I popped one of my earbuds out politely to hear him say, 'I think you're funny.' He explained that he had come from the gym and had stopped by the same gig. That's why he was wearing a grey tracksuit when, 'Usually, I am dressed much better.'

I wondered why his clothes mattered and felt pestered by this line of forced conversation. Like an idiot, I said, 'Tracksuits are great. Nice to meet you.' And put my headphones back in. He kept talking. He leaned in, making intense eye-contact when he spoke. My first instinct was that this guy was an asshole – and I really should have listened to that – but somehow, after he got off the train, I was left feeling flattered that he had seemed so invested in me for six whole stops.

Later, I accepted his Facebook request based on our mutual friends and the fact that he was a musician so he knew a lot of venue managers who could get me booked on comedy gigs. At this time, my comedy career had started to bring in a bit of cash for the household and it felt like a lifeline to me. I went into the friendship with good, professional intentions and though he flirted with me, he knew that I was a mother and in a relationship, so I put it down to harmless fun. After all, he flirted with EVERYBODY. He kissed men on stage, had sex with strangers in toilets, hooked up with women he'd met online – a few who paid him – and even a grandmother who'd given him a ride home from a concert once. I naively assumed his transparency about these liaisons meant that he wasn't romantically interested in me or else why would he be sharing so much? I certainly wasn't into any freaky business. But then he kissed me in the rain after a gig one night and I liked it. He told me that I was an angel and it felt nice to be put on a pedestal during a time when my relationship at home had gone sour.

Comedy provided the perfect escape from my situation and Then-Boyfriend because I could be present for my daughter all day long and then disappear as soon as she went to sleep. I'd found the ideal balance of being a great mother and a shitty girlfriend. I was genuinely working but also started to socialise more while I avoided my real relationship. A few months later, I had sex with The Overlap 'to get it out of my system', justifying it because I'd been unhappy for so long and maybe this was the shock I needed to go back to my regular life. It didn't work of course and, crucially, I'd conveniently forgotten that I was incapable of casual sex.

Now we were 'in love'. I thought about him all the time and felt revitalised in my comedy writing; I skipped through my day-to-day errands with Violet and I was less of a nag at home. All of a sudden, I didn't care where TB was going or when he'd be back, so we stopped arguing. I had more energy overall and the world looked brighter – as it always does in your twenties when you think you're smitten with someone new. I'd elevated The Overlap to a symbolic status where he represented all the opportunities that were still available to me. Prior to our dalliance, I'd subscribed to the idea that I was 'damaged goods' because I'd had a baby but now I believed that I was desirable. I started to feel a bit like my old Toronto self – renewed by potential. I reasoned that I was even becoming a better mother because I was generally happier, but that happiness was underlined by a deep insecurity, vibrating below the surface.

The Overlap kept seeing other women and telling me about them but just having his voice on the other end of the phone made me feel happy and desired in that moment, so I kept things going. It broke my heart whenever he made a point of describing the details of another hook-up he'd had in my absence – 'It was so great, babe. After you left the club, I brought this girl home and I was fucking her from behind wearing nipple clamps and the vibrator against her clit . . .' His words honestly made me sick but I felt like whatever pain I experienced was my own fault. I was the Bad One who was trying (and failing) to leave my broken relationship. I was the fool who'd moved to a foreign country and had a baby with someone I no longer loved. I wanted to be happy but I also felt like I deserved to be hurt. It was a frustrating paradox. Besides, The Overlap was aggressive and I thought having him on my side would come in handy if my ex had a negative reaction when he finally accepted that we were finished.

The Overlap would say, 'One day, we can be a family and I'll stop acting this way because you're proving to me that you're kind, and you're gentle, and you're entirely selfless.' Something inside me screamed whenever he said it. I wasn't selfless! I had needs and growing ambitions of my own, but it was becoming clear that those would never matter to him.

I didn't and I don't value pure 'selflessness'. You can be thoughtful and generous without abandoning your goals or yourself. I was interviewing a family recently about their adult daughter for a show, who was being sent on holiday to reward her selflessness. Before meeting her, I asked her parents to describe her personality on camera and they offered things like, 'She puts herself dead last,' and 'She's always doing what she can for us.' Okay, sure . . . but could they share what they loved about HER?

'She spends all her time helping her brothers, never thinking of herself.' My God. Out of the corner of my eye, I could see the show producer beginning to panic. I asked firmly, 'Has she got any hobbies of her own?' and they offered, 'Yes. Cleaning and looking after her grandmother.' I death-stared this fucking family for a solid minute before the producer explained my mental glitch away as a 'sound problem' and we all moved on to introduce their beloved doormat daughter.

I'm unrecognisable now from the pathetic person I'd allowed myself to become at that low point of my life. It's difficult for me to fathom how quiet my inner voice had become but I had so many tough choices to make and became swept up in their momentum rather than taking responsibility for my decisions in an adult way. Instead of speaking up, I just kept moving forward and hoping for the best. I got comfort from the idea that if The Overlap thought I was selfless, maybe he was taking care of me.

* * *

After a few months of torture trying to juggle the beginning of my new relationship with the end of my old one, The Overlap became my boyfriend. I'd been hiding in plain sight for so long that TB eventually discovered what I'd been up to and finally agreed to move out. It hurt him deeply. I was heartbroken and ashamed to have acted so callously towards him. I felt both terrified by how he might react but also relieved that this could be the beginning of things getting better.

I've never regretted ending that relationship for a split second so I wouldn't say things ultimately got 'worse' . . . but my situation definitely took on a new incarnation of being shit for a while. I suppose I look at it as earning my freedom back by spending some time in jail. Community service at the very least.

The Overlap still slept with other women but now he lied about it and I'd find out from other people. I think he tried to do it less, which was a shame because it meant that I was left responsible for his sexual satisfaction. It made me happy to make him happy – I was 'selfless' in his eyes after all – but everything he liked sexually made me deeply uncomfortable. It started with him sending me photos of himself. These were more than nudes – they were full-blown pornographic images, like him covered in, ahem, 'fluid'. I'd receive several of those daily and he'd get angry if I didn't respond, or if I didn't respond correctly.

I learned that he expected nothing less than an immediate, glowing review. He was clear that making him feel rejected was the worst thing that I could do, so I promised never to do it. He asked for photos of me in return and I hoped that he might accept smiling pics of me holding a coffee at the park. I sent him a selfie with a duck once and he wrote back 'NO', so I ended up sending the nudes he wanted. They were hot nudes too, and I absolutely drew the line at touching myself, so I stand by them as having been tastefully produced. It was never enough though and he'd sometimes grab his phone to film us having sex. Each time, I'd stay quiet about it and then delete the videos as soon as he went to the loo. Of course, I was reprimanded as soon as he discovered them gone but he wasn't a complete rapist so I guess he understood that he'd have to respect my boundaries somewhat, even while trying to gently chip away at them anytime I was distracted. There was one occasion where I woke up in the morning and he proudly showed me photos he'd taken of himself wanking over me while I slept. Cute. I rarely got angry. I really wanted him to love me.

I guess because he was a desperate show-off, he'd gone to the trouble of creating a character called 'Adam Diablo', who bedded women every time the two of them went out together. Deep down, I always knew that Adam Diablo didn't exist and that it was my boyfriend openly cheating on me and then telling me about it through the guise of a fake friend, but it sounds so insane when you say it out loud that I never called him out on it. He'd ring me up at 3am and say, 'You wouldn't believe what Adam Diablo got up to after the show tonight' – right, I wouldn't – 'He shagged the hottest one from your favourite girl band in the toilets!' Funny that both he and the elusive Adam Diablo (whom I'd never actually met but seemed to turn up every time I wasn't around) had matching penchants for having intercourse in public loos.

Coercive control doesn't happen overnight. It can creep up on you through a series of tiny humiliations or degrading acts. He criticised my underwear drawer, saying that I should only wear matching sets and that I should think of him every morning while choosing which ones to put on. He said he couldn't understand why women didn't exclusively dress in lingerie with hold-ups. I was like, 'Dude, I'm poor with a young daughter so I don't care.' He hated that I never went for pedicures and wanted my toes to be higher on my list of priorities while I struggled to pay my rent. He didn't like the way I chopped vegetables or the way I organised my flat. He said that I didn't do a good enough job of waxing my bikini area so he gave me the number of his personal waxer instead. Yes, he was the kind of man who had entirely smooth genitals and, once, I caught him spreading his arse in the mirror and looking back over his shoulder into his own abyss.

He resented that my career was miraculously taking off but needed to make a big show of supporting me anyway so that he looked good. He came with me to gigs and, one night, after carrying my heavy garment bag from my dressing room, he kicked off in the taxi. 'This is bullshit! I should be the one having my shit carried for a show and here I am carrying YOUR SHIT instead.' I hadn't asked him to carry it – he had insisted and now I was in trouble. His reactions tainted the success that I should have been able to enjoy because I just felt scared of what he might say every time I got a new job. He'd agree that I had talent but told me that most of the opportunities I had were only offered to me because I was a woman. According to him, if he were a woman doing my job, he'd be more successful too.

He wanted me to call him 'Daddy' in text messages and also to his face without laughing. He started biting me and being quite rough in bed, bringing his collection of sex toys over, which I HATED, and even suggesting he pay a couple of sex workers so that we could watch them have sex in his flat. He reasoned that this wouldn't be cheating because he would just be WATCHING them, 'like a king'. I was horrified and flatly refused, which of course left him 'disappointed' in me.

I still wanted to make this relationship work somehow, even though I'd managed to alienate my entire family by being with this man. They hadn't been the biggest TB fans but they utterly despised this new prick. Mum, who'd previously been able to moderate her commentary regarding my romantic selections, couldn't keep quiet about this one and even started seeing a therapist regularly to deal with the grief his presence in my life was causing her. The Overlap called me a cunt once in front of both my dad and my sister Kerrie. Dad was so angry that he withdrew completely to stop himself exploding, while Kerrie took the opposite approach of spitting in my boyfriend's face. I wasn't used to having my family look down or take pity on me, so I mostly stopped ringing them while I sorted my life out.

I figured that, as bad as things got, if I managed to turn it all around and prove them wrong, then it would be as though none of it had ever happened. So I stubbornly dug my heels in and resolved to fix everything for everyone to save myself the indignity of admitting that I'd been an idiot. More than getting my family on side, I needed to show myself that I was strong and successful and that I had the power to carve out a happy life for Violet and me. It bothered me that I might fall into the category of 'failed' women with a string of random boyfriends. Surely a smart person like me could never let that happen. So why was it happening?

A huge part of why I'm so passionate now about empowering single mothers is that I understand what it feels like to be embarrassed. There's a pervasive assumption in society that single mums are irresponsible and unwanted; that we are a burden of the state and that we raise our 'mistakes' to be aggressive and ill-mannered. That's a difficult and unjust identity to be marked with when you know it isn't true and I wish that I'd been strong enough to see how much better off I'd have been alone, despite the scarlet letter that would invariably accompany my independence.

The Overlap loved telling people about my daughter as though she was his own accomplishment. He'd say how 'fulfilling' his life had become since meeting us, even though he didn't know the first thing about being a parent and was actually still banging random women over at his bachelor pad. How you raise someone else's child from across town with a Tinder date straddling your face, I'll never know. I guess that's multitasking.

One surprising benefit of the relationship was that there was no room for my audacity in it, so that part of me had to find somewhere else to set up shop. It found its place on stage and, as I was shrinking at home, my stand-up voice became more powerful and self-assured. I'd start with a true story about how I'd recently been knocked back, then fantasise about how I'd handled the situation with an admirable feminist riposte. I became a walking contradiction as other women seemed to feel emboldened by my newfound strength on stage. I even felt inspired by it! Deep down, I knew the right thing to do was to walk away from this toxic relationship but my actions were working on a delay behind my intuition. Sometimes you need to hear yourself speaking sense out loud a few times before actually following your own advice.

Being with The Overlap whipped up frenzied joy now and again but ultimately the relationship was making every aspect of my life more difficult. I got chatting about my problems to a lovely make-up artist backstage on a job and she recommended her own therapist to me. I reached out to Pam via email right then and there for an appointment. Initially, my aim was to learn how to better manage my relationship with a view to sticking with The Overlap and making it work between us. Pam turned out to be a godsend because she steered me away from my obsession with his infidelity and slowly made me see that there were other, more dangerous qualities that made him a dolt. I argued for my investment: 'But I've spent a whole year working on this relationship!' She made me see that the only thing worse than wasting a year with the wrong person was to waste a year plus one more day.

Without my career and my friends, I don't think I would have ever gotten out. Those resources afforded me just enough self-esteem to keep my head on straight and recognise that letting go isn't the same as giving up. That part was key for me. I had confused commitment and resilience with toxic co-dependency. I thought that walking away from this faux partnership would make me a failure but that's just as stupid as if I'd kept my head submerged in a bowl of water forever when I could easily stand up and take a breath.

Fixing this relationship wouldn't absolve me from having left my daughter's father in a messy, deceitful way. I was a cheater no matter what. I needed to forgive myself for acting so cowardly and move forward. This is exactly why I've counselled divorcing friends recently not to rush into their next romance too quickly. You've got to settle all your shit before starting something new, otherwise you carry hurt and expectations with you that impact your ability to think rationally.

Making a 'proper family' with this buffoon didn't guarantee that it would be a happy one. Even if I could get him to stop lying or sleeping with other women, he'd still be the kind of dullard who'd fake an accent over the phone while pretending to be his own music agent. He was a bad investment and a serious creep. So, just like that, I confronted my uncertain future and let him go.

He retaliated when I wouldn't answer the phone by texting a bunch of odd selfie videos of himself crying, while angrily repeating, 'You're damaged! I'm damaged! We're doomed!' And I thought, 'Nah, mate, YOU'RE doomed on your own.' He also sent a few very long, rambling emails calling me 'a silly, stupid girl' before I googled how to block his address for good. (Beware of anyone who sends mega-long emails.) I blocked his number, blocked him on social media, email, everything. I even moved out of my flat. And I never looked back.

But before I went . . . I grabbed a few of his external hard drives that I thought probably had some compromising photos of me on them. I plugged them in with the intention of deleting the pics when, to my medium surprise, I found several labelled folders: 'Laura', 'Jane', 'Harriet', 'Martha', 'Zoe' (like a Mambo No. 5 of data) and also a lengthy Excel spreadsheet naming the hundreds of women The Overlap had slept with before me and during his time with me, too. Well, he'd been able to remember most of their first names. Some entries were just, 'Leeds Festival, Red Bikini'. It seemed he kept digital trophies, you know, like a serial killer would do.

I had been terrible to some of the women he'd slept with during our relationship. I'd blamed many, confronted others and pretty much slut-shamed the lot of them in some form. So by way of apology, I deleted everything. I expected they'd want their pictures to disappear as much as I wanted mine gone. One by one, I dragged their vag-laden folders to the trash and emptied it. So, ladies, if you once had an entanglement with a blond little simp from a failed indie collective whom you regret sending nudes to, I'm sorry if I acted like a dick and our photos no longer exist.

My voice came back shortly after that. And, tragically, The Overlap died in a freak face-sitting accident.

"

My relationships are like most female homicides: I already knew the guy.

"

How to Attract Toxic Men . . .
AND Keep Them Interested!

O ne of the pitfalls of working in a male-dominated industry
is that there are single men around all the time. In the early
days of doing stand-up especially you spend hours together on
trains, in green rooms, at festivals, and they become your close
intimate circle of friends. Too much to drink one night and, bam,
you've sucked off another colleague. Because of my responsibilities
to Violet, I was usually rushing home and I certainly wasn't
getting hammered, so I avoided the spontaneity of any one-night
stands but that didn't stop me from accidentally falling in love
with my friends now and then. My relationships are like most
female homicides: I already knew the guy.

I moved swiftly along into a new relationship, this time with
The Sketch Actor, who I got close to – you guessed it – after
several months of friendship that escalated one night at a festival
gig. The Sketch Actor, despite being consumed by hatred for
Russell Brand, looked a bit and dressed A LOT like Russell
Brand. That part was confusing. He wore more skull rings than

he had fingers for, the tightest British trousers I'd ever seen and torn-up vests that always showed his nipples. My mother adored him. Just kidding; she hated him like she hated the others. I introduced them on a video chat once and she later remarked that he was the filthiest-looking man she'd ever seen and she found it disrespectful that he hadn't bothered putting any clothes on and conducted the chat in his underwear.

I thought he was funny and sweet so I quite liked him until we went on holiday. For a start, I never, ever wanted to take a vacation in the first place. If Violet was with her dad for a weekend or for Christmas, my preference was always to catch up on sleep or work by myself. It felt very unnatural to be without her and certainly wasn't something that I wanted to celebrate. Also, when you're freelance, as I considered myself to be, it's prudent to be available for any last-minute jobs that might be offered to you. Being home was my priority but I could see how this made me a bad partner, and I acknowledged that other women my age could just pick up and travel, or, at the very least, show their boyfriends the undivided attention they craved in a new relationship. I added my inadequacy as a girlfriend to the growing stink of shame that clung to me and reluctantly agreed to spend New Year's Eve with him in Morocco. I made a speech about how irresponsible it was for a single mother to spend money on a holiday, so he compromised by picking somewhere very affordable and paying for half of my share. Still, everything in my being told me not to go.

On our first night abroad, I experienced what I can only describe as a panic attack and it never really went away during the entire trip. My chest got tight and I'd burst into tears out of nowhere, crying like a child who wanted to go home. Then I'd be alright for a few hours and teeter on the edge of tears before losing it all over again. The poor man was having a terrible time, managing my breakdowns with walks through the market and ice cream, but I couldn't escape being viscerally sad. I hated not 'behaving' properly because I was able to clearly see that I was ruining the trip but I honestly couldn't help acting like a nightmare. I felt trapped and since my head hadn't done the simple job of keeping me home, my body was showing me the consequences. My advice is to listen to your body at all costs because your intuition is a lot older than your intellect, so it's always smarter than your head. Ignore it and it'll usually find a way of taking you out. I didn't relax until I was in the boarding lounge on the way back to the UK and, as a wave of relief swept over me, I quietly suggested we never go on holiday together again. Without the distractions of regular life, I just hated being in The Sketch Actor's distilled company.

He wanted to be made a priority which, looking back, was fair enough but I couldn't place him above Violet, work, sleep or food – the true loves of my life. We'd agreed to hang out late one evening after one of my gigs, and I hadn't eaten all day, so was hungrily biting into a burrito I'd saved while he shared some important story. Apparently, the wrap was preventing me from listening well enough, which hurt his feelings. 'You won't even put down your burrito and look me in the eyes!' he said. Well, no. Because I needed it to live.

It was 2013 and, later that year, I was offered a huge opportunity to perform at the Just for Laughs Festival in Montreal, Canada. I'd been invited to be part of Whitney Cummings' gala line-up and she had long been one of my favourite comics so it was a massive honour for me. Violet had just turned four and we were both excited for the adventure and for the trip back home to see family. The Sketch Actor was less than pleased that he hadn't been invited by the festival and I did worry a bit about the pattern of jealousy from my previous relationships resurfacing in this one. He had lots of friends and things to keep him occupied, though, so I went ahead with a clear conscience.

Sitting in the empty auditorium for the gala tech rehearsal waiting my turn was almost an out-of-body experience. I watched Bridget Everett – who I admittedly hadn't known before then but have since been OBSESSED by – bring the entire crew to tears of laughter while she blasted through her set list, checking microphone levels for her songs. Neal Brennan was also in the show along with Tom Papa and Jim Norton, and I just felt so incredibly lucky to be there watching a private performance of their craft.

Suddenly, my phone started vibrating. It was The Sketch Actor but I had to ignore the call. He rang back, and back, and back again, until finally I slipped out the stage door to answer. 'Babe, I was marching along a canal holding a wine bottle and I accidentally fell in,' his voice explained. 'The glass shattered through my hand and I'm off now to get stitches.' I could tell that he was 'merry' if not completely drunk and, since he was with a bunch of friends and there was really nothing that I could do transatlantically to help sew his tendons shut, I offered my condolences and hung up. With his remaining hand, he managed to send texts throughout the rest of the rehearsal, announcing his disappointment that I hadn't put everything on hold and been more available to comfort him in that moment. I came offstage after my own tech run feeling like a shit girlfriend once again.

Mum and I went out for a celebratory dinner with Violet, then got her a babysitter at the hotel so that Mum could come watch my set that night. I felt very proud to have her there and to be making real strides in what had become my full-time, thriving career. Just for Laughs was another big step forward in comedy for me and I was getting better at setting boundaries with partners so that I didn't get distracted from my new goals or my fresh confidence that I could achieve them.

I returned home a few days later and then almost straight away travelled to another festival for work. British festivals have an element of 'camping' though, as a Canadian, it's very difficult to call it that since it's just tents stacked side-by-side next to portaloos in a field and there aren't any bears. They're amazing fun though – with food, music, comedy – and sleeping outdoors is a novelty when you're four years old, so I packed up a wagon, a backpack, a tent and my daughter for the weekend. I was scheduled for two shows each day and the rest of the time would be ours to dance in the child-friendly music tents and enjoy the perpetual hen-do that was our relationship. Dinners, dresses, games, train rides, adventures . . . Violet and I were having a great time, all the time.

She was entrenched in the gang of my female comedy friends and would regularly sit with Harriet Kemsley, Sara Pascoe, Tania Edwards, Aisling Bea, Tiff Stevenson or Roisin Conaty while I took my turn on stage. She loved them and I feel so lucky to have been able to expose her to their influence. 'Listen, Roisin,' Violet would say, 'you know this first part is true and then my mummy's going to change it at the end. She does that for the comedy.' She was savvy to our shtick.

I'd managed to smooth things over with The Sketch Actor during the couple of days that I'd been in London and I accepted his assertion that I'd been wrong for behaving so coldly when that idiot had bloodied himself in the canal. But as soon as I'd arrived at the festival grounds and finished the laborious task of setting up the tent, I received another phone call from him, this time letting me know that his X-rays showed severe muscle damage and the doctor was recommending surgery on his hand first thing the following morning. Fuck. I knew that he expected me to be there. It wasn't like me to disappoint Violet or to ditch a gig but I'd made a commitment to be a partner to this man I could hardly stand, so I set about finding a replacement. My friend and fellow comic Angela Barnes heroically offered to take my spot, though this meant switching her timings with a male comedian who had a separate conflict. Between the three of us, we could make it work. I fed this back to the promoter while pleading my 'family obligation' to the clumsy boyfriend back in London but he flatly refused to make the switch, writing in an email that, 'Having Angela swap in would render the comedy bill too female-heavy on that day and that doesn't work for me.'

Even from the start, when my principles went way beyond my budget, gender disparity at work got my back up. I found it especially infuriating when the gatekeepers were brave enough to put it in black and white so, after receiving that email, I left. Here I was, humping my ass on a train throughout rural England with a four-year-old child whom I financially supported 100 per cent while simultaneously trying to soothe a man who'd stupidly sliced his own hand open acting like a pirate, and I was deemed less capable than my male counterparts? People didn't want 'female-heavy' comedy line-ups back then. And many would still prefer not to have them today.

The Sketch Actor milked his injury for a long time. I'd given birth to an entire person without any family or drugs to help and I just couldn't stomach his neediness. I'm happy to put myself forward as uncaring partner here. I cared about my boyfriend but didn't feel safe bonding with him or fully letting him into our lives. I would qualify his existence to Violet by saying, 'He's our friend but he isn't our family,' which she immediately seemed to understand. It wasn't long after canal-gate that he very sensibly started dating someone who could stand to be alone with him for more than a few hours. I was single again but instead of being empowered, I felt eerily defenceless.

Still a coward, I accidentally started dating The Comedy Producer after we'd spent a few weeks shut in writers' rooms together. I've basically got the same criteria as a giant panda for new relationships, in that you put me in close enough proximity of a potential mate with adequate resources for long enough, we'll eventually give breeding a go. He was nice but during this relationship, a terrible thing happened that it's taken me nearly a decade to tell only a handful of people about because it's the single biggest threat I've ever faced.

While nearing the end of the Edinburgh Fringe Festival, where I'd been working for the month of August with Violet, I received a phone call. 'Is this Katherine Ryan?' the voice asked. 'Where are you? Where is your daughter?' Confused, I asked who was calling and why. The woman didn't give details but calmly stated that she was with the Child Protection branch of my local council authority and that she was investigating a report related to Violet.

'WHAT REPORT?!' I demanded to know.

She seemed annoyed that I hadn't responded to two letters that had been delivered through the door in the last week while I'd been away in Scotland. Refusing to tell me who had made the referral or what the context of it was, she set up an interview in my home for the following day. Taking it all quite seriously, I rang Kitty, my agent, who put me in touch with my agency lawyer for advice. I booked last-minute plane tickets and rushed home with Violet for the meeting. I spent the whole night awake crying, absolutely mortified that someone would try to hurt us in the worst way.

I'd had personal wobbles over the last few years and I hadn't always made the right choices for myself but I was confident of one truth: the solid and irrefutable fact that Violet was impeccably looked after, protected and loved. I didn't dare fully entertain the nightmarish thought that she might be taken away. She was only small and, setting aside how I felt about it, she found being without me for a day to be so traumatic that I brought her everywhere instead. We were closer than close.

Still unaware of exactly what they were investigating, I opened the door the next morning to two stoic ladies holding clip boards and wearing lanyards. They came inside, briefly spoke with a cheerful and oblivious Violet, looked at a few of her drawings on the wall and coolly inspected my tidy little flat. They declined my offer of tea and sat down at the kitchen table. The main lady asked about The Comedy Producer I was dating. She asked a few more questions about me, about my level of support from friends, my babysitters and just generally tried to get a sense of who I was. These people are good at their jobs. I cannot fault them for acting swiftly on any potential issue related to the safety of a child, given whatever they had been told. Even as I sat there shaking with hurt and fear, I had the presence of mind to appreciate the work they did.

After a couple of minutes, they both closed their file folders and their postures visibly relaxed. The main one smiled gently and said that her initial assessment was that Violet was not in danger but that perhaps there was someone in my life who might want to vindictively hurt me. She said that people who want revenge will – in extreme cases – try to threaten the things you most cherish. For every parent, this is obviously their children. She said that as part of procedure, Violet and I would both have to visit a health centre to meet with a nurse and that The Comedy Producer and I would also have to go to a government building in Wood Green for an interview so they could meet him.

Finally, she put me in touch with a support service for people who might be victims of such malice. I could tell that whatever allegations had been made weren't a random mistake and I knew exactly who had made them and why. It was threatening, controlling and a way to get my attention. For this reason, I made the decision that I would NEVER confront the person who caused this. It would give them too much satisfaction to know that they'd succeeded in wounding me as deeply as they had. Being investigated by Child Protection Services was the single most frightening and embarrassing event that I had ever faced but it was my resolve to deny this person the gratification they wanted that actually kept me quiet. I wouldn't gain anything from confronting them. What was I going to say? Get angry and ask them why? The answer didn't matter and would probably have been a lie anyway.

I told no one. Which meant I had no one to talk to. If anything, it brought me closer to The Comedy Producer because I obviously had to confide in him so that he could attend the interview. Weirdly, we had a common enemy now so he became very protective of me and the whole thing only served to force us closer together. He seemed more than happy to open his life up to the local authority and defend his virtue.

Days later, Violet and I took the bus and her little scooter into Highgate, north London, to see the health visitor. She tootled along carefully like she always did and we stopped several times to admire a snail or to splash in a puddle while I worried about what could be waiting for us at the nurse's office. Would she just want another chat or was I subjecting my daughter to a full physical examination? I suppose that under different circumstances, it could very well have been the latter, but thankfully when we got there she just wanted to talk with me generally about dangerous relationships. Thankfully, everyone 'official' that we encountered seemed to unanimously understand that Violet was happy and well, but they had concerns for my safety. I had always considered myself to be strong so I hated being treated as though I might be easy to manipulate. In fairness, it was hard to maintain any shred of self-respect when I'd clearly been stupid enough to find myself in a health visitor's office addressing a Child Protection referral initiated out of spite.

The final step before closing the file was to attend the interview with The Comedy Producer. I couldn't believe he wanted to go through with it. Dating a single mother is one thing, but dating a single mother whose antagonist has prompted an investigation into you possibly being a nonce is a whole new level of baggage. I had never felt lower.

It was storming hail on the September morning of our meeting and I wore a smart tartan raincoat over what I guessed were basically 'church clothes', as I'd never had to consider what one would wear to court. Was I going to court? Once more, I didn't know what to expect.

The offices were disgusting and rammed with sad people. It was the bleakest place I'd ever seen. Upon arrival, we were led to a small room that contained a table, a few chairs and a couple of discarded plasters that I'd also noticed stuck to the legs of those chairs. The same two ladies who'd visited my home were there with their clipboards and file folders, ready to ask The Comedy Producer the same types of questions they'd asked me. In addition, they asked him what his future intentions were for our relationship. He became romantic in that moment and spoke about how serious he was and how he wanted to marry me. I firmly told him, 'Do not propose to me HERE.' The ladies' eyes widened and they shook their heads at him with disapproval. This was NOT the kind of setting anyone wanted to reminisce about at the rehearsal dinner. I felt trapped. Overall, he seemed a lot more blasé about the whole thing than I was. He leaned back in the chair with his legs wide apart. They asked him whether he had any criminal history and whether he'd ever dated underaged girls. Trying to be funny, I think, he started actually flirting with them and said, 'Absolutely not. I'm more into older women,' and winked.

The Comedy Producer was a dweeb and I wanted to let these women know once and for all that my priority would always be my daughter and that, sure, I'd made some humiliating decisions when it came to men who interacted with ME but I would lay down my life before letting anyone or anything hurt her. I felt like my entire life was an exhausting marathon of vigilance and sacrifice when it came to my relationships with men and all I really wanted was to be left in peace so that I could focus on Violet alone. I was breaking my back to create a safe, happy and fruitful environment ALL FOR HER. Our life was going to be better than good. It was going to be very special. In that moment, I blurted out, 'You know, I don't need him. I don't need anyone for anything! I am not a vulnerable person who would make excuses for a bad man just to keep him around. Who do you think I am?' I liked the way it sounded out loud.

This entire mess was caused by me. No, I hadn't invited legitimately predatory men into our lives. But I had developed a pattern of bringing in jealous, controlling, diabolical or just plain weird men who wanted to waste my time or push me around. And that had to stop.

The Child Protection ladies closed the case as evidence showed that neither I, nor The Comedy Producer, posed any danger to Violet. Duh. I buried the shame of having been through that indignity as deeply as it would go and I became an absolute fucking dragon after that. No men. No thanks. I embarked upon a trauma-induced journey of hyper-independence entitled, 'I don't need anyone for anything'. I was on high alert. I pushed The Comedy Producer away until he eventually disappeared.

By now, I was on TV semi-regularly, so I started to get a few athletes and reality stars sliding into my DMs. Nothing explicit, just straightforward invitations to get drinks or else the suspicious and much-dreaded 'How's you . . . ?' without context. There was a famous athlete in particular who I'd only seen dating glamour models publicly, so when he reached out, I wondered what the hell he could possibly want with me. I'd always assumed that my job would put off 'normal' men because of course I'd been led to believe that women are only funny when they're laughing at your jokes, not when they're making jokes themselves. I started worrying that men might see me on a comedy panel and get a false sense of knowing who I was or that they might try to sleep with me as a prank. I could tell that the growing public consensus was that I was some sort of wild dominatrix character – that because I had a sharp tongue on stage, I must also be crazy in bed and 'high maintenance' as a partner. I wasn't really that way at all, I was just standoffish as a reflex, but I didn't care if people got the wrong idea. I never corrected them. A male friend from work once said to me, 'You're basically undateable. Because some of the men you've been with are so awful, if you took interest in someone new, that would be an immediate sign that he was a prick. Nobody decent wants to be that prick.'

A balanced level of independence is a wonderful thing. Being alone is how I learned the value of my own company. I became okay with silence, peace and the idea that if I never built a traditional 'family' unit for Violet, she would be fine. I started writing comedy about the many joys of being single to try to encourage shamed women who might've felt stupid and wrong like I had. I was offered even more professional opportunities and was able to take Violet to Los Angeles, Australia and New

York as she grew up. In 2016, I bought us a flat. It wasn't until I knew we were settled and strong, just the two of us, without the bullshit and distractions that I once thought I had to tolerate to be the 'right' kind of woman, that I finally relaxed. My pendulum finally landed in the middle.

"

All our lives,
women are
warned about
turning 35.

How to Have Another Baby:
Part One

I'd just turned 35 and as my birthday present to myself, I'd booked a private appointment at the Portland Hospital in London to investigate my fertility. All our lives, women are warned about turning 35. 'Your fertility falls off a cliff' has a distinctively violent ring to it – conjuring up images of Damien's fatally possessed nanny in *The Omen*. Why the cliff? Couldn't they have chosen a gentler idiom, like 'passes out in a sun lounger'? Nope. Your fertility, according to actual doctors, has to suddenly plunge towards its demise like a cartoon coyote with dynamite in its teeth. Seems true, though, at least from the graphs I've seen online. So, in that case, we'd better all hurry up and sort things out in time to determine our entire biological legacies before most of us are able to buy a house. It's bullshit. It's an infuriating gender injustice.

I'd known for a long time that I wanted to have more than one child and I was fine with the idea of doing it alone. I figured nobody comes to the end of their life and thinks, 'Yeah . . . but I wish I'd had fewer children.'

This is sort of where the inspiration for my Netflix series, *The Duchess*, came from. One afternoon, I just started laughing to myself about all the hypothetical approaches that a single mother with a unique worldview might explore to grow her family. Would she adopt? I thought that if she stomped around town with a smart mouth and worked erratic hours like I did, she probably wouldn't qualify. Would she employ a 'better the devil you know' logic and have a second baby with the same man who fathered her first child? That worked best for the series because it made them adversaries with a common goal. (Though I'd personally never consider doing that. Gross.) After what she'd already overcome, she couldn't possibly trust a whole new man and risk repeating the entire cycle that follows the 'inevitable' relationship breakdown, so it would be challenging for her to have a child with a new boyfriend. Or would she do away with men altogether and go it alone?

In my real life, the choice was clear: sperm donor. My fertility tests had come back with flying colours and the doctor advised that I should feel no real rush to proceed with egg collection and freezing unless I wanted to, but to come back every year to check how much my egg supply diminished. It was still – however slowly – plummeting from a vertical rock, maybe towards a crashing ocean coast with even more sharp and exposed rocks. This was a constant ominous threat.

By now, my Netflix special, *In Trouble*, was streaming worldwide and I was about to release *Glitter Room*, my second stand-up hour for the platform. I was a homeowner and I regularly toured nationally and appeared on UK television, so I was in a privileged position to be able to afford treatment. Sperm clinics offer donor profiles online. Anyone can create an account to look through the descriptions and most places have a list of optional criteria to narrow the search fields. You can pick ethnicity, religious background, education, height – it's what I imagine dating apps are like but straight to the transactional point of making a baby. There are photos but they're childhood photos of the donors, which actually makes sense in terms of anonymity but came off as creepy to me in the context of buying semen. Essentially, you're looking at a toddler from the past in view of purchasing his adult jizz of the future. That dissonance never sat well with me. Clinics also include a sales pitch-style blurb about each man – usually something along the lines of, 'Ronald enjoys playing a variety of team sports and hopes to help people achieve their dreams of having a child. He's a barrister with strong, broad shoulders and a warm smile'. I didn't like reading about their smiles when I knew full well that they were turning up to jerk off for cash. Of course they were smiling! I wanted a donor with enough humility to come in looking suitably at the floor, like I would do if I was entering a paid masturbation centre.

A lot of them were super-clever biomedical engineers or architects. Their write-ups often came across to me as bordering on the narcissistic side of noble and, remembering what my friend once warned about 'diabolical men', I decided those donors didn't appeal to me. 'Who needs a clever baby?' I thought. Violet was a super smart baby and it didn't do me any favours. It meant that as a newborn, she was awake, frustrated and alert for hours on end. I might not have time to teach this baby the soothing independence of sign language and I figured that Violet's good nature as a toddler was probably an anomaly that wasn't passed down by me. I didn't want to be a mother to the next Elon Musk, or worse, an evil Nazi scientist. Intelligence can be a burden that I worried might make a person more likely to experience mental anguish. Besides, the documentary *Forrest Gump* proved to me that simple folk could lead perfectly successful and happy lives. I just wanted to raise a kind, happy person.

I expanded my search to Seattle Sperm Bank because they have a relationship with the London clinic I was browsing, as I figured I'd find more laid-back hippies there. I based this theory solely on my experience of the chilled American West Coast, and also the sketch comedy television series *Portlandia*. Portland, Oregon, isn't far from Seattle and I reasoned that, since the programme spoofed the city's reputation as a haven for eccentric hipsters, that there'd also be beatniks up the road in Seattle. Good enough logic for me.

I logged in and, immediately, my attention was drawn to Bodhi, a 20-something college student whose bio said that he loved his mom, his skateboard and his guitar. Bingo. His childhood photos looked a bit like he could be related to Violet and he had a real mix of ethnic heritage, which was good because I'm far too Celtic and couldn't be having babies with another 100 per cent Irish person. I needed Violet's sibling to be able to sit in the sun with her for more than five minutes without breaking out in a rash. I'm terrible company on holiday.

When you see a donor you definitely like, you've got to reserve their frozen specimen for £900 straight away because there are strict limits on how many families they can 'contribute' to in each country. I suppose they want to avoid siblings populating an entire town and getting married. Bit judgey, but makes sense. I'd discussed having another baby with Violet, who was thrilled with the plan, but I didn't involve her in any of the specifics. I valued her opinion when it came to most things but I wasn't about to go into details or risk getting her hopes up until I was ready to pull the trigger. For the moment, everything I was doing was just for insurance; I was setting myself up in a feminist chess match against mother nature. I felt safer knowing that I was entering the post-35 egg shortage with sperm in the freezer (like, at the clinic, not at home next to my ice cream) and enough of a biological grace period egg-wise to consider my next move. At that time, I was writing scripts for *The Duchess* and knew that it wouldn't make narrative sense to have just given birth or be pregnant during filming for the series so, at the very least, I'd need to wait until that project was finished. My career was also definitely a consideration and it's terrible to acknowledge, but I wasn't sure whether I was in a strong enough position to be 'forgiven' for what pregnancy would do to my body. Ugly sentence to write. Uglier reality to navigate.

In addition to the fertility cliff edge, potential irrelevance is another obstacle women face at 35. This is especially true in the entertainment industry. I've actually overheard decision-makers rejecting suggestions for female contributors on the basis that they'd be 'too old for our audience', then booking male comedians in the same age bracket instead. You only need to look at the lingering panel show trend of casting six male headliner comedians next to one or two 'beautiful entertainer' category women who've never delivered a single line of stand-up in their young lives to see that female comics aren't valued in the same way as our male counterparts. I've been instructed by producers through an earpiece to 'smile more', specifically at the very serious man sat next to me. I've had frank production chats about wearing my hair down to look 'softer'; I've had my wardrobe scrutinised while half the boys can't even bring in a clean shirt and I'd be a fool to think that my carefully crafted glamorous image hasn't been at least partly responsible for my success. Oh, I've also shared a table at an awards show with a big-time producer who got drunk and made loud MOO-ing noises at a young woman while she accepted her trophy on stage. If we complain about any of it, we're branded forever as 'difficult'.

The thought of getting fat as well as old simultaneously was professionally scary. It would force people to change their understanding of 'what I was' as an entertainer and give them the option to reject me instead. People don't love change. I get that I'm a comedian, not a pop star, and that appearance doesn't matter in the grand scheme of things, but it does matter on TV. Even in comedy . . . at least, when you're a woman. I promise you that it matters to some of the people deciding whether to continue to give me opportunities or not. There's a certain echelon of experience and familiarity where they'll make an exception for you but, most of the time, it's just easier to pick someone else. Preferably, a young actress or a bubbly presenter who laughs a lot.

I'm not proud that I was afraid of losing my career in the event that I got pregnant. Every comedian I know considers themselves to be freelance so, in a way, we're all scared that every job might be our last – and the pandemic certainly didn't help quell those uncertainties. But I want to be honest about my fears because I'm actually very protected. I've got lots of television projects, a national tour coming up and, of course, I'm writing this book, so really, I'm fine. But the women rising up in the comedy ranks like I was a few years ago may not be fine. They'll be overlooked like I was when I was first expecting Violet. And I'm not even bulletproof now.

People who've seen *The Duchess* have asked me whether it's true that I have intentions to grow my family soon. That question has swiftly been followed up by, 'And, if so, will you cancel your tour?' Tell me, how often do you reckon they've asked a father that same question?

"

I tried to have a one-night stand with my high school boyfriend and accidentally married him instead.

"

How to Marry Your High School Boyfriend

Going off what I've seen from the eccentric older ladies I often meet in the park, I think a lot of women wait until later in life to let their freak flags fly. By contrast, I've gone the other way and I'm absolutely certain (and you, having reached this stage in the book, might be, too) that I'm now the most boring and ordinary that I've ever been. I'm very relaxed and surprisingly well-mannered. I go to bed early, I avoid red meat and gluten, I've been solidly pregnant for about a year and a half at time of writing so I can't even drink and I get excited about trips to Costco. My slide to all this started in January 2019, when I tried to have a one-night stand with my high school boyfriend and accidentally married him instead. No one could have guessed that I'd turn out so desperately contented.

It says a lot about society that when people see my husband, Bobby, they immediately suspect foul play. As a culture, we are really not used to seeing a beautiful man married to a woman his own age unless he's been trapped with a baby or is using her for commissary money while in jail. Bobby works out so, naturally, people would feel more comfortable with him dating a 20-year-old Instagram model off *Love Island*. I can assure you that, like any sane adult, he would rather scoop out his own eyeballs with a hot spoon than spend a day in the company of most 20-year-old girls. I've absolutely nothing against younger women but, having been one myself, I know first-hand that in 99.9 per cent of cases when an older man is showing you attention, it's either because he wants to dominate you or because women his own age won't fuck with him. He'll tell you you're special, he'll tell you you're smart, but I'm telling you that, as special and smart as you are, those qualities will only increase with age. So step away from the old man's penis. You're not actually smart until you can see him clearly for the loser he is.

When Bobby and I met in Year 11 at Northern Collegiate, he 'got me' straight away. He could see that I was gentle and he found me to be funny and sweet when hardly anyone else did. It was a relatively small school but, for some reason, he wasn't on my radar at all until the day I saw him at a basketball game and realised that we had mutual friends. His face was entirely painted half red and half black in our school colours and I knew that he was going to the same post-game house party that I was. I climbed up the bleachers at halftime and pointedly told him I'd see him afterwards and that was it. We'd never met before but we just decided out of nowhere to be in love that day. We spent the entire party kissing in a laundry room and I went home with school colours on my face and my new boyfriend's phone number in my pocket. Bobby was gorgeous, a football star and popular in the same way that I was – we were well-liked in our circles, but anyone who didn't know us thought we were dicks. He made me laugh and, crucially, I could tell that he thought I was funny – it was a quality he valued.

Bobby was known as a 'thousandaire' – meaning he was one of few boys his age with a job and that he had saved up over a thousand dollars. He worked weekends at a small Italian restaurant clearing plates and washing dishes. I respected his work ethic and I admired his strength after losing his dad very young and having to grow up protecting his mum and three sisters. The 'man of the house' trope is so heartbreaking. I cannot imagine looking at a little boy and suggesting that he should take on the responsibility of being head of the household as the oldest surviving male, but that was the reality of toxic masculinity and people said it to him a few times when he was small. His parents had gotten together as teenagers and I took it for granted that we would obviously get married as well.

We were 16 and so had started going out to clubs with fake IDs and drinking. One night, I arrived late to a party after a musical theatre show and Bobby was already there, tipsy. I went over to kiss him hello and he stopped me, saying we needed to talk. I was blindsided when he broke up with me. 'But WHY?!' I begged. He said he couldn't remember the reason, just that he'd made a promise to himself earlier in the evening that he would end things and that he was a man of his word. This was the stupidest thing I'd ever heard, especially as we'd been getting along perfectly well up until that point. I knew how important his friends were so I quickly tried to negotiate. 'How about if I don't take up any of your free time and we just have sex when we happen to be at the same parties?!' This is called desperation and it's not cute. Bobby stood firm in the promise he'd made to himself for reasons he couldn't remember. He tells me now that he would've recanted the entire silly thing by the following morning but by then I had FREAKED the FUCK out and it was too late.

I ran from that party in floods of tears. I'd just gotten my driver's licence and hadn't been there long enough to drink so I climbed into my car followed closely by my concerned girlfriends and sped all the way home. It was so dramatic. I screamed the whole journey that my life was over and I didn't care whether I lived or died. My friends in the backseat preferred that we all stay breathing, if at all possible.

Home and disappointingly alive, I fell into my bedroom and sobbed myself to sleep. Unable to face Bobby, who'd RIGHT AWAY started casually seeing some awful girl who smoked, I refused to go to school and I ate nothing but Cool Ranch Doritos for an entire month. You'd maybe assume that a diet of crisps would cause one to gain weight but I doubt they actually contain any nutrients because I lost two whole stone that I couldn't afford to lose. My mum and sisters were afraid of the skeleton that now lurked in their basement so nobody dared nudge me to quit wallowing and just quietly left bags of crisps at the top of the stairs instead.

It might seem callous to stick a teenager in the basement but don't forget that Canadian properties are sprawling by UK standards and we finish our basements beautifully. I liked being down there. I had a huge wardrobe, privacy, a cable television and my very own phone line. My bedroom was next to the laundry room so it always smelled of fresh linen softener. I'd moved to the basement aged 13, just before starting high school, so that Kerrie and Joanne could have their own bedrooms upstairs next to our parents' master suite. I'd been allowed to paint the walls whatever colour I wanted, so I chose to keep it a clean, crisp white but kept a border around the entire room for my girlfriends to draw pictures on and write messages. It looked like a strip of graffiti before the ceiling and it was always in a state of change and being overwritten.

My dad had just moved out at this point and, one day, while he'd taken my sisters for ice cream and I was laying on his floor wishing it would swallow me up, the building's fire alarm went off. Result. Unmotivated to evacuate, I stayed there being soothed by the siren. My dad returned home to find a hundred tenants outside next to fire trucks and assumed the worst had happened. It was a false alarm and I wouldn't have jumped anyway, mostly because I didn't have the energy. I was still inside, still laying on the floor. I was in a very bad way and nobody knew how to help me. Over the next several weeks, I pulled all of my eyebrows and eyelashes out from stress.

Then, one day, I woke up and wanted to eat an apple and go outside. It happened just like that. For no reason other than the passing of time, I slowly started to feel okay again. I wish that I could grab every depressed teenager and let them know that when all seems hopeless, you've just got to give yourself time to sprawl out on the carpet and trust that there is light at the end of the tunnel. It always gets better.

I returned to school and almost immediately got back together with Bobby. I shouldn't have taken him back so easily after his heartless behaviour but what can I say? I wanted to. These were simpler times and it turned out that Bobby didn't like smoking and missed my sweet, sweet banter, so he started passing me notes in class again and ringing my house after school. I let him put in a solid three days' graft before we drove to a secluded park and had sex in my car. (We didn't know about the culture of 'dogging' and I still don't think that exists in Canada. Teenagers just have sex in cars because we aren't allowed to do it in the house. Why British people conflate that with voyeurism is beyond me . . .)

Bobby and I spent the rest of the year being blissfully back in love and he apologised for having been so careless with my fragile teenaged heart. We turned 17 and went to prom together. We'd been drinking beforehand so neither us can remember exactly why but, once again, Bobby broke up with me. This time on the dance floor and while my favourite Nelly song was playing. I hadn't thought you could get dumped in a tiara but the events of that night proved me wrong. Instead of being sad, I harnessed the power of alcohol and got even. I marched into the after-prom party with my girlfriends and told them to 'watch this'. That's never a sign of good things to come when spoken from the vexed heart of an idiot teenager who's just grown her eyelashes back. This time, I needed to throw a grenade into my relationship with Bobby so that we'd never get back together. I'd spotted a very large security guard towering over the beer kegs. He was not only the biggest man at the party but the biggest man I'd ever seen in my life. I'll confidently go out on a limb and say he had an anabolic steroid problem. Anyway, I walked over and started kissing him. Bobby saw. Everyone saw. And, just like that, I was back to self-harm as a failed method of revenge.

I started seeing this 30-year-old bouncer. We only had sex a handful of times but I recall his entire body was spiky like a cheese grater because he shaved it. Rather than sensibly using condoms, he'd pull out and finish into hats, shirts, socks – whatever was laying around in his flat. He loved the comedian Jeff Foxworthy, whose punchline to most of his jokes was ' . . . then you might be a redneck!' If you do this, you might be a redneck. If you do that, you might be a redneck. He'd put the DVDs on while I was over there and it made me think, 'Hmm, if you're a 17-year-old high school student dating an adult man who models himself on Dolph Lundgren and jizzes into baseball caps, YOU MIGHT BE A REDNECK, KATHERINE.'

It didn't help that Mum's new boyfriend was much younger than mine. She'd started a relationship with 'Abe the Babe' from her work, who was something like five years older than I was. Our collective inability to respect social norms made us targets for public ridicule in our small town but I learned not to care. I'd developed an incredibly thick skin for tolerating the fuckery that people launched in my direction and I just couldn't wait to get out of there. Bobby, his friends and his sisters were annoyed with me because, of course, Bobby couldn't remember breaking up with me at prom, so assumed I'd cheated on him in plain sight with the bouncer. I'd had it with him, with Sarnia, with being 17 in general. Things fizzled out with the 30-year-old and, based on his lifestyle, it seems quite unlikely that he'd still be alive today. Probably crushed to death in a car-lifting competition, where the prize would have been free entry into a hot-dog eating contest. Abe the Babe, on the other hand, turned out to be cool and he's my stepdad now.

Twenty years went by before I properly spoke to Bobby again. Being from the same town, you keep mutual friends in common, so I heard bits of gossip about him and I knew when he had gotten married. I was actually at the park with my baby daughter when I saw it pop up on Facebook and felt jealous for a second before realising that I was pushing a swing that contained another man's child. Bobby had messaged me on social media on a few scattered occasions just to say that he admired my work. We always had a similar sense of humour and I felt butterflies each time he got in touch but I kept my responses to just one or two words because I knew I shouldn't be speaking to him. I'd come too far in my life to start flirting with my high school boyfriend, especially as we were both always in other relationships.

In December 2018, I recorded my second Netflix stand-up special, *Glitter Room*, which was all about discovering the power of independence and being happily single for the first time. I meant every word I said and felt excited about living a long life without the tedious baggage of a man in it. While in LA for the taping, I appeared on *The Late Late Show* with James Corden and Bobby shared a clip of my stand-up on his Facebook with the caption, 'My first crush. Congratulations, Kath x'. I could tell that he was single because I'm a woman and we can always tell your relationship status by how you conduct your social media at any given time. I commented under the video, 'It will never be too late for us xx', but mostly as a joke. I figured it would be a lovely throwback for our mutual friends to enjoy. I most certainly wasn't looking to start anything and, besides, that was the first contact we'd had in several years.

A month later, I was in Canada filming *Who Do You Think You Are?*, an ancestry show, for the BBC. Producers couldn't tell me how long I'd be in any city for or where I was going next because the idea is that you'll be genuinely surprised when the historians divulge layers of your ancestral lineage along the way. I landed in Toronto to establish the programme at Mum's house and, due to the spontaneous nature of the trip, I agreed to go out for drinks that night with Kerrie. I'm usually more professional but we were pretty certain I'd be flying somewhere else the following day so we popped out to a cocktail bar around the corner. A few hours and glasses of red wine later, Kerrie's chef husband, Alain, was finishing work and en route to join us.

I don't know how my mischievous psychic mind knew but I made a post to half a million followers feigning a need for recommendations on where to go out in Toronto. I was sure Bobby would take the bait. I had noticed that he was living in Toronto and something told me that, even though we'd never interacted on Instagram before, this would give him an opening to come see me. I hadn't thought of Bobby at all before the trip or even on my way there. He didn't enter my mind until the moment I sent out that brief story. I was just being a spontaneous dick with my sister and went with a spur-of-the-moment intuition. It came to me out of absolutely nowhere. An impetuous 15-second selfie video that would change my life.

Bobby replied to the post immediately, suggesting my sister and I try somewhere we had no intention of going. I messaged back that we'd already chosen a bar but that he was welcome to join us. This was uncharacteristically friendly of me and I sort of panicked when he said he was actually coming. I didn't know this man at all! Rationally, I never would have thought to invite him out – I was wearing flats with jeans and a knitted après-ski sweater – but I'd been drinking with Kerrie, so operated on pure Sarnia muscle-memory and animal instinct.

When Bobby walked into the bar, my first thought was . . . 'Wow, I'm definitely not a paedo.' It struck me how much better-looking I found him as a fully grown man than as a teenager. Men are so annoying because we accept them as being more attractive with fine lines and greying hair, while many of us gals are suffering under lasers and needles so that we don't get kicked off TV. (Just me . . . ?) My point is, Bobby was HOT and he felt like part of the family as soon as he sat down and started chatting comfortably. Kerrie and I were a bit pissed but my brother-in-law Alain is an especially excellent judge of character and I could tell that he had the same crush on Bobby that I did. Almost immediately, we got into an argument about politics because I didn't know what a right-wing libertarian was and I was trying to now convince one that he should be using his privilege to vote, speak up and demonstrate to protect black women. Just a light opener for our reunion date. The impassioned debate never turned into a fight and, when it settled, we decided to forego the ride home with Mr and Mrs Kerrie and go for a snowy walk instead.

We didn't know where we were going but we both knew that once we parted ways, we probably wouldn't see each other for a very long time, so we stuck it out in the cold. We walked all over the city for about two hours before Bobby said he needed to pop into a kebab shop to use the toilet. I didn't want to get caught in the unforgiving lighting of the neon-lit store, so innocently suggested he come to my mum's house and pee there instead. I swear I had no sexy intentions. I didn't have any plan whatsoever, apart from avoiding saying goodbye.

When we got to the house, I looked in the fridge for drinks and could only find Abe the Babe's vegan power green juice, so poured two glasses of that. I sat on the countertop (always my favourite kitchen seat) and chatted until it got too late to delay Bobby's departure any longer. This man went as far as to call an actual Uber and waited until he received the text to say it was in our driveway before he kissed me. Unbelievable. Don't get me wrong, I think this brand-new phenomenon of men obtaining consent is wonderful but this hesitation to make a move must be costing millions in rideshare cancellation fees. I only meant to kiss him back for a minute but I never ever wanted him to go, so I suggested he stay over instead. We agreed that it would be a real missed opportunity not to have sex, so we did. And just like that, my firm plans for a single life were under threat.

The next day, I managed a sore head in an old library while learning how my great-great-great-grandfather's sister caught measles and was surprised to receive a text from Bobby. Refreshingly, he played zero games and we exchanged constant messages every day for the rest of the week I travelled around Canada with the film crew. We wrote nothing special back and forth, just a steady conversation about the R Kelly documentary that had recently been released, Bobby told me about his work and I delivered officially embargoed updates on what I'd been discovering about my ancestry. Nothing juicy – certainly no sexy talk, which I found refreshing – we just had a laugh about things.

He was smart, even funnier than I had remembered and we had an easy shorthand between us. It felt to me like Bobby had always been part of my life and that the 20-year gap had never happened. I casually introduced the idea that he should visit England when I got back. He came a week later and we pretty much knew during those ten days that we should start making permanent plans. On the first night, I looked at him in his hotel bed and taunted, 'You love me, don't you? What a disaster.'

I tried as hard as I could to come up with reasons why I shouldn't be with him but there were none. This was very different from all my previous relationships, where I was justifying why, despite so many obvious problems, I should stick it out. I didn't worry about nine-year-old Violet as I could tell that Bobby would be an asset in her life. His steady, calm energy compliments mine, which I expected would become especially beneficial as she entered teenaged years. I envisioned Violet making better decisions about partners and friends, being more involved in athletics and generally living in a balanced household with Bobby in it. On our own, Violet and I existed in a benevolent democracy. She had as much power as I did and that was fine for as long as she was a considerate little girl, but it felt appropriate to get some sensible back-up before she entered adolescence. Sure, I could have managed a teenager on my own and I certainly don't advocate grabbing any old man just for the sake of it, but Bobby was too good to pass up.

Naturally, Violet was livid when he came back over and she realised he was 'under review'. That's what we called it. I didn't introduce Bobby as my boyfriend, or my ex-boyfriend, or even my friend. I said, 'Violet, this is Bobby and he's under review.' I suppose it was a trial period for all of us. He wasn't jealous of my relationship with Violet the way men had been before and, rather than disturbing what we had built, he found his own space within our family and we all made a stronger unit.

I was starting production on *The Duchess* at this point that I'd written, funnily enough, about a single mother with a twisted worldview trying to decide the best man-free way to grow her family. Filming would last for three months and I wouldn't be allowed to travel within that time, so we needed to make a decision about Bobby's UK visa quite quickly. One option was for Bobby to go back to Canada for several months and apply to return on a fiancé visa or as a resident. The other was to fly to Denmark for the weekend and get married, then re-enter the UK on a spousal visa. The latter made the most sense, so we calmly moved forward. I don't know how else to explain it, other than to say that it just wasn't a big deal. It was exciting in that we were planning a mini-holiday but the getting married part was just like breathing.

We booked tickets but days before we were meant to leave, I caught some kind of parasite from kissing the dog and got sick. The doctor had warned me not to kiss the dogs as they get their noses into all sorts of things outside, so it was akin to 'rimming a fox', but I never listened. Luckily, it had passed by the morning of our departure and Bobby still seemed to want to marry me. He crouched down to pick up my suitcase and stayed on one knee holding out a ring and proposed. I'd wanted to marry Bobby since I was 15 years old so of course I laughed and accepted this formality. Besides, we'd already booked our slot at the city hall and my simple mint-green Valentino dress was gently folded and packed.

I'd invited Caitlin and her husband, Simo, to fly in from Finland where they were now living to be our legal witnesses.

Violet was with us too, even though I predicted she would lose her shit at the civil ceremony. We weren't having a wedding *per se* so I could have easily disappeared for the weekend and lied about it, but I'd always told Violet what I felt was the age-appropriate truth. This would have been a big event to keep secret from her and I was confident in my decision that it would ultimately be good for us both. I straight up told her before we left that we were going to have a civil partnership ceremony and that Bobby and I were agreeing to be partners forever. We googled it and I explained that it was a lot like a wedding, but that it was more low-key. Still, she cried and got angry.

Violet had always been in the driver's seat and I could understand why she didn't love the idea that she was no longer in control. I had always given her so much jurisdiction because I'd wanted the same for myself as a child. It wasn't often that I overruled her but it was happening now. Violet has this easy-going quality where she's seldom cross but on the rare occasion that she does get mad, she only stays that way for an hour, tops. She was in much better spirits on the way to Denmark and was thrilled to be spending time with her Auntie Caitlin. We swam in the hotel pool, mooched about Tivoli Gardens and had a posh champagne brunch on the morning of the ceremony. It didn't feel like a day too out of the ordinary and Bobby seemed as relaxed as I was. I think we mostly tiptoed around the tsunami of Violet that we knew was coming.

Inside the courthouse, Violet suspiciously eyed up the many women milling around in white wedding dresses. Some posed for photos with big families, others clutched ornate bouquets. Without exception, they all looked desperately plucked out of TLC's *Say Yes to the Dress*. I'm sorry but I absolutely hate traditional wedding gowns. I'm sure yours was beautiful but I've personally never seen one that I liked enough to justify their arbitrary mark up. Buy a dress in any other colour, wear it more than once and pay a quarter of what you would pay for a white one. Why should it be white in the first place? Are you an innocent virgin? Didn't fucking think so. Me neither. But you go ahead and be given away by your father to a man who had to ask his permission to keep you, then fill out a bunch of paperwork to change your name like you're going into hiding after witnessing a murder.

Violet has had to listen to me harp on about this kind of thing all of her life so, predictably, she hit the roof as soon as she heard the officiant use the word marriage. 'NO!' she cried, 'This is not a marriage!' The intense fear of change flooded out of her in that tiny room and she sobbed loudly, marching around the perimeters in circles like a trapped cat. Caitlin chased after her with tissues and attempted to console her while I laughed. I have a problem where I laugh any time I'm uncomfortable. I've done it at funerals, at the opera, while breaking up with people, while attempting to tell a lie. Sometimes I cry when I'm meant to be laughing. I could research more into what this says about the dodgy wiring in my brain, but . . . actually yes, I'll do that quickly now.

Okay, shit, it might be a minor case of something called the pseudobulbar affect, which could be from a traumatic brain injury. If I've had one, I don't remember it, which is exactly what someone who'd had a traumatic brain injury would say. I guess I prefer to just leave it. Most of the people who know me have come to accept my cry/laughing as part of my charm. It doesn't happen often but I laughed for the full six minutes of our civil ceremony while my daughter cried. I'm lucky that Bobby loves us the way we are.

Immediately after the ceremony, Violet put on my large black Chanel sunglasses and draped Caitlin's black leather jacket over her shoulders and sat alone on a bench in Tivoli Gardens looking forlorn, and sort of like one of the Olsen twins during Paris Fashion Week. We left her to it for a bit and took pictures that she refused to feature in. Soon, she realised that everyone was behaving exactly as they had behaved before we'd been to the courthouse and that nothing major had really changed.

In her trademark recovery style, Violet's spirits lifted and she directed us all to the hotel rooftop pool for a final swim before departure. I couldn't get in the water as I had to attend a charity gig as soon as we landed back in London that evening and wouldn't have time to redo my make-up. (Yes, I worked on my wedding day and wore the same dress.) She readily accepted Bobby's offer to swim in my place and, together, the two of them choreographed a synchronised swimming routine that they performed for us as a duet.

Bobby and I will have been married for exactly two years when this book is published. Violet and I are smitten with him. We both know we can always count on Bobby to get in the water.

"

I learned to judge
by her eyes when
it was time for me to
gracefully bow
out of an evening.

"

How to Cut Off Your Problematic Auntie

My auntie was the coolest. Growing up, I admired my mum's cosmopolitan younger sister because, unlike Mum, she didn't settle into small-town married life. Instead, she lived abroad and periodically brought back exotic gifts, interesting stories and toasty tanned skin. She was gorgeous, playful and funny in a borderline irresponsible way that I adored. One of my first memories of having laughed until it hurt is after I had chosen a small stuffed monkey in a basket for her Christmas gift. I was five years old and remember picking it out and wrapping it carefully in anticipation of her trip home for the holidays. When she opened it, she said, 'What's this? Mon-chi-chi?' I laughed and said, 'No, MONKEY.' She repeated, 'Mon-chi-chi?!' so I held her cheeks in my little hands and yelled, 'MONKEY!' The mon-chi-chi bit became our thing for a while and, for some reason, it made me so happy to hear her say it wrong over and over again.

Whenever she was out of the country, she'd call to speak to my mum on Saturday mornings and, since I'd been bestowed with the honour of being named family secretary, I always answered the phone. 'Good morning, it's Mr Jones,' a voice at the other end would say. Mr Jones was my friend, a character played by my auntie for the purpose of my entertainment whenever she called. I remember not fully knowing whether Mr Jones was real or not but he'd speak to me for up to an hour before being handed over to Mum and he made me laugh, so I dared not question his authenticity.

My auntie lived all over the world but recharged at my grandma Dorth's house whenever she happened to be in town. I'd go from seeing her intensely to missing her loads. In the late 1980s when I was four, she moved to New Zealand for a year, which seemed worlds away from my room where I'd often sit gazing into my map, imagining what her life must be like there. One morning, Mum brought us round Dorth's for a mid-morning surprise. Upon arrival, she revealed that my auntie had come home and was sleeping in her bedroom. So while Joanne had snacks in the kitchen, I waited outside her door, desperate to rush in at the first sign of rousing so that I could sit on her bed for a chat and a laugh.

My aunt always kept beautiful international boyfriends and I loved answering the phone when they rang her because I'd get to hear their different accents and comically mimic them back to her. She let me watch R-rated movies that sometimes gave me nightmares, taught me how to measure her whiskey properly by lining up my chubby fingers against the glass and let me eat Reese's Peanut Butter Cups until I puked. I loved when she was home. It felt special to make my auntie laugh and, even from a young age, I respected and admired how unique she was. Plus, she was funny, and I loved when funny people loved me. I looked up to her as a 10/10 legend.

Drunk driving wasn't such a big deal back then but she'd been caught doing it so many times while in Canada that she had to spend weekends in jail that summer. Conveniently, the women's prison was just down the road from our house so on a Sunday morning, I'd climb on the back of the couch and look out the window early enough to see the raccoons playing and wait for her discharge. At around 6am, she'd cheerfully stroll up our driveway waving, wearing sandals with her glamorous silk nightrobe. She'd taken to wearing it into jail on Friday evenings because it was comfortable and, to this day, I've never related to someone more. It was baller. I admired her for doing something that was viewed as so innocuously strange in the eyes of boring people.

However, my auntie could be mean and Mum taught me to avoid her at those times. She said never to answer the telephone after 8pm in case it was her sister in a bad mood. One evening when I was nine years old, the phone rang and I picked it up without thinking, or perhaps just not caring about the rule. I was thrilled to hear my auntie's voice but she immediately cut me down by sneering, 'You think you're so fucking special, don't you? But you aren't. You're a silly little cunt.' She hadn't mistaken me for someone else on the line. She definitely knew who she was speaking to. And she was right. I did think that I was pretty fucking special, usually. I could tell that she'd meant it.

My mum was across the room, carefully watching my face, and she immediately ran over to grab the receiver out of my hand. She took over the call so I went and picked up my phone-answering footstool, put it away and went to bed. My mum loved her sister very much but she'd told me stories about how difficult it had sometimes been to grow up alongside her. They'd both had a hard time and Mum had covered up and normalised her behaviour to some extent out of sympathy. I knew that Mum loved her just as much as I did.

While the phone call had stunned me a bit, I didn't entirely mind it because I had caught glimpses of family gatherings descending into this type of alcoholic darkness before. My own sisters and I would usually be hustled off to bed at the first sign of vitriol but I'd stay awake and listen to it from my room. Being personally targeted by my auntie sort of meant that I was starting to be included in the grown-up banter. It hurt my feelings but it didn't change how much I idolised her. I'd just have to be more vigilant next time.

I was at my grandma Dorth's playing cards the next weekend. Mum let me sleep there some Fridays so that my grandma and I could perform our ritual of staying up eating Oreos and playing gin rummy or backgammon until 10pm, then retiring to bed to watch the American television news magazine show *20/20*. Those were some of the most blissful nights of my life. On this particular Friday, my auntie had been in the other room watching a film on her own and decided to wander in and join us. It didn't take long before she was berating me again, talking some nonsense about how she knew what a bitch I would shortly become and that I was going to get 'the rag'. My grandma scolded her, saying that this subject was for my mother to tell me about. With that, I pieced together that it had been a period reference. I slipped away and decided that the auntie I loved was also a werewolf – to be avoided entirely after dark. (I'd seen a *20/20* episode about that phenomenon.)

I think Mum ended up reading her the riot act because she came round to apologise with the gift of a newly released Sheryl Crow album. My auntie explained how amazing this artist was and how she felt like I could appreciate her music. I felt special for owning it as the only other CD in my collection was the *Aladdin* soundtrack. She'd give me very specific compliments that felt meaningful to me, like, 'You have unique colouring in your hair and face,' or, 'You have very cold hands and that's an excellent quality in a woman.'

A few months later, my auntie turned up to take me out for the day. We went for lunch, to the cinema and drove to an outlet mall in a different city to empty the coins from her vending machines. My auntie had many side-hustles and called herself 'a drifter'. She used her stunning looks and inimitable charm to sell huge quantities of new products at trade shows – vegetable choppers, heat-resistant ironing board covers, household gadgets and 'as-seen-on-TV' inventions. She was a genius and I found her adventures super-fascinating. She had contracts with shopping centres to operate vending machines filled with toys and candy that contained actual living fish between the tubes. Real fish that were fed and cleaned on an automatic timer! Hanging out with her was the most fun a kid could have. She habitually gave me huge bags of gold Canadian dollar coins called 'Loonies' – a gesture that made me feel like a wealthy pirate. Once, she took two grocery bags filled with cash into a dealership to buy a new car. I can't stress enough how much this woman was the SHIT.

Since New Zealand was so far away, when she left again for work she would be gone for a long stretch of time. There would usually be some drunken blowout with my dad or the other adults before she left. I learned to judge by her eyes when it was time for me to gracefully bow out of an evening but she'd still manage to snipe at me a few times. She was good at it.

* * *

Later on in my life, my auntie moved back to Canada for good and worked as a fashion editor in Toronto while I studied at university there. How lucky for me! My favourite person so close. By then, she was married to another spicy fashion person and they'd settled into a chic, big city version of family life with a baby. Still a bit of a kid myself, I slept over whenever I could. They fed me and let me spend the night on the softest designer duvets I'd ever touched. I cuddled my cousin who was young enough to be my nephew and tried on my aunt's amazing outfits and electric blue eyeliners. Their home was a gentle place to land anytime things got lonely in the city.

The drinking that I'd witnessed growing up had been replaced by a keen attention to wellness and I'd usually walk in to find egg white omelettes cooking on the kitchen stovetop and organic baby food being prepared. They were a fancy, funny, beautiful couple who influenced what I wanted for my own family.

One day, my aunt let me tag along on a glossy magazine photoshoot and I made some observation about how so many people in Toronto were Asian. I'd just come from an essentially all-white town and had never been a minority. In certain Toronto circles, I now felt like one. My aunt held her sketchpad and poked a small dot with a charcoal pencil in the middle of it. 'These are the world's white people,' she said. Then she widely circumscribed it nearing the edges of the page and said, 'These are the non-white people. You've got to get some perspective.' She'd always known about music and culture, and now I saw her as being aspirational and 'woke'.

Their marriage started to break down and episodes of turbulent fighting indicated that the drinking had come back into her life and escalated. I left university shortly thereafter and became the out-of-town auntie to their child by disappearing to England myself. Wrapped up in my own life, I never took the time to be present for my cousin in the way that my auntie had been for me. I didn't take the time to create characters who'd call him on the telephone; I didn't send birthday cards or letters or anything creative in the place of conversations.

When I arrived in England in 2007, my generation had moved on to texting as our main method of communication, which

I used as an excuse for my self-absorbed laziness. By 2009, I had Violet. For the next decade, I rarely visited home and was generally just a shit big cousin. I'd receive bits of information here and there from Mum and my sisters, and I ascertained from those that the pattern of my auntie being lovely for a few weeks then drunk and disorderly for a few weeks had continued. Everyone was living closer together now, so the contact was more regular – which meant that opportunities for conflict were more frequent.

Eventually, I'd been disconnected from the family for so long that I started to feel uncomfortable at Christmas gatherings at Mum's when people started to get drunk. Don't get me wrong – I love a few drinks now and then but I didn't inherit the sinister drunk gene that seemed very unique to that side of the family. A few of them could be like snipers and the more removed I got from it, the less I could tolerate.

I'd dread coming downstairs in the mornings in case my moody auntie was still there. I'd normalised tiptoeing around her as a child, waiting out the bad behaviour for all the good that was promised in between them, but they seemed to be getting harder to stomach. It bothered me that my little sisters were now often targets for verbal abuse since they'd both become adults and were sat at the bar drinking alongside her. That was always the most dangerous place to be. I hated it even more that they shrugged it off again and again, and that they'd learned to do so from Mum, who bore the brunt of her sister's vile outbursts.

It felt to me as though my aunt liked me a whole lot less since I'd become a successful 'uppity' feminist comedian. I imagine

BLUEWATER MUSICAL PRODUCTIONS
"FESTIVAL BY THE BAY"
AUGUST 31ST 1997

"YOU MAY GROW UP TO
BE A STAR"

Left: Reduced to an ensemble – singing with my sisters in matching pigtails.

Right: Slaying the competition in an unbeatable nineties look.

Left: Thinking my hat was the most unacceptable thing about this photo…

Above left and right: Taking any gig I could get.

Right: 'Perform like it's for sale and the rent is due tonight.'

Left: Creatively posing in what I knew was an adorable sailor suit.

Above left: Ugly stepsister with my actual sisters.

Above right: Cancelled: being harmlessly Asian in *The King and I*.

Sexing it up in high school, hearing the pop star messaging loud and clear.

Left: I'll Be There For You: our interpretations of the nineties 'Rachel' hairstyle.

Right and below left: Orange for prom with my BFF, Caitlin, and my future husband, Bobby K.

Right: Loved him from the start.

K Squared.

And so my love affair with teacup dogs began.

'Girls are flattery operated' – loving my time at Hooters.

Meeting Jessica Simpson and being fooled by 'Paris Hilton' – that's hot.

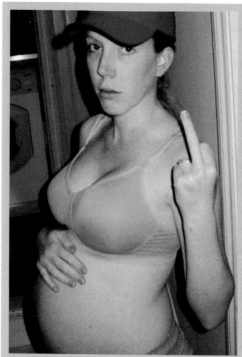

My babies.

Left: Meeting Violet in 2009.

Right: Laughing en route to a festival gig.

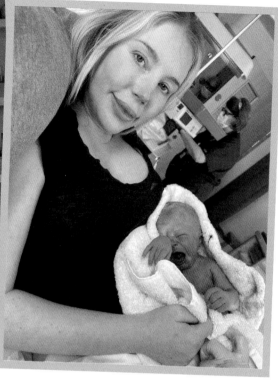

Left: Then And Now: in my exact same maternity dress.

Above: Meeting Fred.

Left: Family of four: heart full, iron deficient.

The Audacious Life
Chose Me.

it seemed to her as though I thought of myself as being 'better' than she was – and that's exactly how I felt. Any Christmas that I bothered to come home after about 2015, she'd call me a socialist, say that feminism had gone too far or generally try to bait people at dinner into circular arguments about trans rights or whether 'an all-meat diet is best for the human body', for example. She started identifying as a 'Trump Patriot', even though she's Canadian (which I keep having to explain is NOT American), and she exhibited a lot of internalised misogyny that I found to be hurtful and confusing. She'd say that white men were the most marginalised people on earth, which I always thought sounded funny coming from a 'settler' to Canada who'd never be viewed as an immigrant. Maddeningly, she'd automatically accuse women in the media who'd said they'd been raped of lying. It was difficult for me not to answer back and I'd have to remind myself that these were not debates, they were traps.

Sometimes, it was nothing at all that set my aunt off. You'd be laughing and drinking then she'd snap for no discernible reason and call everyone at the table a 'weak cunt'. She'd usually apologise the next day and I'd be left incredulous as to why she was so easily forgiven. Mum loved her. We all loved her and it was important never to exclude her son, so I think that's why Mum especially made an effort even though doing so came at an emotional cost. My aunt wasn't a bad person, just someone who could be quite hurtful due to what I would personally class as a disease. I can't comment on everything that happened after I moved away, as it's sort of hearsay, but it all sounded messy to me and, as I grew older and stronger, I had less energy for Mum's acceptance of it and the visible hurt it caused her.

* * *

In recent years, my aunt has become darkly silent whenever I'm around, which I find oddly to be more unsettling than being berated. Christmas 2019 was the last straw for me and when I decided I could make a choice to lovingly cut her out of my life completely. My thoughts, the use of my time, my words and my responses are all within my control, while other people's feelings, beliefs, illnesses and actions are not. I've known this deeply and applied it to my relationships successfully since my therapist, Pam, helped me see it after my relationship with The Overlap but I continued to make excuses for my aunt – probably because the length of time I'd known her eclipsed the time that I'd known these rules. There's something infantilising about being around people who were powerful when you were small, even when you're grown.

Perhaps foolishly, Bobby and I had arranged for a private function back in Canada so that our friends and family in Sarnia could all properly catch up and celebrate our recent nuptials with us. Bobby's extended family were there, loads of our mutual friends showed up and my family all came – apart from my dad and his wife because Dad refuses to be in a room with Mum and he also happens to avoid my aunt. Mum wore a stunning Sies Marjan blue wool sweater, embellished with a silk organza rosette. I knew it was lovely because I'd given it to her. Nearing the end of what had been a fantastic night, my aunt (who'd been more than pleasant until that point) made some comment to me about Mum's outfit choice, really harping on about what a stupid-looking sweater it was. Quite happy, drunk and unknowingly pregnant at the time, I'd momentarily forgotten myself and defended the sweater, saying it was gorgeous and that maybe my aunt didn't know everything about anything. In an instant, that descended into accusations that I'd performed stand-up on Netflix about my aunt's cancer, which I'd been unaware she'd had. It was true that I had made some comparison on a panel show between the growingly popular saying that 'feminism is cancer' and actual malignant cancer cells, but I promised that it had been a coincidence that both applied to my aunt. No one had told me about her diagnosis until afterwards. That hurt me too. I think it had hurt both of us that I'd been so removed from my family that I didn't even know that my childhood hero was sick until after she was better.

'I NEED DATES,' she yelled, now with her iPhone in my face, filming me, just like I'd seen in viral videos of deranged women in Walmarts across America. 'When was the panel show recorded and ON WHAT DATE did you learn I had cancer!?' It was surreal. Feeling shocked and frustrated, I started to cry. 'Oh, you're the victim now? You're a VICTIM?!' she hounded. Everything she said to me seemed to be straight out of Fox News.

I managed to stay relatively calm and let her continue to film me crying at my party, knowing this video would be the last record she'd ever have of us interacting. I stood firmly in front of her and tried to quietly explain that I'm different in my actual life to how I am on stage, and that she couldn't take anything she saw on television as a completely accurate representation of my personality – I was often embellishing to make a point. Suddenly, it dawned on me: it was none of my business whether this woman understood me or not, so there was no sense in explaining myself. It wasn't normal that I'd grown up learning to constantly manage the erratic behaviour of the people I loved the most. I felt annoyed with myself for having been drawn into the altercation in the first place. I felt stupid for having allowed myself to cry. Then I got angry thinking about how many times Mum had been in the same position and cried, and about how many more times she'd be here crying again. We'd been offering excuses and empathy to alcoholism, and we'd keep feeling stupid for as long as we continued to allow it.

My aunt emailed me to apologise the next morning and I replied that I understood and that it was fine. I meant it. I empathise and I don't blame her for the way that she operates. I think she's special, intelligent, layered and a ton of fun when she wants to be. She's a great mother and I wouldn't be who I am today without her audacious, no-fucks influence growing up. I love her so much but I don't have the tools to be around her anymore, to carry on any kind of relationship alongside alcohol abuse, so I'm out. Why should I? I don't have to. You don't have to. As I've said before, letting go isn't the same as giving up.

We'd have a huge problem if she ever spoke to my husband or to my daughter the way I've seen her speak to other people or the way she's spoken to me, and I'd rather not see that happen. The difference between Mum and me is that she cares deeply about whether or not she's properly understood because she's a good, fair person. She instinctively forgives and makes new attempts to articulate herself, in hopes that others will finally come round to her perspective in disputes, which I think is a very natural response to conflict.

Conversely, I don't care what my aunt thinks of me anymore and it's not about fault. Now, I can peacefully walk away from a source of harm in my life without any resentment or second thoughts. I can love her and still say that enough is enough. It's a shame but it's necessary for me and I think my mum needs to see it. Mum could use a bit more of the trademark no-fucks attitude that I learned from my aunt growing up. It's one of her many admirable qualities and, in a big way, having the confidence to remove myself from my aunt is a strength that I inherited from her in the first place.

I let go of my aunt but, back in high school, I gave up on my grandma too.

It was **entirely** too much for me, so I **ran off** to be a selfish **little bitch** instead.

How to Be a Real Piece of Shit to Your Grandma

My mum's mum was my 'person' for a long time. When other eight-year-old girls were asking for sleepover parties together, I just wanted to stay at my grandma's – though we didn't call her 'grandma'. My sisters and I called her by her name, Dorothy. We started as babies with 'Derf', then 'Dorrthhhhh' and finally graduated to 'Dorth' when we were old enough to say it properly. I think we called her Dorth partly because her mother, who died before I was born, was 'Nanny', so that favourite name felt taken and no other maternal nomenclature quite fit in her mind.

Mum spoke to Dorth on the telephone every day. I memorised her number by the time I was about 18 months and I would wait until my parents were asleep to climb out of my crib and call it. I'd say, 'Derf? I can talk now. Everyone's in bed.' Dorth did characters and voices that made me laugh and we'd either gossip or she'd tell me stories until I fell asleep myself. Kids won't believe this but landlines in the 1980s would stay engaged unless both parties hung up, so whenever I accidentally left the receiver off the hook, Dorth would drive to our house in the morning and hang it up so that she could use her own phone again.

All special dinners happened at her place and she came round to ours all the time to visit or chat to Mum. She had a sense of humour with me before I had one of my own. When I was about seven, I'd been sitting at the kitchen table, drawing a pair of legs wearing snow boots with my colouring pencils. I excused myself to go to the toilet and when I returned, I saw that Dorth had sketched a bare bum onto the legs. For some reason, I lost my shit that day. I crumpled the page and cried under the table, refusing to be Dorth's best friend for the rest of my life. Looking back, I think I'd felt that the joke hadn't included me, but that it had been infantile and at my expense. I stayed cross for about a week, which really upset my grandma and, though she apologised, she held her ground that the bum was not intended to cause offence but to make me laugh. This was rare, though: Dorth and I had very few disagreements and people often commented on how alike we were.

Dorth was the family's nucleus, so when she was diagnosed with breast cancer in her late fifties, I never imagined that she would get progressively sick and die. The cancer didn't kill her but a post-operative allergic reaction to the staples in her lumpectomy wounds unleashed infectious poisons into her body. She was treated at home but suffered from digestive issues and mysterious auto-immune problems after that. But my grandma didn't look sick. She always looked glam when she went to the doctor's office and I think her youth and beauty worked against her in getting a proper diagnosis. One day in 1996, she asked me whether I thought she'd be okay and I said, 'Don't be silly; you've got at least five good years left,' thinking at age 13 that five years was basically an entire lifetime. Dorth laughed and said she hoped she'd get more than five, so I followed up with, 'Oh, yeah, yeah, but I'm saying let's just think about the first five as guaranteed.'

Dorth was eventually admitted to palliative care in hospital with stomach and bowel perforations that allowed more seemingly unstoppable toxins to infect her bloodstream. I didn't like that and I hated the stress it put on my mum. I was becoming a teenager and I withdrew from the heaviness of what was happening with Dorth. Her organs started failing. One night, she called me from her hospital bed for a chat, the way I used to call her as a baby. She said that she loved me and asked if I would say, 'I love you, Dolly Lou,' back to her. I thought that sounded weird and foolish, as earnestness wasn't our usual method of discourse. She insisted, so I rolled my eyes and said it sort of through gritted teeth. I didn't say it properly. I didn't want to. I stopped accompanying Mum to the hospital when Dorth was intubated and could no longer speak to us at all. On one of my last visits, though, I remember Mum putting Dorth's make-up on for her, then holding up a small mirror and asking whether she liked it. Dorth shook her head 'no' while looking so little and vulnerable in that bed. She wanted the tubes out.

I'd tried to be a grown-up all through my childhood but still lacked the basic maturity to handle the sight of the two strongest women in my life looking powerless. It was entirely too much for me, so I ran off to be a selfish little bitch instead. I didn't want my grandma to see me anyway. I had crazy teeth with complex orthodontics at that age and was the angriest and ugliest that I'd ever been. I focused on that, as though it would have mattered to her at all under the circumstances. I wasn't there to support my mum and I certainly wasn't there for Dorth either.

She didn't make it to my 'guaranteed' five years and died aged 63. At the time, I rationalised the loss by deciding that 63 must be very old indeed and that I should accept that people you love get old and they die. I never allowed myself to acknowledge or grieve her death properly. It was so much easier to shelve that for 20 years.

Lucky for me, Dorth is a very forgiving person – even in death – and she hasn't held a grudge over the time I let her die alone while also abandoning Mum in the process. I think she ultimately understood that I was a stupid and emotionally repressed teenager. I didn't hear from Dorth until well into my adulthood, then, all of a sudden, around when I turned 35, I started getting signs of her presence in my life. It's not that she appeared as a ghost in my bedroom or anything, I just started thinking about her constantly as though she was around and generally feeling her spirit. I think communication technology in the afterlife is very similar to that in mid-1980s Sarnia, Ontario. As long as one of you has the receiver off the hook, the line stays open.

"

I personally
have never
stolen anything
in my life.

"

How to Get Robbed by a Masked Man

I've been robbed a few times and I'm pretty sure I can remember each event, though it's difficult because I do get over things quite quickly. I'd be an ineffective judge because, with the time it takes for the accused to be tried in court, I'd be mostly frustrated that everyone hadn't just moved on and end up dismissing every non-violent crime on the grounds of 'not really worth arguing over, is it, guys?' What I'm absolutely certain of is that I personally have never stolen anything in my life. Not sweets as a child, not cosmetics as a teen, NOTHING.

Though, actually, I did borrow cash from the prom committee money box to pay my share of the vodka run happening after school, with the full intention of paying it back. But on my way out the bursar's office with the 20 dollars in my right hand, my left thumb landed inside the door latch and got stuck as my body continued forwards. In what I can only describe as an absolute freak act of karma, the momentum against the sharp latch sliced my thumb open so deeply that blood spattered up the wall. I was able to pass the note off to my waiting friend, securing the alcohol purchase for later, then wrapped my thumb and drove to the doctor to have it glued shut. I've still got a horseshoe-shaped scar reminding me to never, EVER steal (or even secretly borrow) again.

People who haven't had the good fortune of cutting their teenaged thumbs open do steal, though. I first became a target for muggings after Violet was born. Word around Crouch End, north London, was that thieves purposely sought out mothers of young children walking alone in my neighbourhood because they're distracted and will never give chase. I was mooching about the high street one day when a couple 'accidentally' bumped into the buggy, jostling it enough that it briefly tipped to the side. I apologised to them like any Brit (or transplanted Canadian) would do, and hurried round to the front to check that Violet hadn't been too startled. That's when they snatched my nappy bag off the handle and ran. I had just been to sort out a bunch of admin related to Violet's new life on Earth, so it happened to contain my bank cards, my passport and even cash (gifts) in three currencies! Madness for me to replace but a very fruitful day at the office for the couple. The rumours about new mothers were true – I definitely didn't give chase. It's a decent scam if you're looking for one.

The second episode was a true snatch-and-grab mugging in the very traditional sense. By this time, Violet was three years old and we were walking hand-in-hand back from the bakery on a slow Sunday morning. I'd slung my handbag over my shoulder and she was carrying an old clutch purse that I had given her. Inside were some little plastic ice cream toys – the kind of shit they glue to the front of those horribly overpriced magazines that drive toddlers wild with desire. Seemingly out of nowhere, a man appeared behind us and grabbed my bag. Instinctively, I locked my arm and held on to it. I think I probably crushed Violet's hand as well. I just buckled down and held on as tightly as I could to everything in case my brain confused my hemispheres and I released the side holding Violet. The man screamed 'LET GO!' and, during what felt like moments but was probably just seconds, I genuinely tried to drop the handbag but couldn't.

Not wanting to hang around, he gave up on me and snatched Violet's little purse out of her tiny hand instead. He ran off with it down a side street. We both burst into tears from the shock as he fled and huddled next to a woman walking with her own toddler on the opposite pavement. She very kindly walked us the rest of the way home and came inside while I rang the police to report what had happened. It felt very weird to me that this neighbour zeroed in on the kettle and set it to boil with such a noble sense of urgency. But I would later learn that tea solves all British problems, soothes all negative British emotions and that it was simply her national duty to make tea for me in a time of personal trauma. Whether I understood its expression or not, her care was noticed and appreciated.

The lady left with her child once the tea was made and the policemen had arrived. Violet was the one to actually give them the statement as she felt quite violated by the entire altercation.

She explained the whole thing probably better (and in more detail) than I could have done and asked me every day for probably six years after that whether the man had been arrested. Kids are ruthless in their sense of justice but, in actual fact, I think the thief was probably quite unwell. Besides, he went to all that trouble to get the world's worst plastic toys. Having stepped on many of those myself, I'm confident that realisation was punishment enough.

I was robbed of £20,000 the next time. YEAH. Twenty thousand! Violet and I had moved into our own home during 2016 – a period of success where I quite evidently had a lot of money. It was Christmas and I'd been paying a lot of removal fees, travel expenses, mortgage stuff, tax, gifts and just generally transferring funds around to pay for different things all at once. It was a bad time for keeping track of things.

Then, in January, my accountant rang me and asked why I'd spent so much the month before. I gave the annoying artist's answer of, 'Um, I dunno . . . How much do you mean?' She pointed to a specific cheque made out to a name that didn't match up with any invoices. I hate discussing money and when there's a discrepancy, I always assume that I've been wrong. I went through a small existential crisis when I learned that I'd been careless enough to forget writing a cheque for £20,000 to someone whose name I couldn't remember. My accountant insisted that I go to the bank to procure a copy of the cheque and when I did, I could tell straight away that my signature had been forged. Racking my brain to come up with who had access to my chequebook, I remembered that there had been two men in my house delivering furniture who'd seemed overly friendly and asked for my autograph. But it surely couldn't have been them or the signature would have been a better match to my own. I had left them alone for a bit but then I was moving house so I'd left several people alone – cleaners, packers, removal guys, everyone! I had no way of tracing who might've stolen the cheque but I vowed to be more careful after that and, it's a shame, but you just can't trust strangers in your home. Thankfully, the bank refunded the money and I learned a valuable lesson about security.

A year later, another incident started out as an attempted home invasion, though I'm still not sure how to properly classify it even now. I'm no expert and I hate unsolicited reviews myself but if he was a burglar, he was quite shit at his craft. I had just come back from a tour gig at around 11pm and dismissed the babysitter. I relaxed into my usual night-time routine of checking on a sleeping Violet, making a snack and popping on a catch-up episode of *Love Island*. All of a sudden, the dogs started freaking out by the front door, which was massively out of character for useless adorable teacups. My yorkie, Manny, in particular was ANGRY with the front door.

I crept down the corridor towards the front of the house and saw Manny leaping at a man's hand coming through the letterbox, reaching around for the latch. With more calm curiosity than fear, I approached the door, which had a porthole feature window in the middle. A man's face was pressed against it and, when he saw me, he jostled the door and said, 'Let me in.' Even though it was nearly midnight, he had sunglasses resting atop his shaved head. That was weird. He wore jeans with a suit jacket and I felt like his whole vibe was office casual. For a moment, I thought he might've been the driver who took me home from work and had perhaps forgotten something. I simply answered, 'No, I can't let you in, sorry.'

He started pushing on the door again which annoyed me more than anything else. I told him, 'Ugh, I'm going to have to ring the police if you won't leave – look.' I dialled 999 and held the phone up to the window so that he could see I was serious. He stumbled back and walked off, so I concluded that he was probably drunk. My little maisonette was in a gothic church conversion and ours was the front door entrance, so I figured he was probably just looking for God.

I needed to get to bed though, so I asked the police to come by just to check he was gone. They came a few moments later and said they'd had a drive around and couldn't see anyone. They left and I settled Violet, who had been awakened by the barking and commotion. (She loves a drama.) I washed my make-up off to get ready for bed and, on my way back to the bedroom, I was startled by the man's face back in the porthole window.

That exact scene – a man's face in the window – was honestly my worst nightmare growing up. I'm sure it was a regular cinematic device in horror films. One minute, there's no one in the kitchen, then the heroine opens the refrigerator door to grab a juice and when she shuts it, THE KILLER APPEARS BEHIND IT. I'd always hated jump scares as a teenager and now here I was, walking one way past an empty window, then turning round and BAM, there was a man's face pressed up against it. However, as an adult, it just annoyed me again.

I rang the police back and, while I was doing so, I could hear Violet speaking. She had taken the liberty of calling her dad who lived down the road. The man disappeared once more but when Violet told me that her father was on the way, I envisaged him running down the street in pyjamas, wielding some sort of blunt instrument and ready to be a hero for his child . . . which certainly wouldn't deescalate the ongoing situation. Great. I was about to have two uniquely unhinged men fighting in my front garden when all I wanted was some rest. I know my daughter's father. He grew up on a farm and is no stranger to an axe. Plus, a confrontation like this one was exactly the type of glory he dreamed of. With my head in my hands, I wondered how I'd let the simple mistake of a lost man seeking refuge in a church spiral so wildly out of control that my daughter would soon see her trouserless dad being taken down by the cops in a case of mistaken identity.

Just then, flashing blue lights poured into Violet's room through the windows. As predicted, we heard shouting and sounds of a struggle out front. 'This is it, Katherine,' I said to myself, preparing for the satisfying moment when I'd finally see my ex in handcuffs. I went to the door and squinted to make sense of all the blurred silhouettes moving through the strobing darkness outside. Then BAM, another face inches from mine in the window startled me backwards. This time, it was Violet's dad's. 'Looks like they got him!' he said. I opened the door to see that the police had apprehended the man from before, whom they'd found trying to climb round the back of my house through the garden. Violet joined us to catch a quick glimpse of the action before inviting her dad in to regale him with a dramatised version of the nocturnal unfoldings. 'You're safe now, kid. Dad's here,' he boasted, as though he hadn't just stumbled upon an arrest and dragged an actual sledgehammer into our home. Fine. He was wearing shorts, I'll give him that. I'd expected him to be pants-less. And I was glad that Violet had the comfort of knowing he was always just a quick jog away with a weapon.

I chose not to press charges against the man because, having considered the circumstances, I really do think he was confused. The police said he'd spend the evening in custody getting sober and then be released, hopefully in time to visit an open and operational church in the morning.

* * *

Our most recent burglary was the real deal. It happened two years ago in 2019, right after Violet and I had moved into our new home with Bobby. Violet and the dogs were spending the weekend away at her dad's, which seems, in retrospect, a little more than coincidental. I mean, maybe it was random but Bobby and I both had a bad feeling about the cleaning company we'd been using at the time. Each week, they'd send three or four different people to blitz the house. We hardly ever saw the same people twice. I felt uneasy having that many strangers in our home but I was working a lot and felt we needed the help. It's one thing to have a dedicated professional learning your routines and going through your cupboards but it never felt right giving a rotating squad access to the house keys. I could never have outright accused them of any wrongdoing, as the woman in charge was so amazing and kind, but something didn't feel right about it. And you know how I am about intuition . . .

Bobby was making dinner around 8pm one warm evening in September and accidentally splashed spaghetti sauce on his shirt. In the same situation, an absolute scrub like me would have left it there for the weekend but Bobby has more self-respect than I do so he paused the cooking and ran upstairs to change. I stayed put with a glass of red wine, watching *The Politician* on Netflix. I'd been filming my own Netflix series at the time and marvelled at the obvious discrepancy in our respective wardrobe budgets. After a few minutes, I heard banging and running around upstairs and assumed that Bobby must've caught the cat with a hamster in her mouth. She had eaten one of them already that month, which we had to replace after holding a funeral for it. Security on the hamster habitat was tight but one never knows with Violet and I half expected a breach.

The stomping continued for longer than a cat chase should take and seemed a little intense so, to be safe, I went to the front door and unlocked it, pressed the button to open our automatic gate and waited at the bottom of the stairs for instructions. Bobby immediately came flying down shirtless and shouted, 'There's someone in the house!' He then ran past me through the door and out the gate, leaving me alone in the house.

Mobile phone and wine still in hand, I fled behind him but tactfully turned left down the street rather than right as he had. I'd decided that if there was a murderer in the house, he wouldn't be able to split himself in two and pursue us both on foot. Frantically, I flagged down a car while ringing 999, who put me on HOLD. I didn't even know they could do that! I actually sat on hold for several minutes while crying to the kind motorist about the intruder in my house. That's when I saw a police car go past, rather than pulling into my gate. In the beam of its headlights, I could see that there was a fight between two men happening in the street. One of the men was my shirtless husband!

I ran over to see what was going on just as 999 came back on the line. I politely berated them for leaving me on hold for so long. Still crying and confused, I said, 'Listen, I know that you're underfunded and understaffed, but when someone tells you there's a man in their house, I don't think you're meant to make them hold the line. That seems very irresponsible to me!' It was hardly the time or the place for a mum lecture, but I felt quite passionately that they shouldn't be so blasé with the next caller facing an intruder. I had paid a lot of tax that year and I think I was mostly frustrated with the Conservative Party and their budget cuts. The whole situation was sooooo Liberal-elite: a shoeless white woman holding a glass of Merlot while crying in the street about cuts to government funding and trying to be polite about her house being robbed.

Throbbing with animal adrenaline, the most jacked version of Bobby I'd ever seen prowled up the pavement towards me, holding what looked to be my laptop. He had scratches on his naked chest (and, just like that, it's a romance novel) and blood was pouring from one of his bare feet. Breathless, with eyes wide like a predator, he explained that he'd been upstairs changing and noticed that his wardrobe was open and his cufflinks were scattered on the bed. These cufflinks had been gifts he'd hated and had never worn, so he wondered for a moment whether I'd been sorting through some things and chucked them there. Something didn't sit right though, so he stepped outside his room into the hallway, where he was met by a man in a skeleton mask and gloves holding my computer. They'd startled each other and Bobby said the man went, 'Oh fuck!' before turning around towards Violet's open bedroom window that he had obviously entered from.

The way Bobby describes it now is that he switched into 'American football mode' and just went after him as though he was an opponent holding the ball. They scuffled in the bedroom for a few seconds after the man threatened, 'I'll fucking kill you!' and Bobby pushed him out the window onto the first-floor roof. Their altercation continued up there before the man jumped off via a side wall and into the neighbour's garden. Bobby studied which way he was going and that's when he ran down the stairs past me and out into the street. When he'd shouted, 'There's someone in the house,' I guess he'd meant to say, 'There WAS someone in the house,' and this is why grammar is important. Though really, there could have been others in the house but the skeleton man was the only intruder he'd seen and confronted. During my wait on hold and ensuing monologue for the 999 dispatchers, Bobby was down the road stalking along the bushes that he'd calculated the man had to emerge from to make his escape. He heard rustling and, sure enough, out popped the masked man still holding my laptop.

Bobby leapt at him, tackling the man to the ground, thus freeing my property, which skidded across the pavement as they wrestled. The police car that drove by wasn't a result of my 999 call but a routine traffic patrol who happened to see the fight and stop. Bobby had apprehended the man for them and so thinking the police already knew what was going on and had arrived to take over, he released him. When the officers didn't get out of their car right away, Bobby went to grab the man again but this time the burglar reached for the knife that had been hidden down his trousers and repeated, 'I'll fucking kill you.' With the laptop recovered and the police on the scene, Bobby backed off and decided not to risk serious injury or death over a break in. He gestured to police that they needed to catch the man who was now running away, so they gave chase in their vehicle for a few minutes but eventually lost him down a narrow alleyway. In the cops' defence, they only had seconds to react to what was essentially a total surprise. Afterwards, forensics came by the house to take shoe prints, which we were told were 'just like fingerprints' – an absolute lie. We went through every room slowly and found that, while Bobby had managed to get my laptop back, the burglar had taken a couple of handbags, cash and jewellery – specifically, he'd taken Bobby's National University Championship American football ring. I loved the poetic foreshadowing of a man finding a football ring, choosing to steal it, then, moments later, being tackled by the owner of said ring. It was annoying but strangely satisfying at the same time.

It was a scary event and Bobby had a few sleepless nights after it, but today, we're sort of indifferent to the man getting away. He was in his twenties and probably got the fright of his life. Bobby and I hoped that he'd maybe take the opportunity to learn from how close he came to being arrested and having a police record for aggravated burglary which, due to the weapon involved, is quite a serious charge. I know from *Love After Lockup*, my favourite reality show where people fall in love and start relationships with incarcerated criminals, that once you've been to prison, it's very difficult to escape the cycle of crime.

Also, 'stuff' is just . . . stuff, right? My dad reached out to the jeweller who'd made Bobby's football ring and had it replaced due to its sentimental value, and I was glad to have my laptop because I had work and pictures on there that I hadn't backed up, but, overall, the outcome was positive. We learned that we absolutely cannot leave first-floor windows open and we were thankful that Violet wasn't at home. Bobby solidified his role as sexy heroic action-man heartthrob superhunk protector of our family and now we keep the cameras and alarms on 24/7.

In the days that followed, we had detectives in and out of the house a couple of times just to look through the one distant camera that we did have on and to speak to neighbours about their CCTV as well. One afternoon, a man came to the door asking to see the footage and we assumed that he too was from the police. He wasn't in uniform but the detectives had also been in plain clothes. I couldn't hear through the intercom whether he identified himself as police or not but we certainly were under the impression that he was a detective. After this man walked all through the house and asked a few odd questions, Bobby requested his card and he cheerfully told us that he was a journalist with a tabloid newspaper.

'What?!' I instantly sobbed. 'But how do you even know where we live?!' I imagined the article he would write, saying how stupid and spoiled we'd been, next to photos of our brand new house. I felt violated all over again and, while I'm usually quite impervious to criticism, I really didn't want my home published in a tabloid days after it had been robbed. My fault for speaking about it publicly, really. Refreshingly, the journalist totally understood and was really nice. He promised not to write about his visit or the burglary and he stuck to his word. That surprised me. Finding work in print media is tough these days and it's worth mentioning that there are some decent journalists out there who may not subscribe to the values of their shady employers.

But just know this: Murdoch and his ilk have your address. They have all our addresses for if and when they want them. If you ever decide to go on *Strictly*, they'll be outside snapping pics while you're taking out the bins, so you'd better have your knickers on. Or not – depending on the outcome you're after.

"

For the first time in a while, I didn't have to hold everything together in my life all by myself.

"

How to Have Another Baby: Part Two

As preproduction began on *The Duchess* in 2019, and I had reunited with Bobby out of the blue, I knew that instead of pursuing my carefully plotted sperm donor plans, I'd start a family with him instead. It was just that easy. In the beginning, I had cognitive doubts about having a 'traditional' relationship but I couldn't feel any intuitive roadblocks at all. I've learned to trust wisdom above intellectual reasoning, so I knew that being with Bobby was the right thing to do. I was sure of it deep in my bones. So after we were married in Denmark, poor Bodhi's carefully selected frozen sperm were either chucked in the bin or returned to sender.

In principle, it annoyed me that I had to film *The Duchess* before trying to get pregnant, as by now I was now 36 – which I'm told is even more 'geriatric' than 35 – but it made sense. When I had been expecting Violet, I threw up multiple times a day in my first trimester and I understood that it wouldn't be wise to have any distractions like that on set. Besides, I get pregnant the way Kim Kardashian gets pregnant – mostly in the face and boobs, so not easily hidden. Filming would last three months and I considered that I might create a problem for the continuity and wardrobe departments in the unlikely event that it worked straight away. I wasn't sure how long it would take to conceive but I resigned myself to wait as a sacrifice to the show. You know, exactly the way men DON'T.

We wrapped filming on *The Duchess* on 4th December 2019 and I was pregnant the following week. I appeared on *The Jonathan Ross Show* a few days after that and ALREADY people were noticing, so I had to delete comments and messages on my social media asking how far along I was. (*Why* in the face?!) I felt very fortunate not to have struggled, as so many people wanting babies feel the frustration and disappointment of seeing negative tests month after month, but something told me not to get too excited. Obsessively, I googled miscarriage rates and read blogs written by women who'd lost their early pregnancies. I felt more 'out of the woods' with each passing week, especially after our first, seven-week scan showed a strong heartbeat, but I couldn't feel completely at ease. I tried to brush it off and managed to convince myself that ultimately everything would be fine, so it came as a terrible shock when Bobby and I attended our ten-week scan and were told there was no heartbeat. They never use the word 'dead'. I guess everyone feels more comfortable distancing themselves from the tiny life which has ended by discussing it in terms of cardiac activity. But the baby had died.

I'd gathered something was wrong as soon as the doctor started scanning me that afternoon. Her eyes darted around the screen, which she had turned away from us, and she was taking too long to speak. I looked at Bobby's face rather than looking at hers because I knew that I'd have a better chance of reading his reaction first. When she gently broke the news of the absent heartbeat, I did the very British thing of comforting her. I smiled and soothed, 'Please don't worry, that's completely fine. Oh well,' as though I hadn't spent the last two months planning someone's entire life as part of our family. I sat up and had a relatively chipper conversation about how to proceed over the next few days. Bobby didn't say anything. The doctor offered medical management, where I would be given pills to expel the pregnancy; surgical management, where I'd be admitted to hospital for what is essentially an abortion procedure or expectant management, which is the option of doing nothing and waiting to bleed.

I couldn't make the decision and I just wanted to leave the consulting room and get on the train to Liverpool for the gig I'd booked that evening. In that moment, I remember feeling really stupid for having scheduled a comedy show immediately following an early pregnancy scan. Bobby and I quietly cried underneath our sunglasses on the short walk to the station and I rang the babysitter to ask her to stay with Violet so that Bobby could join me at work. I wasn't about to cancel.

I fulfilled all of my bookings, TV recordings and work commitments over the next three weeks of failed medical management attempts. I'm not sure what else a person is meant to do. The collective grief of pregnancy loss struck me hard during that seemingly endless purgatory. One in four women, I now understood, could be working the tills at Morrisons, installing electrics, caring for the sick, driving lorries, policing the streets – whatever it is they usually do – while knowing that the once-growing baby inside them was dead. Before this, I'd had no clue that there was a scenario where a deceased embryo wouldn't come out. I thought that 'miscarriage' always referred to getting a positive pregnancy test followed by your regular period-type symptoms a few days – or more rarely, weeks – later. It wasn't just my own individual experience but the absolute scale of this trauma happening to millions of women that was a head fuck.

In the beginning, I was angry with my body over what I'd concluded was its intentional murder of my baby. After several days of still suffering pregnancy symptoms while feeling like a walking tomb, I got even angrier that my body couldn't even miscarry properly. It was like my mind was battling with a petulant teenager. I'd be telling it, 'Listen, you're having a miscarriage, so you need to respond to this medicine and just let it go.' To which my body would reply, 'Fuck off, I'm FINE. You need to give me as many gin and tonics as you can and get into a fight with a rapper in front of everyone at the NME Awards!' I did that. Then I actually fell down the stairs. I did that accidentally because I'd drunk too many gin and tonics. But even then, it wouldn't miscarry.

The trouble was, I didn't have time to take a day off for the surgery. My mum's sixtieth birthday was coming up and I'd made plans to join her in Mexico with Violet and my sisters. My doctor advised against flying, warning that there was an increased risk of haemorrhage if I finally did start to miscarry at any point, which was probably something that I wouldn't want to experience abroad. We don't take many holidays and I felt like it was more important for my surviving child to see her family, so I asked Bobby to join us as a safety compromise and decided to take my chances with the Mexican hospitals. I updated my insurance and went.

I can't say that I loved the trip and I kept throwing up because, of course, my teenaged jerk of a body thought it was still pregnant, but I'm glad we went. There were fun moments as there always are, even in a crisis. On the third day, a stranger on the beach tapped me on the shoulder to say that she had just taken a photo of Violet, Bobby and me walking along the water and offered to email it to me. She said that, as a mother herself, she knew how rare it was to be included in a photo, so sometimes when she spotted families doing sweet things together, she'd capture the moment for them. I think that's the only nice picture we have together from during my 'pregnancy' and I'm happy we have it. Mums are spooky.

The surgical procedure I now needed was booked at my local hospital for the week we returned home. Covid was just becoming a 'thing' in late February 2020 so I had to wear a mask and take a test, but it wasn't a concern that I had recently travelled. I figured that if I went first thing in the morning, I could be in the car and en route to work by noon, as I had to stay out of town over the weekend for a job. Having had breast implants, I was confident that I would come round from general anaesthetic quickly. (I'm the best at it and it's an underrated talent that I'm proud of.) What I hadn't considered is that on the NHS, arriving at 7am doesn't guarantee that you'll be in theatre any time before lunch. Luckily, I was placed fourth on the list of surgeries that morning and I woke up in recovery at exactly 11:45am. I sat up to leave but the nurse stopped me, explaining that she had to monitor my blood pressure and get the doctor to discharge me properly before I could go.

I'd forgotten about the duty of care part. All I knew was that finally I wasn't pregnant anymore and I didn't want to hang around. I was no longer chemically trapped – I was free! In the politest way possible, I tried to convince the nurse that what I was asking for was NOT special treatment but in fact was an ABSENCE of treatment. I said, 'I keep reading that you are overburdened so I really just want to get out of your hair. I know how to take my own IV out.' I asked her if I could leave no fewer than five times. I was glad to be unrecognisable, wearing a mask, so that she'd never be able to tell her friends that TV's Katherine Ryan is a dick. After a bit of cajoling, she agreed that I seemed to be very awake and took my cannula out for me. I practically ran out of that ward, rang Bobby and met him in the parking lot.

Bobby joined me on this work trip like he had in Mexico. We had to go straight to the filming location and lie about what kind of surgery I'd had because the publicly funded broadcaster who had hired me states very bluntly on their website that they do not insure for any matters of the womb. I loved the production company who were making the show and I'm sure they would have worked around me had I told them the truth but I chose not to risk putting them in that position with the channel or becoming a possible burden to them. It hurts, though. It's bad enough that women make up half the population but are incongruously hired maybe a quarter of the time (and I'm being generous). But then to check the insurance page and see in proud, plain English that our employers don't give a fuck if our actual vaginas fall off on set is . . . it's bullshit.

I suppose that one positive takeaway from this dark chapter in my life was that I gained even more love and respect for my husband. (I definitely thought I'd had plenty enough beforehand but I guess the universe disagreed and sent me a lesson just to make sure.) I watched the way Bobby processed his own grief from our pregnancy loss but what surprised me to see was, despite his obvious pain from losing the baby, how much he actually cared about me. He handled the entire ordeal with a strength and grace that made it okay for me to be really sad some nights. For the first time in a while, I didn't have to hold everything together in my life all by myself. Bobby had all the right instincts and made all the right choices when it came to Violet's wellbeing and also mine. I admired the way he showed great leadership even while he was struggling himself. After witnessing that, I implicitly trusted him as the person I could count on in every situation. I looked up to him and felt safe with him and, though it wasn't an ideal scenario, it brought us closer together.

* * *

By May 2020, I was pregnant again. We were a lot more positive about this pregnancy as we thought, statistically, the chances would surely be low that miscarriage could happen twice, back-to-back. Also, I liked soothing myself with the logic that THIS would be our special baby that couldn't have been born without the loss of the first one, so it all made sense. It felt better to tie everything up in a way that gave a meaning to our suffering. This baby was due on Bobby's late dad's birthday, which I also took as a sign. We had an early NHS scan at nine weeks to check that everything was on track but, by then, Covid protocol was in full force so I went in alone while Bobby waited outside. Before the sonographer could begin, I asked that he please not turn the screen away and to say something quickly because I was afraid of silence from my previous experience. He agreed to my requests and as soon as he applied the ultrasound, I could see a flickering heartbeat. Something wasn't right, though. He examined the screen for a long time, then said, 'I'm going to ask my colleague to come take a look.'

For fuck's sake, not a colleague. I sent Bobby a text to say that the baby was alive but that they had to check something further, and I know it was hard for him to receive that ominous news alone in the car. The colleague entered, took a look at the images on the screen and confirmed that whatever the lead sonographer had seen was correct. I was promptly sat up and ushered through the main reception – away from the mothers of healthy babies – and into 'the Crying Room'. I could tell it was the Crying Room by the bleakness of it: it was a little converted cupboard with a single window that contained just three pine chairs, a tiny table and boxes of tissues.

I stopped at the doorway, spun around and told the nurse that whatever diagnosis she meant to deliver in the Crying Room, I'd prefer to hear over the phone while sat in the parking lot with my husband. 'We've got our own tissues in the car,' I said. Gently, she coaxed me into one of the horrible chairs and explained that she'd brought me to the private room – 'CRYING ROOM,' I corrected – just to say that the baby might have a problem with its abdominal wall but that it was too early to confirm this and it often corrected itself anyway, so I'd need to return for another scan. There was hope but I didn't feel great about things anymore.

I climbed into the car, where Bobby had already been diligently googling 'omphalocele', a condition where the baby's organs don't move from the umbilical cord back into the abdomen properly and is often linked to other genetic abnormalities. Nine weeks is really early to be able to diagnose something like that, so we'd have to hope for the best and see how we got on. We'd felt so positive beforehand, thinking, 'What are the chances?' As it turned out, they were about 1 in 5,000. Pretty low, but a useless statistic when you happen to be the one.

Once again, I had to work quite solidly over the weeks that followed. In between jobs, I went for a Harmony blood test to check for any genetic conditions that might explain the possible problem with the baby but the results came back totally clear. Those tests incidentally told us that I was carrying a boy. I read stories from families whose children had been born with fluke omphaloceles and went on to have perfectly healthy lives but I also heard of many instances of the condition being fatal or requiring multiple surgeries after birth. I had no choice but to wait, try to be as distracted by my job as possible and will the baby to grow out of it. We went for a few private follow-up scans (because they let your partner in the room if you're paying) and, each time, the baby measured a bit smaller than he should have. Meanwhile, the defect kept growing bigger. I hated those weeks but ultimately I feel like they gave me a chance to accept that the baby wasn't well and probably wouldn't become well. Finally, in mid-August, right at the start of my second trimester, his heart stopped beating, sometime around 13 weeks. I had surgery the following day.

This time, I lost about 15 per cent of my blood during surgery for some reason, which is borderline 'too much', so I had to hassle the nurses extra hard to get out of there as soon as I woke up. Sorry to those nurses but you must understand that my impulse to leave hospitals is just too strong to control. I respect you and your work and your checklist for discharging patients but . . . I'm a bit like a feral cat trapped in a garden shed. If there's an escape, I'll find it. I didn't have my phone with me and the surgery took longer than expected, so I knew that Bobby would be having a terrible time waiting in the car. (The poor man must have some form of parking lot PTSD by now.)

I'd decided to be very open about my first miscarriage, discussing it publicly, but I didn't feel the need to repeat myself by talking about the second one. I hadn't really told anyone that I'd been pregnant to begin with so there was little need to announce that I wasn't any longer. The only reason why I had shared my experience initially is because I wanted to help people feel less alone and ashamed. It certainly wasn't cathartic for me and actually made me feel quite vulnerable. Plus, it opened a floodgate of grief as women from all over the world started writing to me daily about their own pregnancy losses. I felt very privileged to have conversations that gave them an outlet and hopefully some peace but it also took an emotional toll that I wasn't prepared to invite into my life a second time.

There were the funny moments too, of course. Like when the tabloid papers ran stories about my first tragedy next to photos of Bobby and me from Jonathan Ross's most recent Halloween party. We were holding hands and covered in fake blood, dressed as Peter Pan and Tinkerbell. The way the page had been formatted, it sort of looked like we were just leaving the hospital in a terrible state. There's also the added layer of Peter Pan 'never growing up' and leading children away to an island of 'Lost Boys'. I mean, how dark do you want to go? Another paper chose a photo of Bobby and me posing like characters from Netflix's hit series, *Tiger King*. I wondered who I'd managed to piss off at the photo agency to have these images run alongside the worst news of my life. 'Let me catch a break!' I thought. But they did make me laugh quite a lot and I do love a humorous twist, even at my own expense.

You can be deeply sad and be able to have a little laugh at the same time. After I lost my second pregnancy of 2020, my friend Elizabeth came round for a drink, put her hand on my shoulder and soothed, 'Fucking men. Too lazy to even drag their organs back in through their umbilical cords.' That was nice. The ironic misandry directed at a helpless foetus was just *chef's kiss* in that moment. That's not to say that it ridiculed the baby's predicament or made light of my trauma, just that it offered us a moment of reprieve from an otherwise inescapable sense of despair. That's what comedy does for me – it finds lightness in the dark. I'd had enough earnest doctors and nurses offering their very kind condolences; it was Elizabeth – a funny person – who really made me feel better.

The main deterrent stopping me from discussing the second miscarriage was that I worried women might find it disheartening to hear about. One was enough. I hated thinking that I might make someone lose hope or steal their happy feeling – the one I had throughout my young, dumb pregnancy with Violet. I wished that I could feel that way again but the innocence of it had gone. I felt like I couldn't add anything useful to the conversation by talking about it all over again, so I just quietly moved forward instead. I'd had a few mini crying fits in the toilets at work, in taxis and in my hotel room between filming during the weeks that we'd known the baby was sick, but after he'd died, I panicked for only two days as the hormones left my bloodstream and then I got over it. I think your body briefly 'looks for the baby', like an animal would, before accepting that it's gone. Having the surgery right away definitely helped my grieving process and that's the route that I would recommend to any friend faced with the same situation.

* * *

By the end of September 2020, I was pregnant for a third time. I know – by this point, I'd been pretty solidly knocked up for almost a full year. People on social media commented nearly every day for months that I looked like I'd either gained weight or had too much filler injected over lockdown. They must have been terribly confused by how I'd never seemed to make it past a certain threshold of fatness to indicate that I was definitely expecting. I can only apologise for the frustration they experienced during what I can only assume was an absolute emotional rollercoaster for them. But mainly, they can all get fucked.

It's not in my personality to passively 'wait and see what happens'; I need to take control and be active. So I threw all the ammunition I had into protecting this baby. My agent, Kitty, had told me anecdotally about a doctor who specialised in recurrent miscarriage and had treated one of her best friends successfully after she'd lost several pregnancies in a row. My instinct was to reject the idea of seeing him, on the basis that doctors had let me down when I'd been sick with lupus, and I resented that this one would probably blame the losses on my autoimmune response and waste my time. Lupus is poorly understood like miscarriage is poorly understood, so I dreaded having to explain to a whole new person that I was dealing with both. I'd managed to heal lupus myself to the point that I was asymptomatic, and I'd carried and delivered Violet successfully right after I'd been my most ill, so it was hard for me to imagine that someone might tell me that I couldn't carry another baby at all when I knew deep down that I could. Besides, the second miscarriage had been caused by an abdominal wall defect and I thought surely lupus couldn't cause that.

In the end, I was determined to try anything, even if it meant being insulted and left without answers. I made an appointment to see Dr Shehata in Harley Street and I'm so glad I did. Kitty told me to expect tests for specific antibodies and over-active 'killer cells' that could be stopped by Dr Shehata's treatment from attacking a growing embryo as a foreign invader. The NHS doesn't investigate miscarriage until a mother has had at least three and, even then, don't offer real intervention during the crucial first trimester, so I was excited to hear what Dr Shehata might try.

He and his team were lovely from the very first appointment. I was sent for blood tests which were returned quickly, showing increased anti-thyroid antibodies and moderately high activity of natural killer cells. Dr Shehata was very clear that his private treatment plan was not proven to work but that he had a lot of confidence in it. I'd already read reviews online from women who'd suffered years of infertility and who'd experienced several more miscarriages than I had, and credited Dr Shehata with the subsequent births of their healthy children. I understood going in that many alternative treatments are unproven, simply due to lack of research funding or official testing.

There's an excellent book called *Invisible Women*, written by Caroline Criado Perez, which exposes data bias in a world designed for men, and I think it offers good insight into why this blind spot in medical research might exist. Or maybe it's just coincidence that they're putting so much energy into Viagra instead. In any case, I was prescribed blood thinners, steroids, aspirin, vitamins, intralipid infusions and an increase in my existing hydroxychloroquine prescription for lupus. The aim of this cocktail was to increase endometrial receptivity, so that the embryo could deeply attach itself into the uterine lining as the placenta developed, and to modulate my immune system to stop it from potentially rejecting the baby.

I gained two stone in a month. Yeah. That's 28lbs or 13.6 kilos, just so everyone understands. That's in addition to the weight I'd already put on while being pregnant and recovering from surgeries over the past ten months. But being bigger didn't stop me working in the way I had feared it would, and I started to value my body for its function rather than how it looked.

Throughout my life, I've hurt my body by sticking breast implants inside it, and tanning, burning, lasering, injecting and waxing my sensitive skin. I'd cursed it in my twenties for not being small enough, not being cute enough and not dancing well enough to be cast in a Sean Paul video. Now, I was asking my body to work the way I wanted after wasting so much time pushing it to look the way I thought other people wanted. I found it liberating, actually. I focused all my attention towards accepting that the steroids were going to change the way I looked for a while, but also hopefully keep this baby alive.

* * *

I'm editing this paragraph three days before my due date, in June 2021, and I feel like it's all going to be fine. I'm sure the publishers would have cut this part out if it hadn't been, so safely assume that if you're reading this, I had a baby in the summer. I love the third trimester because it's really the first time I haven't felt sick in over a year, so zero complaints from me. I've been turning up to work quite visibly pregnant and very few people have had the balls to mention it to my face. They've been refreshingly cool about it too. Surprisingly, I got to keep two amazing jobs – one with Amazon and one hosting a new dating show for ITV2 – despite having to tell production I'm pregnant! I was worried about being replaced but everyone's been super accommodating, so times are changing indeed.

Bobby and I have posted a few photos in the last couple of weeks but have opted to proceed pretty discreetly otherwise. I've learned that pregnancy announcements can be quite triggering for women going through loss but sometimes seeing happy announcements gives hope as well. It's not a secret but it's also not news.

In the event that you find yourself expecting a potential future child, I'd recommend that you never reveal your due date – not to anyone. It's the first question people ask and it's the last I will ever answer. Staring off into space and musing, 'I don't know,' in response bamboozles strangers and leaves them with nothing else to say. It's fun both in the moment and for the entire duration of your pregnancy. They are unable to comment on your bump size and can't spot you nearer to the time and offer quips like, 'Where's the baby?', 'Any day now . . . !', or, my personal favourite, 'Still pregnant?' FUCK OFF, GLORIA. This hack has been my biggest stroke of genius. The other day, a close family member asked how many weeks along I was and I offered her my trademarked, 'Not sure.' Visibly offended, she accused me of mistrusting her and thought my worry was that she would go to the tabloids. 'Not at all!' I reassured her. 'It's not that I think you'll tell anyone, I just don't want any texts from you on the day.' I am an asshole, but watch – I'll be blissfully left alone when I deliver while you're fielding phone calls all week long from your mother-in-law.

I can't say for certain whether following Dr Shehata's plan for the first 12 weeks was the magic ingredient or whether my third pregnancy of the last year would have been the one to 'make it' regardless, but I think alternative investigations are certainly worth looking into if you're searching for a potential solution to recurrent miscarriage. Losing a baby hurts so much every time. Personally, I'm not sure I could have done it again and bounced back with the same enthusiasm. I'm very privileged to be able to afford private care and it infuriates me that alternative treatments aren't available to everyone. What exactly do I pay tax for in a compassionate society otherwise? I hate being told that it's going to the NHS then hearing about an MP giving yet another unfounded million-pound contract to his equestrian BFF or – better yet – his mistress. Just because something's common doesn't mean it should be tolerated. But enough about Nigel Farage . . .

Women are being made to carry their dead embryos around, then being casually advised to 'try again' as though they might not be walking the same gauntlet. If that can be somehow avoided, I firmly believe that's worth fervently exploring.

Celebrity is **nothing new.** (What do you think **Jesus** was?)

How to Impress Famous Celebrities

To me, it's very comforting and tribal to share mutual friends. You've seen the look on a stranger's face at a party when you say, 'Oh you know Wilma from college, don't you? She and I work together now!' They'll be instantly more receptive and likely to open up. If you're lucky, you might even get a bit of gossip, like, 'YES, Wilma. Hasn't her husband just moved out because he was allergic to the cat?' followed by hefty SIDE EYES all around.

The culture of celebrity is no different as far as I'm concerned. Celebrities are people that we (think we) know in common and it can be fun to spark up conversations surrounding their perceived circumstances, experiences or behaviour. Yes, I've heard the saying that, 'Great minds talk of ideas, average minds talk of events, small minds talk of people,' but anytime I discuss celebrity, I'm trying to get at bigger ideas – like the social customs or cultural trends they embody or represent. I'm mostly fascinated by what and who we think celebrities are – the space between the actual person and the persona – and what the consumption of that through our media and our suspended disbelief says about us.

Celebrity is nothing new. (What do you think Jesus was?) I hate the way it's sneered at and commonly viewed as being shallow or low-brow. Sure, some of it has run away with itself in recent years and has become icky consumer-driven capitalist trash, but overall, it's fun! And even the toxic elements of celebrity make for an enthralling discussion with the right person. If you don't see that, I think you're a snob and it makes me sad for you that you're missing out on exciting subjects like Bennifer.

I was very lucky to meet Jessica Simpson in 2005, when I was 22 and still living in Toronto. She was a huge star at the absolute pinnacle of her reality TV career, after bursting onto the music scene to rival Britney and Christina as the 'preacher's daughter' pop star who abstained from sex before marriage. Tanned, talented and beautiful, she married boyband hunk Nick Lachey and won the hearts of every All-American girl with her hit MTV show, *Newlyweds*. There was something disarming and extra lovely about her, like if Stacey Solomon was blonde and from Texas. Young, pale women like me got to see Jessica Simpson break away from her record label's constructed image of the sexy virgin as she was shown relaxing at home in tracksuits, one time memorably asking her husband whether tuna was chicken. I fucking loved her. I wanted to be sweet and ditzy like she was. I wanted the tiny body she worked for, the gay hairstylist she travelled with and the tiny white dog she carried around (who would later be tragically eaten by a coyote, RIP). I honestly thought that every element of my life would be better if only I were Jessica Simpson.

I was offered the opportunity to dress up, along with four other girls, as Daisy Duke, the character from the iconic *The Dukes of Hazzard* TV series, which had just been loosely remade as an action comedy road film starring – my hero – Jessica Simpson, in denim booty shorts as the lead Southern belle. Much Music, the channel where I'd been working as a podium dancer, was hosting a TV press event for the movie and thought it would be funny for the cast to choose 'Canada's Daisy Duke' in a quick-fire pageant during their interview. Each of us would strut past the stars wearing our best attempts at Daisy Duke-inspired outfits in front of a live audience. I couldn't wait. I prepared by starving for a solid week and painting my skin what I can only describe now as a borderline offensive shade of tan. I covered the entire surface of my head with blonde hair extension clips and paired size zero jean shorts with the leather cowboy boots that I obviously already owned and wore around daily. Walking to the studio on the morning of the event, I felt so joyfully nervous and almost faint with hunger. Upon arrival, the other girls and I were packed into a tiny dressing room together where we fizzed with excitement. Nobody cared about winning. Equally, we weren't bothered about Johnny Knoxville or Seann William Scott (the other stars of the film), we just wanted to meet Jessica Simpson.

Moments before we were due to go live on air, I heard footsteps and voices coming up the corridor. I actually held my breath. I'd never properly met a celebrity before and I was seconds away from possibly becoming lifelong BFFs with my absolute favourite one. First, I saw security guards, then the boys and, finally, Jessica Simpson herself appeared at our doorway. She looked me right in the eyes and then her gaze fell immediately to the floor. She smiled and mumbled a shy 'hello' before being whisked away to the stage.

That was it. But I'd seen everything I needed to see. I'd been able to download so much information from our brief encounter: I could instantly feel that she was introverted, tired, sort of uncomfortable and definitely even more starving than I was. The world would later find out that her marriage was falling apart at this moment but all I knew was that while Jessica Simpson was indeed special and beautiful and lovely, she was also just a person, not a deity, as I had imagined. She seemed timid and sad. It's not that meeting her was a disappointment; it simply provided a clear and instant realisation that, given the choice to swap places, I'd rather be me. I couldn't believe it. I would rather be strange, flawed, nobody me, than be JESSICA ACTUAL SIMPSON. Well, I wanted to be the version of me who dressed and acted like the constructed version of Jessica Simpson, but still, it was something.

I didn't win the Daisy Duke lookalike stunt but afterwards I trotted down the road to Hooters and rewarded myself anyway with a beer and my favourite buffalo chicken strips. Food used to taste so good back when I let myself get hungry.

Meeting your heroes is excellent, especially during your formative years. It gave me perspective and humanised someone who I'd previously thought to be some type of perfect, problem-free unicorn. Since then, a few other celebrities I've met have seemed sad too. Maybe existing in a suspended place between your genuine self and your manufactured self does a number on people's mental health.

*   *   *

In 2006, I went with my friend Amy on a trip to the Playboy Mansion in Los Angeles. Amy was an actress and model who was always up for interesting adventures, so when she invited me to Hugh Hefner's annual Kandyland Party, I jumped at the chance to go. If you're not familiar with the Playboy brand, it's a men's magazine at its core, which exploded into an international brand of clubs, television shows and more or less a lifestyle. The Playboy 'Bunnies' are fit young women in lingerie-inspired bunny costumes, complete with ears, cotton tails and a trademark 'hop'. Playboy bunnies fit with the aesthetic of that time, so I couldn't wait to experience this once-in-a-lifetime invitation to Hef's iconic fancy dress party.

At the time, Hef famously 'kept' eight girlfriends at his mansion, who'd been whittled down to the main three – Holly, Bridget and Kendra – to star in the hit reality series, *The Girls Next Door*. They all had little dogs, their own bedrooms (apart from Holly, who was Hef's number one and slept in his bed) and a weekly beauty and clothing allowance from their famous octogenarian boyfriend. Some girls say that sex with Hef was part of the deal; others maintain that it wasn't. They all certainly showed him physical affection on the show and at public appearances. I personally believe the words of former girlfriend Izabella St James whose account in her book, *Bunny Tales*, says that they all basically had to bang him Wednesdays and Fridays. That book is full of details involving Quaaludes and a wet penis cloth between shags. That's basically my Amazon review.

The Playboy Mansion party was both fun and unsettling at once. I saw musician Dave Navarro there and the big actor from *The Green Mile*. A random German man offered to 'fuck me in the ass for sport', which I politely declined, and Amy and I spent most of our time with some truly nice and very religious football players we'd met at the hotel who played for The Denver Broncos. One of them spoke at length to me about blood health and how shellfish are bottom feeders so therefore we shouldn't eat them. I swam in the grotto and stayed relatively sober because I just wanted to look at things and dance.

The dress code for women at the Playboy Mansion is 'nude', or a variation of nude, like a bikini, lingerie or body paint. My candy-inspired outfit for this candy-themed party was RED. That's it, just the colour red. Amy and I had been shopping for lingerie and I'd just picked the thing that I thought looked best on me. 'What candy are you?' people would ask. 'RED!' I'd say. I was every strawberry liquorice, Twizzler, cherry bomb, cinnamon heart, candy cane and Swedish berry rolled into one. *JE SUIS RED.*

The biggest celeb at the party was Hugh Hefner himself but I liked the girls. It was a time in my life defined by and dedicated to beautiful women on reality TV shows and I just wanted to see them, gain proximity and maybe come out of it a little more like them. I could tell that they were positioned around Hef as a job. For them, this was less of a party and more of a disturbance in their back garden. (Not a euphemism for Wednesdays and Fridays.)

Of course they smiled and posed for photos but they didn't want to be there. I could tell. Hef sat between them all in a glorious sultan's tent wearing his trademark silk night robe. One of the world's most legendary journalists, a champion of racial diversity and transformer of sex culture in 1960s America was now perched on a hired velvet sofa inside a branded marquee, singing listlessly along to the chorus of 'Who Let the Dogs Out?' waaaay past his bedtime.

* * *

Today, I have a rule not to speak about any interactions with celebrities that happened in private spaces. Jimmy Carr taught me that speaking about house parties should always be off limits as a matter of general decorum. He's one classy babe, that Jimmy Carr. And he believes in human beings being entitled to their privacy. Having said that, I have special permission to share two stories because I acted like a monumental prick in both of them.

The first was when I'd arrived late from a tequila-sponsored podcast event and bumped into Kourtney Kardashian at a party Jimmy was hosting in his garden. I enjoy a cocktail here and there, or maybe a glass of wine at a patio lunch, but I'm not usually drunk. The boys on the podcast had been doing shots of white tequila throughout the recording and I'd reasoned that I could participate by mixing a little into an iced soft drink and be fine. I was not fine. I was tipsy at best. As soon as I spotted Kourtney, I confused television with my own life and assumed she was my close personal friend. Note: Just because you've watched someone obsessively for 20 seasons doesn't mean that you know them at all or have any business butting into their personal lives.

I walked right up to her and said, 'Kourt, you need to leave Scott for good.' (You probably don't need the context but if you do, Scott Disick is the father of her three children who – while being very handsome and charismatic – never treated Kourtney with the respect I felt she deserved. They have now been separated for some time and he's proven his douche status to me by dating a roster of teenagers.) Rather than rightly telling me to fuck off and mind my business, Kourtney very sweetly said, 'How? He's staying at my house right now. Who else would I even date?' to which I replied, 'Burn your house down and date literally anybody you want. How about Prince Harry?' (He was single at the time and I stand by it as a suitable match.) She tolerated me with all the grace and charm that the Kardashians have become famous for. Everyone says they're on time, easy to work with, lovely and disarming. That's true as far as I could tell.

My second incident as a party prick was when I was introduced to Professor Stephen Hawking and started flirting with him. I'd learned from the film about his life that he was something of a ladies' man so naturally fell into the rhythm of chatting him up.

Why not? He's an icon! Due to motor neurone disease, he used a smart tablet to help him communicate through his well-known computer-generated voice. After a few short words with me, he fell silent. His personal assistant informed me that, regrettably, Professor Hawking's tablet had run out of battery power and that our conversation would have to end. They went away and I smelled a rat. I'm nowhere near as clever as any professor but I know when I'm being blown off. This man was clearly using a pre-rehearsed excuse to get out of having a conversation with me! When they said he was a genius, they weren't kidding. That's exactly what I'd use my tablet powers for if I had one. I'd never respected anyone more. Later that night, I did some online research into how Professor Hawking's voice system worked. Sure enough, there's a backup battery for the tablet in the wheelchair power. If the chair is moving, the tablet is working. I KNEW IT. Not only did I try, and fail, to pick up Professor Stephen Hawking but rather than taking the L with some dignity, I went away and found actual evidence to support his rejection of me. It's always good to be sure.

* * *

Suffice to say, I've never had a 'type' and I was never drawn to celebrity men as life partners. I went off-piste a few years ago and dated a really nice guy who worked in Hollywood. He was deeply skilled at schmoozing and had zero qualms about interrupting the meal (or probably even wedding, funeral, any major life event) of any famous person he spotted who he wanted to speak to. Being Jewish didn't stop him from following Mel Gibson into a lift and asking him to autograph a completely-unrelated-to-Mel-Gibson book he happened to be holding. He always described his keen interest in conversing with celebrities as a simple appreciation for anyone outstanding in their field. To be fair, he did the same with authors, playwrights and pretty much anybody notable we happened to bump into. He knew a lot about a lot, so I believe that he was innocently drawn to fascinating people, but bothering strangers annoyed me. We'd be leaving a restaurant and I'd hear him say, 'Elvis Costello?' then launch into a conversation with the unsuspecting singer-songwriter who was sat eating with friends.

In 2018, I was in Los Angeles filming Netflix's *The Fix*. One summer afternoon, Violet was swimming in our hotel pool with some really sweet kids when their mother walked over to deliver a countdown to lunchtime. Hollywood Boyfriend immediately recognised her as Tina Fey and flew out of his chair to go over and discuss some iconic *30 Rock* joke. I love Tina Fey as much as anybody but I stayed with the towels.

HB had Lindsay Lohan's phone number; he made friends with famous musicians, comedians, actors, models . . . I'd say 80 per cent of his friends were celebrities. Most times that I'd ring him, he'd be dining at a famous magician's private residence, hiking with a film star or sleeping on someone's tour bus. Maybe it's just how Hollywood works but he never wanted to leave anywhere at the risk of missing out on something, and I was usually too tired to care. One late night at a festival bar, he was introducing me to yet another American actor at 2am and I put my hands up and said, 'I'm so sorry, sir, but I absolutely cannot meet another new person tonight,' and took myself to bed.

Of all celebrities, dramatic actors in particular frighten me. I'm sure they mean well but I find the lifelong pursuit of pretending to be someone else VERY creepy. These are highly trained liars who win awards but should really be punished – possibly with jail, or even snakes. How could you trust them? How could you DATE one?! They might as well be Russian spies, if you ask me. I once chatted with a man from a superhero film and he suggested we play a game where we say the first thing that popped into our heads. He cheerily explained, 'You just speak! You don't think about it. Just say the exactly what you're thinking and then I'll go next, and so on. It'll be fun!' My blood ran cold. 'You . . . you mean . . . You think it's a game to . . . Have a human fucking conversation?' I asked him, while pawing at the table behind me for a sturdy candlestick or knife with which to defend myself. 'Yes!' he insisted, 'it's HILARIOUS!' That's when I knew I had to get out of there. But how would I be able to fool him with an excuse? Many actors are so talented that they can read facial expressions, however subtle. This is the real reason I get Botox: to make myself impervious to their evil powers. My greatest fear in life is being alone with a serious actor.

I let it happen again on a sofa in the corner of a hotel bar in London. The place was crawling with celebs as a big awards show had just wrapped nearby. Prince Andrew was actually there (pre-controversy) and I hate to add anything to the man's denials of guilt but I did see him chatting up a well-known woman in her forties. If I hadn't known who she was, I might've guessed by the look of her that she was a teenager, though, so it's sort of neutral information.

Anyway, next thing I know, a legendary big blockbuster star – someone your dad and your grandad both definitely love – sat next to me with a ukulele and I wasn't able to get a hold of my phone quickly enough to call the police for help. This man was so famous that he was able to light a cigarette and smoke it in plain view of the staff without anyone coming over and asking him to put it out. My grandpa used to do that regularly at the bank but people would try at least three times before they gave up trying to stop him. Nobody challenged this guy, not once. He offered to play me an original song he'd written. I declined on the basis that, 'Oh, I just do comedy, so music's not really . . . ' and with that, he started strumming on the instrument. He said that I'd definitely enjoy the song as it was funny, then sang a few bars before looking up at me expectantly.

'You didn't laugh,' he prompted. 'I'll do that part again because you didn't hear the funny part.' I'd heard it. It was a misdirection joke; the song was about a female love interest who surprisingly turns out to be a man at the end. I'm not too hard on the older crowd for failing to fit into today's 'woke' agenda. It's confusing and difficult for them – I get it; it takes time to evolve and adjust. He hadn't meant any harm and I wasn't offended by it, but I saw the punchline coming a mile away for a start and I just didn't think it was funny. But if I wanted him to stop singing, I'd have to deliver the greatest performance of my career. He played it again and paused for my reaction. This time I laughed and laughed, then apologised for not hearing it properly the first time. He didn't buy it and he didn't like me. He left and I was alone again in my own blissful company. I owe that solace to my bad acting.

I'm so lucky to know comedians who, I am pleased to report, you can have actual normal human conversations with. The divide between their personalities and personas is only very slight compared to proper celebrities, if existent at all. I've had brief encounters with Kathy Griffin, Amy Schumer, Ali Wong, Dave Chappelle, Wanda Sykes, Mel Brooks, Bill Burr, Kevin Hart, Sarah Silverman, Whitney Cummings, Neal Brennan, Chelsea Handler and Gary Gulman, and I get to be ACTUAL FRIENDS with all my favourite British comics too. These are the people I like and feel safe with.

There's an easy shorthand between comics where they shave out the crap and dive into deep conversation without a moment of small talk. Generally, I'd say they care less about how things look and more about how things actually are – something that seems to be getting increasingly rare. They're often ridiculous and uncensored and they ask loads of questions while trying different answers because they aren't afraid of being wrong. I love them. The novelty of this job will never wear off for me. It's wild that I get to hang out with strange, funny people and that we're all fortunate enough to travel around speaking candidly from the heart and behaving like dickheads.

I still love Jessica Simpson. She went through a hard time and eventually gained her own authentic voice. Meeting her when I did helped me skip a whole bunch of steps towards cutting the shit and moving towards this amazing life that I never thought I wanted. God knows what might've happened to me otherwise. I could have ended up as one of Hef's girlfriends or – worse – a trained dramatic actor.

I expect **most** of us were taught **growing up** that it's wrong to put someone down to make yourself feel better.

How to Survive Controversy

My persistent refusal to 'cancel' anyone seems to make my generation angry. I generally don't believe in discarding people because I think it's unreasonable to expect that everyone should live their entire life without acting like a massive asshole at least a few times along the way. These days, a popular method of trying to end someone's career is to comb through their social media posts from a decade ago searching for banned words or a sentiment that clashes with present standards of wokeness. Listen, I'm not saying that I agree with her – I just don't think that J. K. Rowling's stance on trans rights automatically means that all Harry Potter books are shit. Equally, I don't think someone deserves to be fired from their job for challenging the rollout of a new vaccine. I recognise that Chrissy Teigen tweeted some way-over-the-line nasty comments to a vulnerable teenager before she became mega-famous but every American magazine was doing exactly the same at the time. We evolve. Accountability is very different from total erasure.

That's the thing that confuses people whenever I defend the subject of their outrage. I consider myself to be awakened and alert to the injustices in society. But I'm also an advocate of empathy. I know that I've said things in the past for shock value and I've held beliefs that have since evolved into better, more informed ones, and I feel fortunate to have been surrounded by intelligent, compassionate people who've pushed me to think critically. It's perfectly acceptable to hold people accountable when they've been wrong but I'd argue against the leap to aiming to get them fired for a fleeting thought they tweeted before Obama had even become president. That feels like centuries ago.

I've loved being wrong. Maybe not so much in the moment but on reflection, at least. I value the lessons I've learned and feel lucky that I had the relative anonymity in which to make them. Those times have made me sad, reflective and ultimately humbled. But I've nearly been 'cancelled' for being right too. I've been misinterpreted (or wilfully misinterpreted) and it hasn't felt great.

In 2013, I made a joke during an appearance on the BBC satirical panel show *Mock the Week* that managed to upset almost the entirety of the Philippines and ruin my sister Kerrie's vacation all in one go. There are games on the programme, and I was playing a round of 'Scenes We'd Like to See', which you might recognise as having a similar improv format to *Whose Line Is It Anyway?*, the American TV show. The scenario was 'Unlikely Things to Hear from a Cosmetics Company' and comics took it in turns to jump forward with answers. Jokes come in many styles. I chose to expose the sanctimony of Western corporate consumer culture that presents an image of virtue while exploiting workers behind the scenes. My answer was an angel-faced, 'We don't test our products on animals, we use Filipino children instead.' A spiky attempt but the UK audience mostly got that it was aimed at corporations, not their casualties, and it remained in the edit for broadcast.

A few days later, I logged into my social media to be greeted by a flurry of rape threats, death threats and your basic calls to bring me to justice. An isolated clip from the show had been shared worldwide and been taken badly out of context. People were demanding that I shut down my cosmetics brand and stop hurting children. I mean . . . I think it's fair to say that's a misunderstanding of epic proportions. Those who didn't take it literally thought instead that I was making fun of Filipino children. 'Why not say a different race of child?!' they asked. 'Why not an ugly white child like your own?' Well, that's because I'd recently read that there were nearly two million child labourers between the ages of five and 17 in the Philippines and I thought that was a really bad and exploitative practice that Western greed was at least partially responsible for. I also do not own, and have never owned, a cosmetics company.

Formal complaints were made and a handful of families attended a physical demonstration outside the BBC headquarters in London. The irony was that a British dad actually pulled his own children with Filipino heritage out of school and made them stand there holding handmade placards all day. I was, like, *facepalm*, let them go be kids for fuck's sake, they don't even watch panel shows in the first place! It went away and then resurfaced again around 2017, and more recently in 2021. Different age groups are discovering my timeless comedy in steady waves, I suppose. I really didn't mean any harm by what I said, and I do appreciate that the avenue I chose was a deeply spicy way to get my point across. I expect that incident will continue to come up every few years until I'm either successfully cancelled or dead.

When it first happened, though, one of the reasons the Philippines was at the forefront of my mind was that my little sister, Kerrie, was on holiday there meeting her Filipino partner's extended family for the first time. She saw the controversy unfolding on the news over someone's shoulder in a bar and thought, 'Um . . . this isn't good for my visit.' Kerrie had to navigate Manila wearing basically my face, as we look so alike, but thankfully her relatives understood the joke and weren't offended by it. If they had been, it might've ruined my sister's relationship and she wouldn't be married to Alain, the love of our lives, today. Their children will be part Filipino and I promise to never, ever make my nieces and nephews lift a single finger. My non-existent cosmetics company is shut for good.

* * *

I was blessed to co-host the NME Awards alongside incomparable broadcaster and cultural curator Julie Adenuga in February 2020.

I'd been a guest in 2016 so I knew it as a raucous good time punctuated by messy rock and roll moments. In 1966, The Beatles played their last UK live performance at the awards. Unbelievable. In 2011, the Foo Fighters went on to play a song and continued for over two hours. Wild. There have been many instances of climbing on tables, crashing of glasses, injuries and requisite hangovers. There's spontaneity in comedy the way there is in live music, and that's part of what makes it so magical. So when about halfway through the show, up-and-coming British artist Slowthai shouted something from the audience, I answered back on my hosting microphone, hoping that we could have a funny exchange. He playfully accused me of flirting with him, so I went with it and agreed that indeed I wanted his body. It was funny! This escalated from both of us because we were equally committed to our 'performance characters' who each needed to maintain status in the room.

The first rule in improv is called 'Yes, and . . . ', which means that when one performer makes any statement on stage, you agree and add to it. For example, if they said, 'I'm taking a cake out of the oven,' you'd never respond with, 'No, that isn't a cake,' you'd say something along the lines of, 'YES, and we should decorate it for Grandpa's birthday!' to keep the scene moving forward. I apply this to improv in my stand-up a lot of the time. Slowthai and I were simply 'Yes, and-ing' each other. How uncomfortable would it have been for everyone if I'd taken some moral high ground and shut down his quite innocent heckle?! I was grateful for the interaction – it was in the spirit of the evening. Eventually, we were locked in an embrace which was filmed on smartphones and uploaded to the unforgiving internet.

The lad had a terrible few weeks of online abuse and rage-inducing articles, but, like every Twitter storm, it eventually blew over and he was thankfully strong enough to withstand it, later releasing fresh music about cancel culture and mental health. Meanwhile, I found myself on the receiving end of criticism for my failure to participate in his attempted takedown! People questioned my feminist credentials and were quite intolerant of my interpretation of events. 'You're the entire reason women are victims of sexual assault!' some said. Hmm . . . not sure that's accurate. Strange how when women say they've been assaulted, they are disbelieved and when women say they've NOT been assaulted, they are disbelieved. Silly women. What are we like?

I expect most of us were taught growing up that it's wrong to put someone down to make yourself feel better. That's where I think cancel culture has come to in 2021. People sit at home and do fuck all but wait for someone else to make a mistake so they can feel better about themselves for exposing it. Being so focused on catching people out for their wrongdoing and demanding their blood isn't advocacy at all and I think it's become ego-serving. There are situations where crimes have undoubtedly been committed, like in the case of Harvey Weinstein, and I was glad to see him dragged out of Hollywood on crutches. May he be the first of many to disappear. But we have to draw the line somewhere and make room for growth when it comes to less severe infractions.

I created *The Duchess* mainly for women – specifically for underrepresented single mothers because I'd never seen any version of my own situation articulated on screen. The lead character, Katherine (because, whatever – Seinfeld didn't change his name), is a woman who has the professional and financial needs in her life fulfilled but is so hyper-independent that it has somewhat warped her worldview. I wanted her to be a 'bad person' but a good mother. Journalists have asked me on live television, 'How do you justify your dirty mouth to your child?' and I've chosen to respond with, 'How did Frankie Boyle answer when you asked him the same question?' Of course, they hadn't.

The show was spicy. It had to be. I wasn't trying to follow the current popular format of making a comedy half drama, I just wanted a bunch of unusual characters and jokes to build this unique shape of a family for people to enjoy. And it mattered a whole lot to me that she should be RICH. That annoyed audiences and producers alike. 'But she's an artist – how come she's got so much money?' Because, bitch, I'm an artist too and look at my house. We can do it! Nobody questions why the serial killer character in the Netflix series *You* has multiple properties in New York and Los Angeles yet works as a librarian and part-time barista. Actually, someone in a writer's room must have questioned it once which is when they added the scene where he needs cash, so he magically fashions a fake first edition novel together out of some garbage and sells it for four grand. Sure. Nobody's asking why Ricky Gervais' character in the excellent Netflix series *After Life* works for a local print newspaper but lives in a four MILLION pound house in Hampstead Heath. Bafflingly, he explained that away to me by saying, 'His wife made all the money,' as though it's some kind of feminist checkmate. YES, maybe his wife bought the house but my point is that he didn't have to offer any narrative explanation of that in the show. People were generally fine with him living there without interrogation. However, women on screen aren't allowed to have money. In real life, up until very recently, we didn't even have pockets!

Before its release, *The Duchess* was reviewed by a man who'd recently adopted a newborn baby. Suffice to say, he didn't like the show. He hated it so much, in fact, that he went against the critic's usual code of conduct and revealed the entire ending in his article. He took particular exception to an explosive scene in episode three, where Katherine is rejected by the adoption agency so retaliates by flying off the handle, hurling as many insults as she can think of at the agent. In what I intended to be an ironic exposition of a position, Katherine denies ever wanting to adopt a baby in the first place because they're basically damaged. The story being told is that Katherine is the one who is damaged and she clearly cannot handle rejection at all. The very next scene is a quick cut to where everything she said during this tirade is undermined anyway by her biological daughter being admonished for bad behaviour at school. I thought that was clear. It wasn't.

The adoption agent happened to be played by a black woman and this reviewer took offence at a white woman berating her on screen. My feeling on that issue is that we cannot exclude minority actors to make ourselves look good. This woman performed the best in her audition and was the strongest for the role – period. Katherine was a dick to almost everyone on the show, so should we have cast it all-white? You could call me a capitalist feminist – I don't care how I looked, I just care that this woman got paid. And the adoption agent subverted TV stereotypes by being in a position of status in the scene and never losing her cool.

We all have different ideas of what's progressive, I guess. I'm sure I'll be admonished for something I'll create in the future or, far more likely, for something I accidentally uttered into a drive-through window in the far distant past. That's showbusiness, nowadays. I want to make as many people happy as I can while hopefully offending the fewest, and I've been dutifully practicing that for the last 37 years. I should be getting good at it sometime soon.

"You can **fine-tune** who you are but you can **never** escape your true **self entirely.**"

How to Redefine Family

I'm not great at keeping in touch with extended family. There's something about genetic links that I've never fully grasped as a fundamental concept. I just feel like people can be closely or distantly related and still be polar opposites, so what's the point in clinging onto those relationships on the basis of heredity alone? Isn't all human DNA quite similar to a banana's anyway? Having been held by a stranger from your haplogroup a few times as an infant doesn't automatically mean you should meet up with them as an adult if you happen to be passing through their town. 'Oh, your second cousin Melvin lives in Plymouth. You should stop by!' Absolutely not, Dad. I'm on a tight schedule.

My detachment likely stems from growing up so far away from the whole of one side of my family. It wasn't easy to ring your grandparents in Ireland from Canada in the 1980s, so my sisters and I used to gather round the futuristic speakerphone in the kitchen once a month to briefly say hello. I think it cost something astronomical, like six dollars per minute! I drew pictures for my dad's sister, Auntie Mary, sometimes that my dad would fax to her office from his. At some point in early primary school, I placed a card with an original poem on my dad's nightstand that said, 'You left your home to find a mate. You left your home at a quarter to eight. Your mama cried and your papa too, but you left home anyway. Boo hoo hoo.' Atop quite a culturally insensitive caricature of a leprechaun-type young man. He thought that was funny enough to fax back home to the family, who loved it and marvelled that I'd even coincidentally got the time right. I certainly knew my audiences.

Whenever Dad's parents, siblings or uncles came to visit us in Canada, they'd stay for three to seven weeks at a time and it was a bit of a culture shock on both sides. My nana would crank the air conditioner up full blast and also open all the windows in the middle of sweltering July because she didn't understand North American central cooling methods. I've lived in the UK for 14 years and I still don't get why you'd heat up a small metal radiator in the corner of one room and expect it to warm the whole house, so the cross-continental confusion is mutual.

One warm summer evening, Nana had knocked out the screens from the sliding window in the basement, which Canadians need to keep mosquitos, flies and wildlife out. I remember being awakened by her small voice calling up the stairs to say, 'Barry? There's a big black cat down below!' (My dad's name is Finbarr but people call him Barry as well. I think Finbarr is better. I call him Dad, Fath or, my personal fave, Barfin.) My dad grumbled out of bed and flew down the stairs to deal with the cat that had snuck in through Nana's open window. He crashed around after it for several minutes before I heard him scold, 'Mam, how many times have I got to ask you to CLOSE the windows?!' The chase continued for a while downstairs until cheers indicated to me that Dad had successfully grabbed the feline intruder. The celebrations soon turned to disappointment and cries of, 'But you TOLD me to CLOSE the window!' followed by more hunting chaos. I later learned that while Dad had initially snatched the cat up by the scruff of the neck, when he moved to toss it back out the window, it whacked against the glass with a THUD and scurried back off into the darkness of our basement. Nana had shut it too soon.

* * *

Living in England, I describe myself as being 'the right kind of immigrant', meaning that I obviously wasn't born here but I don't experience the xenophobia or racism that immigrants from other countries can. Being white and Canadian seems to put me on some arbitrary 'good list'. I find it odd that society changes its mind every few years about which are and which aren't 'desirable' places to come from. As I'm sure most people know, being Irish carried its own stigma in the 1980s, when my dad decided to emigrate from Cork. It wasn't bad as far as I noticed growing up in Sarnia but there were certainly people who playfully called him a 'dog' or 'the Irish Dog' in front of me. Things were much worse in England, where hostility towards Irish workers would have been palpable, but now people seem to have swapped that rancour onto Eastern Europeans FOR ZERO REASON. I wonder who'll be next? That's why I find it so annoying when people are quick to call me a 'plastic Paddy' and question my right to my heritage, simply because I wasn't born in Ireland. Irish families who moved around the world when it wasn't such a welcoming place for them paved the way and absorbed a lot of nonsense so that Irish immigrants can have a much easier time today. And you want to insult their children? I'm not sure what that makes me then . . . Canadian? Because violent colonial history shows that you can't be ethnically Canadian and also white, sorry.

I love watching xenophobes get all muddled up whenever I appear on political satire programmes with my friends and fellow comedians Nish Kumar or Romesh Ranganathan. I see social media posts from trolls telling us all to 'GO HOME' or some version of 'BACK TO WHERE YOUS CAME FROM' and it's like . . . Romesh's parents are Sri Lankan but he was born in Britain. Nish is of Indian descent but was born in Britain too. Where exactly would you like him to go? Wandsworth? Did the racists mean to indicate my friends' ethnicities when directing them back to their places of origin because, if they did, my ethnicity is 100 per cent British and Irish, so what should the destination on my plane ticket be, please? We cannot all 'go home' by that contradictory logic and it makes me wish I could ask the natural follow-up questions. But by the time I see the trolls' messages, I suppose they're usually passed out in a pool of cider under the stairs.

My sisters and I visited Ireland often as kids but didn't get anything near the experience that my dad had growing up. He was born in 1952, in Montenotte, Cork, and recounts stories about robbing orchards, hiding his new shoes so he could run around barefoot, being shot at by farmers and the priests belting him for bad behaviour at school. I'd gathered my dad was something of a menace but judging by the film *War of the Buttons*, I actually think that's just the normal way all little boys acted back then. In contrast, anytime we were in Cork, we had to stay close to my parents. Rather than drinking naggins and loitering around Penneys alone as we'd have liked to do, we visited with crowds of older family members who all sang karaoke from their own speaker equipment that they'd bring along to functions. They were a very large, very musical family. There was certainly no roaming around or any freedom for my sisters and me because, apparently, everything in Cork city was now 'dangerous'.

I know nothing of my dad's dating history but I do have a theory about wild, belligerent boys who grow up to be fathers: the universe reprimands them by giving them little girls. Imagine wanting a boy and instead getting turbo-feminist ME, plus two extras! Dad must've been a literal tormentor of the female sex to warrant such karmic backlash. Though I'll go out on a limb and say God maybe went too far giving him me.

I was always happy to get back to our house. I could feel that being in Ireland stressed my mum out because we'd all have to squeeze into my nana and papa's spare room and be without a dishwasher and other modern home comforts. I wasn't used to being around so many people all at once and, though I loved the adventure of going to see them, I preferred the familiar quiet of my own space with just my sisters.

My immediate crew are the family that matter most to me and the only people with whom I've felt a true closeness. Kerrie, Joanne and I are quite different but they give me context and grounding. If there's anything I dislike about them, it's the eerie feeling of gazing into a funhouse mirror I get when we hang out. Some of our mannerisms and features are so similar that it gives me the creeps. I've heard this articulated by a TV psychologist as, 'She's got something I just can't stand about me.' It's unsettling. They remind me of my childhood self, of my teenaged self and of my most vulnerable self.

Joanne is three-and-a-half years younger than I am and might be the most earnest, granola person I've ever met. She is the softest and most easily wounded of the three of us. She grew up to be the most artistic and plays several instruments extraordinarily well. Her singing voice is the most beautiful. Her delivery style is different to mine as she's very happy to belt out sincere songs and publish that heart-warming material on the internet. I refuse to perform anything without at least a hint of sarcasm or irony. Joanne is admirably vulnerable and the most easily offended, even though she can be wickedly funny herself. Her hair is amazing but its length suggests that she might be in a sex cult. It's blonde, thick and covers her bum in a way that says, 'My values are timeless and I grow this gift as a sign of obedience to a miraculous God. Also, I know it's sexy and makes me look a bit like Disney's Rapunzel.' Yes, she also dresses up as a variety of cartoon princesses for kids' birthday parties or to read stories for the students she teaches. She has an amazing little body and I've been pestering her to start a foot-fetish OnlyFans account for quite some time. She continues to refuse.

Kerrie is the baby who arrived in 1988, two years after Joanne. I have a clear memory of peeking into her bassinet at the hospital and marvelling at her long fingernails and eyelashes. It wasn't that I particularly admired them, I was more impressed that she had any at all. Six-year-old me thought it was amazing that someone just a few hours old could be so advanced as to have already grown such luxuries as nails and lashes. Where had she found the time? Kerrie is glam, spicy, has been happy to openly challenge authority all her life and even called my dad an 'idiot' to his face once in the second grade. Miraculously, she didn't even get in trouble. She makes me look demure, if you can believe it. I have a filter deep down somewhere but one never knows what Kerrie is going to say next. She's long and lean and could drink me under the table – assuming I'd ever be foolish enough to enter into such a contest. I can be an acquired taste but people unanimously LOVE Kerrie. She manages a skincare aesthetics clinic by day and dances in a body-positive burlesque troupe by night. She's amazing and she misses me the most.

I took a very parental role with Kerrie when we were smaller, then basically abandoned her just as she turned 14. I went away to university that September and stayed for four years, then moved straight to England and never came back. I feel badly about having done that. We grew apart slightly during those first few months at university because I was a preoccupied 19-year-old prick and I found it jarring to be confronted at Christmastime by how quickly Kerrie was changing. She was strengthening her friendships in high school and she'd somehow transformed from a little girl into a young woman over a short semester. I didn't quite know how to pivot as a big sister, so I ended up doing what any responsible adult would and I brought Kerrie with me out to the clubs in Toronto. She'd take the train up to visit some weekends and present my driver's licence to the bouncer, while I'd be next in line with my passport. The smart ones would notice that we had the same birthday. 'Yes, we're twins!' we'd announce, getting away with it every time. Kerrie looked and acted as mature as anyone else my age, and it wasn't as though I was bringing her towards any danger. All we wanted to do back then was drink and dance. I went swiftly from being a sort of motherly figure to being an actual sister, to suddenly being on the other side of an ocean and then someone else's mother instead.

Kerrie has confessed to having experienced mixed feelings about Violet's birth and she didn't love it when I first married Bobby either. Jealousy would be too reductive a term to describe it but I think she's mostly protective of me and perhaps envious of people who spend more time in my company than she's able to. I feel very similarly and, while we now love and accept each other's husbands, I have been quite threatening towards Kerrie's boyfriends and close friends in the past. I showed incredible restraint at her wedding when I stopped myself from dragging one of her bridesmaids from the bathroom, where the girl was crying about her own hair not being right. This chick, who purported to be my sister's friend, was making us late for the church and six-year-old Violet was egging me on to tell her off! It took some time but Kerrie now realises that Violet and Bobby are extra reinforcements and more people to love and protect her as much as I do. I'm grateful that Kerrie has so many wonderful close friends while I'm not there to attend her burlesque shows and her husband Alain is one of my top favourite people on earth. Maybe the universe protected us both when it moved us an ocean apart because we have too much fun when we're together. I'd never get anything accomplished with Kerrie living next door.

* * *

When Violet entered my life, she redefined family for me. She's my special little friend, my most cherished person, The One, who gave me the maturity and wisdom I'd always been searching for. I don't run from people or from feelings like I used to, thanks to her, but I've learned to forgive myself for having done so in my youth.

Violet is smarter and more generally content than I was as a child, and loving her has shown me just how much my parents must have unconditionally loved me, too. I love her because of how much I like her, not because she happens to be related to me. But I know from my own experience that, one day soon,

Violet will grow up and break my heart by leaving me the way I left my family, and that being genetically linked won't be enough of an excuse to make her stay. Even while she's still under my roof, I don't exactly know how to force a teenager to keep being my friend, so I suppose I'll have to sit back and hope for the best. I've really put all my eggs in one basket with her (who knows if I'll even like the new baby! It might be a jerk).

I often wonder whether I've done Violet a disservice by bringing her up away from anyone who's genetically related to us. Technological advancements have mercifully allowed for more virtual contact with her aunties and grandparents but I hope she doesn't grow up to resent me for raising her in isolation basically by myself. I've tried to give us both the best, most fruitful lives and as many amazing opportunities as I could, and do you know what she says to me now? She goes, 'Sarnia is so cool, Mum. They have a Starbucks.'

At least if Violet moves there and starts her own family one day, I'll know how my dad felt when he emigrated all the way to Canada from Ireland so that his children could have a big garden and a finished basement, only to watch me turn the plane around and take it back to the UK. I'll know how Mum felt when she parented herself right out of a parenting job. That's the goal with raising children, isn't it? That if you do it well enough, your babies will become fulfilled and independent.

Judging by my marriage, my secret lust for a fake tan, my penchant for breaking into a spontaneous cabaret musical number and my daughter's affinity for Sarnia, I've decided you can fine-tune who you are but you can never escape your true self entirely. Like it or not, I'm rooted in audacity.

* * *

So, that's a bit about me. I hope it helps you to become more audacious and, if not, I'll be glad if it made you laugh. I had to restrain myself from speaking too much about Violet, her thoughts, her reactions, during many points in our journey because that part of the story is hers to tell, if and when she chooses. Besides, parts of this book are mortifying and I don't want her flipping through it to find the bit about herself and accidentally land on the page where I got off with the taxi driver because I didn't have seven dollars. Have I included that story? Hopefully not.

Oh, and my second baby's been born now, hooray! Mr Fred Ryan Kootstra crashed into this world powerfully just three hours after I finished editing the last chapter of this book. I was booked in to have him at the Lindo Wing (where the royal babies were born) because I'm up myself and think I'm fancy now, but The Universe had other plans. God looked upon me that day and She said, 'No posh hospital for you, Katherine. You're trash, remember?' and then Bobby nearly delivered him in the passenger seat of our car. We made it, though – just barely – and Fred was born exactly 19 minutes after I waddled, sobbing, into the private birthing centre. My consultant wasn't there, it was too late for drugs, and because it was a Sunday evening, the kitchen was closed. Guaranteed they'd have opened it for Kate Middleton, though . . .

Anyway, I'm filming a brand-new show for Amazon and going back on tour immediately, because the hustle never stops. Feminism has massively backfired because I'd sort of love to be home nursing the baby, but hey – never complain, never explain. I'm so blessed to be able to do my job and to have this life and I can't wait to see what's around the corner for my family of four. Thank you for the important role you've played in getting us here. I so appreciate you for coming to see me on purpose, for watching my shows, and for reading this book. I've taken risks and, thankfully, they've paid off, but I'm no more special than anyone else. You can do this too if you haven't already.

But first, you've got to stop apologising so much, stop wasting your time asking questions when the answer doesn't matter or is going to be a lie, and start navigating your life with a self-assuredness that pisses some people off. I tried to throw my own tools away for a long time before accepting that I was better off learning to sharpen them instead. It wasn't until I had nothing that I realised I had everything, and the more gratitude I had, the more abundance came my way. With regards to anxiety and conflict, try to remember that nothing matters very much, and little matters at all. Your peace should not be undervalued. Resilience is half the battle. You don't need a long-term plan or a short-term plan – just wake up every day, wash your face and move forward with confidence. Some people will call that 'audacity'.

Let them.

Acknowledgements

I think a lot about how my work will impact my children in the future. Every parent is embarrassing but, admittedly, I take it to the next level. I appreciate that I don't exist as an island and that everything I share – even with discretion – will result in their public exposure, and that's difficult for me to accept as someone who values consent. I try to mitigate that exposure, but I can't do this job effectively and prevent it completely. I worry that they'll grow to be resentful of what I do for a living, but then I remember that my job bought them a swimming pool, allowed the oldest one to meet Justin Bieber and will send them both to private school, so they can suck it. Thanks, kids, for graciously accepting the many gifts I've bestowed upon you (including life) and try not to be a dick about it as teenagers, please. Your dad and I are doing our best not to humiliate you, spoil you, or ruin your lives, we promise. You're so lucky to have us because we're extremely good-looking, we're in love, and we seriously put you first, even when it might not seem that way from where you're standing (a second-floor Juliet balcony, you're welcome).

Thanks, Mum, for tricking me into believing that I could do anything and everything. I believed you when you told me the bullies were just jealous, and I grew up thinking I was basically the shit because you had high expectations of me and I trusted your judgement. I appreciate that you had better grammar than anyone else in the town and enunciated your words properly. Without your stunning command of the English language, I wouldn't be able to work internationally, as my accent would be too grating. I sound like a posh American, thanks to you – a bit like Meghan Markle, or someone who was raised in Hong Kong but went to a fancy college because they came from family money. I admire the unbreakable spirit that allowed you to spend a quarter-century in Sarnia without succumbing to its basicness. I love that you had the audacity to partner with a much younger man back when only Demi Moore was doing it, and I'm sorry for having kicked up such a fuss about your iconic behaviour at the time. I think you're wickedly funny, very wise and one of the most classically beautiful women I've ever seen. I know you hate getting old but, as you always say, 'It's better than the alternative.' One day, we'll both be old and, hopefully, by then, you'll have learned to care less so we can go on an all-inclusive cruise and fuck shit up in bikinis.

Dad, I love it when you randomly text me the weather report for London, as though I'm not experiencing that climate in real-time from where I live . . . in London. My phone buzzes and

ACKNOWLEDGEMENTS

I'll read your message declaring there's an 80 per cent chance of rain as droplets blur the text on the screen. I'll look up at the sky and think, 'Thanks for the warning, Dad.' Growing up, I didn't realise how alike we are, but I see it now and I really love gossiping about people with you. You're good at it. It's amazing how many times I'll find myself texting Kerrie to say, 'OMG Dad's funny'. She'll agree and remind me that I said the same the week before. Then I'll warn her about snow in Toronto before signing off. Like you, I cherish small luxuries, like going out to dinner and having nice things. I love being the boss and I can sometimes be hot-headed. I always thought I embarrassed you (and I know that on many occasions, I did) but, in recent years, I'm impressed by how little you actually give a fuck what people say. You're great in a crisis and everybody likes you. I often think about the time I'd forgotten my passport at home and missed my intended flight to Ireland for Nana's 75th birthday. When, after having retrieved it, I arrived late to the big party, there was no mistaking your silent rage at my tardiness, but you kept your composure and delivered an incredible welcoming toast. I remember your technique of going round the dining hall, thanking all the different branches of the family by name, peppering your speech with jokes that were perfectly pitched for the room. It was a tough gig considering most of the audience were deaf. I couldn't have worked that crowd, but they loved you. So, it might be your fault that I'm a comedian. The girls and I love Cheryl and you two are a great example of an ideal marriage. Cherbear, thanks for looking after our dad so we don't have to. Oh, and sorry for moving to England. It's not much, but I promise never to support their football team. Up Cork!

Kerrie and Joanne, you're the entire reason I chose to have more children. I can't imagine my life without you and I wanted to give Violet the gift our parents gave to us. Thank you for being my first audience, my sounding boards and my context.

I have wonderful, interesting friends – many of whom I've mentioned throughout this book. My best childhood girlfriends (Caitlin, Alana, Brae, Cyndie, Lori, Kate, Katie, Lynn and Heather) have been so tolerant of who I was then and what I've now become. They've all been incredibly gracious about my Sarnia jokes and I appreciate never having been kicked off their WhatsApp group.

Comedians, I love every single one of you – even the ones I hate. I am so blessed to be in your gang and I wish that we could hang out more. The pandemic has truly highlighted how much life sucks when we're not together. I miss watching your sets, chatting shit in dressing rooms, and greenroom drinks after a studio record. I met my best comedian friend, Geoff Norcott, in one of those greenrooms. Geoff, I'm so lucky our paths crossed that day and I respect you and your work more than I can say. You're hands down one of my favourite comics and definitely one of the people I cherish the most.

The community of female comedians is so strong in the UK. I hope it's clear to up-and-coming young women in my industry that I'll do anything I can to help you. I'm watching your sets online when I can't be there in person, I'm recommending you to bookers and I'm going to employ you every time I get the chance.

My squad, Jen and Fiona, you're my fairy godmothers and my best friends. Having you both come into my life to make my stage persona more powerful and beautiful has had a huge influence on the performer I've become. I admire your creative talents and I love spending time with you on jobs and generally in life. I didn't mention Emily Dean in this book because she exists in a space all her own – somewhere between comedy, life-coaching and spring *Vogue* cover-modelling. Emily, you are the smartest and most special woman I've ever met. Thank you for coming into my life at Jimmy's party and for inspiring me to have a rose-gold kitchen. Somehow, you manage to blend being a uniquely funny genius with being an ethereal fashion icon. Your intoxicating charm is unrivalled. I suppose you're a bit like Kate Middleton, if she had an ass and a sense of humour. You're like George and Amal Clooney blended into one. You're like a brunette Taylor Swift, if she liked football. You're surprising and disarming, and a genuine one-of-a-kind exclusive. Knowing you has made me a better person and I need you to look after my children if Bobby and I have second thoughts about owning them and decide to run off.

Thank you to my managers and agents. Josh and Dave in Los Angeles, you're two of the coolest legends in the business and I have to pinch myself when I remember that you willingly represent me. Thank you for introducing me to Jared Levine, the best lawyer, and Richard Abate, the literary agent responsible for the letters on this page. United Agents in London have covered my ass in every respect. Will Farmer matches me up with my favourite brands and facilitates my darling podcast, Sarah Armitage and Darcy Guiras pitch me for commercial work, Kate Davie sells my smooth Canadian voice, Maria Dawson is the legal powerhouse who keeps everyone in line and keeps me out of trouble whenever I say something stupid. Amanda Emery, thank you for letting the country know when I'm on tour or releasing a new project. Ian Coburn, I'd never be touring at all if it wasn't for you. I love that you speak to me in facts and figures. I've never questioned for a minute that I'm in the safest of hands with you, and I'll never forget you coming to watch my show previews ALL ALONE before anyone else would buy a ticket.

Kitty Laing, ours is the longest relationship I've ever had. We met as little baby children in 2008 and look at what we've built since then. I'm blessed to have you – both as an agent and as a friend. I didn't believe you at first when you said that I could have Netflix specials and sitcoms and I know I couldn't have done it without your influence. Your ABC (Always Be Closing) motto inspires me to work harder every day, and I appreciate you giving me days off when you know I need them, too. We could really show those *Love Island* kids a thing or two, as we've never had our heads turned and have stayed loyal, and it has paid off. Even the people who hate seeing me on TV send lovely tweets and messages about you, saying, 'How did you get booked for this!?! You must have a fucking incredible agent.' And they're right, I do. Isaac, it's bittersweet losing you as you become an agent yourself, but you assisted Kitty with such personality and attention to detail that I knew you'd be outgrowing us soon. We'll miss you. Please don't be a stranger and DO NOT DARE take on any clients who might fit into my bracket and steal my work, or we will come for you like a hurricane.

Thank you to Beth, Susannah and everyone at Bonnier for taking a chance on me and my first book. I hope it doesn't result in a crushing financial loss for you because I've loved writing it so much, and that's down to your relaxed, collaborative style. I don't usually work so well with others when it comes to sharing my deepest secrets, but the rapport we've built and the trust you've given me has made me feel like I could express myself authentically.

My glorious husband, Bobby K. I've banged on about you for an entire chapter already, so I'll just say this last thing: watching you as a dad has healed all the misgivings I had about men. You know how to look after both Fred and Violet in ways that I don't. The other night, I needed your help with Fred then instinctively said sorry for asking, as though he was only mine. You took him in your arms and said, 'Katherine, I'm his dad. Don't apologise, we're in this together.' I've never been comfortable being 'in this together' with another adult, but it's refreshing to be reminded that you and I are truly equals. You have a natural affinity for leadership and, even as a feminist, I'm comfortable calling you the leader of our household. It's very relaxing. Finally, the pressure is off me, and I can trust the person I admire the most, with the finest dick in town, to make wise decisions for the family, while giving me the respect of being able to overrule him if I disagree. I've loved you my whole life, BK. I look forward to our next chapters together.